Reason, Freedom, & Democracy in Islam

Reason, Freedom, & Democracy in Islam

Essential Writings of 'Abdolkarim Soroush

Translated, Edited, and with a Critical Introduction by

MAHMOUD SADRI

AHMAD SADRI

OXFORD

UNIVERSITY PRESS

2000

OXFORD
UNIVERSITY PRESS

Oxford   New York

Athens   Auckland   Bangkok   Bogotá   Buenos Aires   Calcutta
Cape Town   Chennai   Dar es Salaam   Delhi   Florence   Hong Kong   Istanbul
Karachi   Kuala Lumpur   Madrid   Melbourne   Mexico City   Mumbai
Nairobi   Paris   São Paulo   Singapore   Taipei   Tokyo   Toronto   Warsaw

and associated companies in
Berlin   Ibadan

Copyright © 2000 by 'Abdolkarim Soroush

Published by Oxford University Press, Inc.
198 Madison Avenue, New York, New York 10016

Oxford is a registered trademark of Oxford University Press.

Library of Congress Cataloging-in-Publication Data
Surūsh, 'Abd al-Karīm.
Reason, freedom, and democracy in Islam : essential writings
of Abdolkarim Soroush / translated, edited, and with
a critical introduction by Mahmoud Sadri, Ahmad Sadri.
p.   cm.
Translated from Persian.
Includes bibliographical references and index.
ISBN 0-19-512812-5
1. Islam and reason.   2. Freedom (Islam)   3. Democracy—Religious
aspects—Islam.   4. Islam and state.   I. Sadri, Mahmoud.
II. Sadri, Ahmad.   III. Title.
BP190.5.R4S88   1999
297.2'72'092—dc21   98-38231

1 3 5 7 9 8 6 4 2

Printed in the United States of America
on acid-free paper

Foreword

The present collection represents part of my intellectual activities during the last fifteen years, in the aftermath of the Islamic Revolution in Iran. It has been collected, annotated, and translated here according to the discernment of its editors and is presented, in accordance with my wishes, in chronological order to reflect the evolution of my thought along with the social developments in Iran. These essays are partly a reaction to and partly an instigator of social developments in my country. As such, they are, I hope, of interest for the scholars of the cultural and intellectual history of Iran.

It is worth noting that I have reviewed and discussed the translation with the editors and translators in detail. I have found them faithful, meticulous, and rigorous. I should thank my respected colleagues and friends who have encouraged and helped in this project and, in particular, the young scholars who have translated and edited this work: Dr. Mahmoud Sadri and Dr. Ahmad Sadri.

Tehran   ʿAbodolkarim Soroush
April 29, 1998

Contents

Introduction

'Abdolkarim Soroush has emerged as the foremost Iranian and Islamic political philosopher and theologian. His sprawling intellectual project, aimed at reconciling reason and faith, spiritual authority and political liberty, ranges authoritatively over comparative religion, social science, and theology. However, it is only by understanding the local context of his intellectual endeavors that one can appreciate the universal significance of his thought.

The Local Context

The Icon

The persona of 'Abdolkarim Soroush must be examined in light of the iconic tradition of modern Iranian intellectuals. The "iconic" intellectuals are the producers as well as embodiments of ideas and ideals, and as such they are held in semireligious veneration. The main contours of this tradition emerged in the decades preceding the constitutional revolution of Iran (1905–1909). The multiple roots of this tradition account for its unique mixture of what Max Weber called "emissary" and "exemplary" prophecy.[1] In both respects, this tradition marks a radical departure from the intellectual traditions before Iran's turn-of-the-century exposure to the West.

Iran has had a rich legacy of traditional intellectuality anchored in religious seminaries (*ulama*), the patrimonial state (*ommal*), the rural nobility (*ashraaf*), and the traditional bourgeoisie (*bazaar*). Because of its marginal status and growing numbers, this last group was able to appreciate the new ideas and ideals that were being imported, along with samovars and guns, from the Russian and Transcaucasian frontiers. Thus it is not surprising that the lower layers of lay intelligentsia (especially in the northern regions of Iran) quickly absorbed the new ideas and became the carriers of a mission strikingly similar to that claimed by the Russian "intelligentsia" (a Russian coinage, incidentally). Increasingly, modern Transcaucasian, Azeri, and, later, Iranian intellectuals emulated their Russian counterparts in their breathless and tenacious quest to Westernize, modernize, and catch up with the more advanced countries of Europe.[2] Besides the Russian brand of missionary intellectual zeal, the ideal Persian iconic superintellectual evinces exemplary traits that are French in origin. The postconstitutional generations of Iranian students, who received their higher education in France, were profoundly influenced by the ideals of personal commitment, individual valor, and moral courage that shaped the idealized self-image of the post-Dreyfusard French "engaged" intellectuals, a term coined during the Dreyfus affair in the 1890s.

It was the convergence of the models of the French exemplary and Russian missionary heroic intellectuality in Iran's thriving middle-class imagination that produced the hybrid form of the nineteenth-century *monavvarolfekr*, and later, the twentieth-century *roushanfekr* intellectuality. The new self-proclaimed "enlightened" leaders laid claim to—and soon acquired—a patina of native charisma because of their alleged mastery of modern erudition. Taking as their intellectual heroes such archetypes as Tolstoy and Zola, the intellectual leaders of modern Iran demanded of themselves nothing less than an unswerving missionary activism aimed at national progress and an exemplary *j'accuse*—heroism in proclaiming socially relevant truths against entrenched authoritarian regimes. This certainly holds true for the radical Shi'ite version of liberation theology elaborated and personified by 'Ali Shari'ati in the 1970s. In their various manifestos, the contemporary flamboyant leaders of the Marxist, Maoist, and Guevaraist movements of the last quarter of the current century (e.g., the Toudeh Party, the Fada'iyan-i Khalq, and the Mojahedin-e Khalq guerrillas) consider themselves, among other things, heirs to the mantel of leading superintellectuality as well.

Iconic intellectuality implies not only the role of the heroic producers of ideas, but also the equally heroic selflessness required of the consumers of ideas. By the same token, mere professionals, scholars, academics, seminarians, and literati are excluded from the ranks of iconic *roushanfekr* intellectuals. Indeed, the *roushanfekr* is the opposite of Kierkegaard's scholar, who builds public conceptual palaces but might live in a private existential doghouse. Private and public lives of iconic intellectuals are expected to merge to allow a clear view of their calling: leading the way toward reform and setting an example for the rest of the society.

The iconic intellectuals are by definition at least equal to, perhaps, in the case of some laic thinkers, even better than their principles.

The appeal to a common mission and ideal lifestyle did not imply the uniformity of instruments of achieving the designated goals that depended on individual predilections and intellectual traditions. We will argue that three paths emerged in Iran as the nineteenth century drew to a close. Some advocates, notably Akhoundzadeh and Taqizadeh, chose the path of total surrender and assimilation, which we designate as radical laic modernism, while others, such as Aqayev and Talebof chose an accommodative but culturally and ideationally preservationist agenda, reflexive revivalism, thus anticipating the contemporary movement that encompasses Soroush's position. Both groups found themselves confronted with a third front: the rejectionist revivalism of nativist, antimodern, and anticonstitutionalist Islamists.[3] This turn-of-the-century debate is by no means resolved; indeed, in the current cacophony of Tehran's burgeoning free media, the continuing currency of such enlightenment ideals as progress, development, and religious reform underscores the abiding relevance of this trilateral debate in fin-de-siècle Iran. ʿAbdolkarim Soroush is an iconic intellectual who represents reflexive revivalism in this dialogue. Understanding this context is critical for the observers in the United States and in some European countries, where the public intellectual is an endangered species.[4]

Let us remember that Soroush started his public career as a high-ranking ideologue in the Islamic Republic.[5] He was later appointed to the Advisory Council on the Cultural Revolution by Ayatollah Khomeini.[6] In the last decade, however, he has emerged as the regime's enfant terrible and, more recently, as its bête noire because of his trenchant criticism of the theological, philosophical, and political underpinnings of the regime. He has been since summarily fired from his job, barred from teaching, discouraged from speaking in public, and periodically prevented from publishing and traveling abroad. He is routinely threatened with assassination and is occasionally roughed up by organized gangs of extremists known as Ansar-e Hezbollah. Yet, Soroush's defiance is not regarded as particularly heroic in Iran. Selflessness and unbending commitment to the socially relevant truth is par for the course of Soroush's career as a superintellectual. When he went abroad for a few months in 1996, after a series of violent disturbances in his public lectures and in the wake of persistent official harassment, there were no signs that his public would countenance his permanent departure.

The Iconoclast

To say that someone like Soroush fits into a pattern is not to imply that he is just the latest product of a cultural assembly line. He is an original by any standard. But his uniqueness has as much to do with his prodigious talents and extraordinary education as it does with the unique stage of the Iranian and Islamic civilization that he represents.[7]

To demonstrate this, it is enough to compare Soroush to some of the earlier links in the chain of Iranian iconic intellectuals. Soroush belongs to the genre of the *religious intellectuals*.[8] The charisma of the first generation of post–coup d'état[9] superintellectuals like Mehdi Bazargan and Yadollah Sahabi emanated from their mastery of modern exact sciences while maintaining and revising their lay piety in the light of modern science. "Yes," they would aver in words and deeds, "it is possible to be religious, modern, and nationalistic all at once."[10] The immense popularity of ʿAli Shariʿati, who was Iran's most celebrated iconic intellectual before Soroush, was due to his powerful fusion of the Shiʿite tradition of resistance with the revolutionary ethos of the French left in the sixties. Shariʿati's elegant and ebullient style of writing and speech was unprecedented and remains unsurpassed in Iran. His nearly hermetic and heroic lifestyle is also in line with that of an iconic intellectual. Although Shariʿati, like Bazargan and Sahabi before him, was at home with Islamic learning, he was routinely dismissed by the clergy (especially after he challenged their toleration of the vulgarities of mass religiosity) as unschooled in scholastics of the seminary, and when they finally locked horns, he was excoriated as a Western-educated heretic.

Unlike all of his predecessors in the line of religious superintellectuals, Soroush, thanks to his firm grounding in both traditional and modern learning, cannot be ignored by the clerical establishment. On the contrary, he occasionally uses his mastery of the seminarian language of critical discourse to win followers among scholars at the holy cities of Qum and Mashhad. Besides his undisputed claim to the mantle of a *roushanfekr* intellectual, Soroush wears the charismatic halo of a serious traditional scholar. Even the ideologically correct scholars of the establishment no longer challenge his scholastic credentials.

The Opus

Like Shariʿati before him, Soroush is quite prolific. The development of his ideas in the past few years can be traced in a succession of articles that he regularly publishes in Tehran's monthly literary and critical journal *Kiyan*. He also remains close to the pulse of social developments through polemical duels, addressing university students on religious and national occasions, and even delivering occasional funeral orations. The currents of Soroush's revisionist Islam flow in three fields: the epistemology and sociology of knowledge, philosophical anthropology and political theory, and ethics and social criticism.

Soroush's magnum opus is a tome entitled *The Hermeneutical Expansion and Contraction of the Theory of Shariʿah*. It reevaluates the Islamic *shariʿah* in the light of insights garnered from the fields of jurisprudence, history of ideas, hermeneutics, epistemology, philosophy of science, and sociology of knowledge. In this book and in his other writings, Soroush poses such question as, "What can we as mortals hope to know about the mind of God and to what extent ought we take the edicts deduced by Islamic juristconsults as literal and immediate divine commandments?" The clergy who have posed similar quandaries, do not object to these discussions as such. They are, however, outraged by Soroush's recklessness for exposing the laity to such sensitive subjects. But this issue is itself a bone of contention between Soroush and the seminarian establishment. Soroush criticizes the practice of protecting humanly developed dogma by forbidding "scandalous questions" (shobheh).[11]

Soroush's philosophical anthropology starts with the question of human nature. In his rather pessimistic view of human nature, Soroush appears to have been inspired by a modern tradition that starts with Hobbes and finds expression in the ideas of the framers of the American constitution. But his treatment of this tradition is quite refreshing. In his essay "Let Us Learn from History," instead of engaging in philosophical guesswork about human nature or dismissing the question as hopelessly abstract, he takes a direct and empirical route: there is nothing mysterious or abstract about human nature. It *is* revealed to us in history:

> We must warn against the false belief that human history could have been more or less virtuous than it has turned out to be. . . . Our definitions of humanity need to be soberly and somberly reexamined in view of the amount of greed, cruelty, wickedness, and ingratitude that they have caused—all of which they have done willingly and by their nature, not because they have been coerced or perverted.

Here Soroush gives the sober liberal view of human nature an empirical, collective basis. Combining the bare-knuckle realism of liberal philosophers with mystical, theological, and theosophical arguments, he softens the pessimistic edge of this view with verses from the Qur'an and the poetics from Hafez.

> At the dawn of creation, the angels accurately divined that human society could not be devoid of depravity and bloodshed. Nor did God fault them for this judgment, only advising them that their knowledge is incomplete.[12] Hafez restates the protestation of the angels but meekly and with infinite grace:
>
> > How can we not lose our way in the midst of so many harvests of creed
> > When Adam was led astray by a single seed!
>
> > There is no escape from blasphemy in love's bower
> > If "Bu Lahab" is absent, whom can the hell's fire devour?
>
> > Where the Chosen Adam was struck by the thunderbolt of insolence
> > How would it behoove us to profess our innocence?

Soroush believes that Rousseauesque idealism (shared by anarchists, radical Marxists, and Islamic fundamentalists), based on the assumption of the innate goodness of mankind, has the potential of underestimating the staying power of social evil and of fostering the false hope that it can be extinguished. This miscalculation could lead to disastrous projects of social engineering of the kind undertaken by the socialist regimes.

Soroush's political philosophy remains close to the heart of the liberal tradition, ever championing the basic values of reason, liberty, freedom, and democracy. The main challenge is not to establish their value but to promote them as "primary values," as independent virtues, not handmaidens of political maxims and religious dogma. In his "Reason and Freedom," Soroush is at pains to demonstrate that freedom is itself a truth, regardless of its performance as an instrument of attaining the truth.

> Those who shun freedom as the enemy of truth and as a possible breeding ground for wrong ideas do not realize that freedom is itself a "truth."[13]
> . . . The world is the marketplace for the exchange of ideas. We give and take, and we trust that the ascendance of the nobler truths is worth the sacrifice of an occasional minor truth: "As the barrel of wine shall last, let the occasional chalice break."

'Abdolkarim Soroush is also one of the boldest social critics of postrevolutionary Iran. As such, he has not minced words about the questionable office of the clergy (*rouhaniat*) within the Islamic tradition where they perform no sacraments nor mediate the relationship between man and God. He has also criticized the hegemony of the clerocracy in general and also in so far as it threatens the autonomy of the academia in Iran. Some of these points are quite evident in his "What the University Expects from the Hawzeh." In another essay, "The Three Cultures," Soroush denounces utopian reconstructions of the "true identity" of Iran at the expense of its Islamic, Iranian, or Western components. In yet another treatise, "Life and Virtue: The Relationship between Socioeconomic Development and Ethics," Soroush launches a Weberian study of the link between economic development and traditional religious ethos.

Soroush sees contemporary Iran as a society in the grip of massive disenchantment. Twenty years ago masses of enchanted Iranians ratified the constitution of the first Islamic republic in the hopes of realizing earthly perfection in government. Those hopes have now turned into despair. The resurgence of Iran's turn-of-the-century varieties of revivalism and modernism could be attributed to these circumstances. They were exacerbated by the disappointing end of the Iran-Iraq war, hailed at the time by the leaders as a do-or-die crusade. Soroush is the intellectual face of reflexive revivalism in Iran. Its social and political face can be seen in the sweeping victory of President Khatami in 1997 (now hailed by the liberal newspapers as the "Epic of May 23") and in the massive turning away of the new generation of Iranians from revolutionary rhetoric.

The Global Context

The Luther of Islam?

The American journalist Robin Wright[14] and many after her have referred to ʿAbdolkarim Soroush as the Luther of Islam. Whatever the aptness of such analogies, they are notable not so much for their historical accuracy as for their power of historical imagination and intercultural understanding, otherwise woefully lacking in the Western media's voyeuristic and orientalist interest in the Islamic world. The point is that neither theocratic rule nor the modernizing movements aimed at religious revival, reform, and secularization should be considered novel phenomena by the heirs of Western Christianity. The Christian West has, after all, lived through the imperial papacies of Gregory VI through Innocent III (eleventh and twelfth centuries) and has tasted the religious politics of Cromwell and Calvin (sixteenth century). Thus, the upheavals in Islamic politics in Iran and elsewhere should seem less like exotic spectacles and more like familiar scenes from Western civilization's recent history. If, as the Christian West has shown, the establishment of, and disenchantment with, a visible "City of God" leads the way toward the "Secular City," then Islamic civilization is on the verge of a decisive and familiar breakthrough.

In terms of his politics, however, Soroush is unlike the reformists of sixteenth-century Europe, even though his writings are replete with explicit borrowings from European theology and philosophy from Schleiermacher and Kierkegaard to Locke and Popper. Here we must take issue with the neo-Orientalists who dismiss Islamic liberalism as an alien and untenable epiphenomenon. Their argument takes Moslem liberals' borrowing from the West as evidence that they are less authentic than the anti-Western fundamentalists. But it should be borne in mind that in opposing such liberal ideals as democracy in favor of an Islamic "republic of virtue," fundamentalism *also* follows a long antidemocratic Western tradition, expressed across the centuries from Thrasymachus's debate with Socrates to Marx's rejection of "bourgeois democracy." The antidemocratic stance of the 1960s Islamic revivalists was less influenced by Islamic theology and jurisprudence than by the French leftist rhetoric against the failings of docile bourgeois democracies. The right-wing clerical ideal of a true Islamic community of virtue is profoundly influenced by authoritarian interpretations of Platonic and Aristotelian thought. The elites who took over the reigns of power in Iran conceived of themselves more as "enlightened despots" than as Shiʿite vice regents of the "occulted Imam." Those who have been quick to point out that in its internal theoretical civil wars, Islamic liberalism has borrowed from mainstream Western liberal theories forget that the Islamic fundamentalists have also borrowed from Western countercurrents of populism, fascism, anarchism, Jacobinism, and Marxism.[15]

Global Secularization and the Work of Soroush

Let us now turn to a comparison of Soroush's project with the social-scientific efforts to identify the nature and role of religion in the post-traditional world. For the purposes of this discussion and in order to better understand the universal relevance of Soroush's position, it is useful to distinguish three interrelated concepts: modernization, secularization, and reformation.

We understand modernization (or, alternatively, "rationalization")[16] as a process of progressive complexity and differentiation of institutions and spheres of life under the influence of economic and technological advances associated with the advent of capitalism. Secularization is an instance of modernization involving the differentiation of religion from economic and political institutions, namely separation of church and state. Secularization can also imply a separation of religion from culture and conscience. The two meanings of secularization can be expressed in the dichotomy of objective versus subjective secularization (profanation).

Reformation (or, alternatively, revivalism) refers to attempts, on behalf of the religious, to anticipate, adjust, or respond to the changes associated with objective and subjective secularization. Thus, according to our sociological definition, not every religious innovation would qualify as reformation or revivalism.

Secularization from Within. Modernization, secularization, and reformation have been indigenous to Western Christianity. Social thinkers did not expect religion to survive the ineluctable forces of modernization and secularization. The founders of the sociology of religion, Max Weber, Emile Durkheim (in his early career), and Georg Simmel, expected secularization to succeed not only in separating religion from the state (that is, objective secularization) but also in eradicating it from culture and conscience altogether (subjective secularization or profanation). The world, in their vision, would become increasingly and inescapably more rationalized, intellectualized, demystified, and disenchanted. They failed to anticipate religion's resilience and its ability to retrench and reinvent itself. A statement in a *Newsweek* article of March 16, 1998, sums up the consensus of the contemporary exegetes of the classical sociology of religion: "Human nature," argued the author of an essay on the new forms of religiosity, "is afraid of spiritual vacuum." Contemporary sociologists have acknowledged the continued existence of religion and have tried to explain the meaning, function, and reach of the new religiosity.

The theoretical convergence of three prominent sociologists of religion—Daniel Bell, Peter Berger, and Robert Bellah—on the nature and future of religion in the posttraditional world, which is indicative of a broader agreement among sociologists,[17] provides a social-scientific perspective from which the views of ʿAbdolkarim Soroush can be better understood. For these theories hold not only for Western societies, but for all societies that confront modernization and secularization. The general sociological consensus concerning the contours of the new religiosity may be summarized in three propositions.

First, the increasing compartmentalization of religion in the modern world as a result of secularization is a foregone conclusion. Religion, in other words, has clearly lost its monopoly on public perception, morality, and conscience. Modernization and secularization have made religious exclusion or absorption of competing ways of life and belief nearly impossible. Hence the inevitable and simultaneous emergence of tolerance and pluralism on the outside and ecumenism and voluntarism on the inside of the religious sphere. Religion has become "deobjectified." It has become a matter of preference in the contemporary "faith market."

Second, secularization has sociopolitical and cultural-psychological aspects. The original meaning of the term *secularization*, that is, "removal of territory from control of ecclesiastic authorities," signifies the institutional separation of church and state. Social and political functions of the church are thus relegated to other institutions. This stage of the process is understood as objective secularization. Subjective secularization or "profanation"[18] involves an infiltration of cultural practices and personal perceptions by the profane. While the pioneers of the sociology of religion found this latter and more thoroughgoing evisceration of religion to be the inevitable result of secularization, contemporary sociologists of religion have concluded that the continued presence and bourgeoning of religion does not support such a strong theory of secularization.[19] Few dispute, either doctrinally or sociologically, the reality and, indeed, desirability of objective secularization in the sense of a separation of church and state. Some thinkers have even gone so far as to claim that secularization is an integral part of the historical mission of religion.[20] It is the scope and depth of subjective secularization or profanation that is in question. It is clear, for example, that the degree of profanation varies with locations, classes, genders, and cultures.[21] There is, then, an asymmetry between secularization of structures and secularization of conscience. Although subjective secularization or profanation has succeeded in the West more than in any other part of the world, its advance, even in the West, has been checked—even reversed—in the recent past.[22]

Third, the new definitions of religion take seriously the desire of human beings for order, purpose, justice, and salvation. These are issues that the founders of the sociology of religion neglected. Daniel Bell attributes the continued success of "campfire evangelism" in the United States (and similar movements elsewhere) to a universal "existential need." Religion is anchored, not in the need for social control and social integration (per Marx and Durkheim) nor in the innate requirements of human nature (Schleiermacher and Otto). Rather, it is rooted in "the awareness of men of their finiteness and the inexorable limits of their power, and the consequent effort to find a coherent answer to reconcile them to human condition." Contemporary sociology perceives religion as a set of coherent answers to the core existential questions that confront every human group. Thus, the social function of religion is no longer its sole explanation.[23]

Is there a future for religion? Contemporary sociologists agree that religion as the sole organizer and arbiter of human society and consciousness has vanished forever. The solid "sacred canopy" has dissolved. It has been replaced by a patchwork of local faiths. The sacred seems irreversibly divorced from the secular. However, the demise of the supernatural in the public sphere is counteracted by its upsurge in the individual and group quest for transcendence. Religion in this sense is not only alive and well; it is thriving.

The foregoing views or the relationship between modernity and religion, their Western provenance notwithstanding, dovetail with those of ʿAbdolkarim Soroush. But there is a significant and instructive difference: for modern sociologists of religion the above conclusions are "descriptive." Secularization is firmly in place but profanation has not followed suit. Religion has survived in new forms, and sociology seeks to explain this phenomenon. Soroush's work, however, is "prescriptive." He envisions the possibility and the desirability of secularization of an Islamic society without a concomitant profanation of its culture.[24] It is not hard to imagine that in the Iranian intellectual milieu such a doctrine would come under attack not only by radical laic modernists but also by rejectionist revivalists. Neither can envisage separation of secularization and profanation, as we shall argue in the final part of this essay.

Secularization from Without. Wherever modernization and secularization are (or are perceived as) foreign elements, we can expect three distinct reactions. First, there will be crusades to "overcome the modern" in the name of preserving traditional identity and truth.[25] Modernization and secularization are thus vilified, even demonized, as unnatural, conspiratorial, and alien intrusions upon indigenous beliefs. Antimodern movements tend to advocate an authoritarian society and culture in the name of preserving the eternal and the sacred tradition. We have identified these, for lack of a better term, as varieties of rejectionist revivalism. They have frequently turned into nativist, purist, and militantly romantic movements with religious or traditionalist overtones. A second reaction to modernism and secularism may be described as reflexive revivalism which aims not so much at overcoming the modern as accommodating it. Reflexive revivalism acknowledges the force and sweep of modernization and secularization and shows a willingness to cast it as a desirable and divinely preordained destiny. It thus tries to separate the universal, inevitable, and beneficial aspects of modernization and secularization from its culturally specific, imperialist, and "degenerate" properties. The third reaction is radical laical modernism that favors the wholesale surrender of the native culture and values to modernity.

Inevitably, the pioneers of reflexive revivalism come under attack both by the guardians of rejectionist revivalism and the advocates of radical laic modernism. Neither of the last two groups believe in the possibility of secularization without profanation. Both consider profanation inevitable once secularization sets in. The rejectionists, fearing the demise of religion, reject the project of secularization without profanation. The laic modernists, for reasons of their own, agree that the two should not be decoupled.

Soroush belongs to a relatively new and sophisticated brand of reflexive revivalism within Islam that has its origin in the works of the late Mohammad Iqbal Lahori. Soroush's views—cognizant of the forces of modernization and secularization, informed by Western history and theology, and influenced by revolutionary and reform movements in the Islamic world—are not only illustrative and instructive from an academic point of view, but are also capable of revolutionizing Moslem theology and mass religiosity. It is no secret that neither the laic modernism of militaristic elites (for whom the Algerian junta presiding over a tragic civil war sets a poignant example) nor the rejectionist populism of traditional leaders (exemplified in certain elements of the Iranian and Sudanese experiences) have been able to offer a viable, durable, or desirable course for the future of the Islamic world. We believe that Soroush's bold synthesis points to an alternative and increasingly popular path.

We are indebted to ʿAbdolkarim Soroush for his generous disposition in discussing the meaning and context of his works and the fine points of translation in the summers of 1996 and 1997 in Iran and during his visit to the United States in the winter of 1997. We must also thank Ahmad Sheikhzadeh, ʿAli Aliabadi, and Charles Kurzman who gave us much encouragement as we labored on translating, annotating, and editing the text. Sincere thanks are also due to Bill Kaufman who has carefully read the manuscript and offered many insightful suggestions.

Denton, Texas   Mahmoud Sadri
Lake Forest, Illinois   Ahmad Sadri
June 1998

Reason, Freedom, & Democracy in Islam

I

Intellectual Autobiography

An Interview

SADRI: I would like to ask you for an account of your intellectual development. I am certainly interested in whether you distinguish any turning points, watersheds, or distinct periods in the evolution of your thought.

SOROUSH: In the name of God the compassionate, the merciful, thank you for giving me this opportunity. Let me first offer a sketchy account of my life. We can then talk about anything you feel needs further clarification.

I was born in 1945. My childhood years went by rather uneventfully. The only noteworthy aspect of my early life is my interest in poetry. I remember one of my classmates who had charming handwriting would make several copies of my poems and distribute them among students during break times. Recently a friend showed me an old copy of one of those poems. It was such a delight to discover a relic of my pre-adolescent years.

SADRI: Do you remember any of the poems?

SOROUSH: I vaguely remember one line that is not entirely disagreeable, even with my current taste in poetry, it is not one of my earliest poems though. It might date back to the last year of my primary school:

> Rosebud has chosen its place atop a stem full of thorns,
> For it's a place redolent with danger, and safety it scorns.

3

The first poet I came to know was Saʿdi. My father was an admirer of Saʿdi's admonitory book of poetry, *Boostan*. He used to read from the book aloud after his morning prayers. I remember hearing his voice every morning as I sat at breakfast. We had an old copy of Saʿdi's complete works at home. It was full of misprints. I still know most of Saʿdi's prose and poetry by heart. Looking back, I realize that my style of writing is influenced by him. This is definitely attributable to my childhood exposure to his works.

I attended ʿAlavi high school, a private institution dedicated to the dissemination of religious ideas. It had a principal by the name of Mr. Reza Rouzbeh who had a master's degree in physics. In addition, he had studied Eastern philosophy and knew religious canon law, *fiqʾh* and *usul*. So he was well versed both in traditional seminary studies and in modern science. One of the most salient attributes of Mr. Rouzbeh was his single-minded devotion to reconciling religion and science. At sixteen I attended his extracurricular lessons on the exegesis of the Qurʾan, where he made an all-out effort to derive scientific principles from religious texts. I had great difficulty convincing myself of the cogency of these arguments. I frequently objected as I found his interpretations contrived and forced. Mr. Rouzbeh would patiently listen to my arguments and respond. But his answers rarely persuaded me. These occasional debates focused my attention on the relationship between religion and science from early on. The only other noteworthy event of these years was a memorable trip to the desert town of Gonabad. There I met the *qotb* or the master of the mystic Sufi order of Khaksari that is also known as Gonabadi. Upon my return, I wrote a fictionalized travelogue entitled "Journey to the Center." This piece was published in the school newspaper. I no longer own a copy of it.

Upon entering the University of Tehran,[1] I approached a famous Islamic philosopher, Mr. Morteza Motahhari, for instruction. He did not have the time himself, but he introduced me to one of his students, a clergyman and the Imam of one of Tehran's mosques, with whom I studied Islamic philosophy for several years. These private instructions proved highly beneficial. It was during these lessons that I became interested in the relationship between philosophy and religion. I distinctly remember that my tutor would initially present a series of philosophical arguments in a thoroughly logical and cogent fashion and then proceed to demonstrate that religious principles and traditions already contained those rational premises. This method of argumentation convinced me, at the tender age of twenty, that Islam is philosophically sound and unassailable, a belief I retained for several years and sought to bolster through further studies of eastern philosophy. What happened to revolutionize my opinion is another story. I wrote my first serious unpublished article, "The Philosophy of Evil," in this period. My mentor showed me the text of an inquiry on the nature of evil and the meaning of suffering. I wrote a detailed treatise on the subject, and my teacher sent it out to the inquirer with some corrections. I still have the manuscript of that essay. It must have been written around 1967.

There were other developments during my university years. I was becoming gradually acquainted with science, taking it increasingly more seriously. Also, these years coincided with the events of 1964 and its aftermath. The rise of political struggles and upheavals in Iran made politics unavoidable for university students. Gradually, the despotic nature of the imperial regime was becoming more evident, and the guerrilla groups were starting to gain popularity. Among these the Mojahedin-e Khalq (literally, the people's holy warriors) had a special allure for the religious-minded because of the religious overtones of its rhetoric. That was when the question of the relationship between politics and religion first caught my attention, especially insofar as it contradicted what I had been taught in high school—to avoid politics, an allegedly complex science that could only be mastered after many years of apprenticeship at the feet of such gurus as Winston Churchill; their exact words! However, the events of that bloody and contentious decade taught me otherwise and awakened my political sensibilities.

My familiarity with the teachings of the aforementioned Islamic guerrilla group persuaded me to study Marxist and leftist thought as well. Marxism made its debut in Iran some eighty years ago and was bolstered after the allied invasion of Iran in 1941 which gave the Soviet Union a foothold in Iran. The influence of Marxism continued throughout the reign of the shah. During most of this era intellectual identity and enterprise was more or less synonymous with Marxism. Although the pro-Soviet communist party of Iran, the Toudeh Party, was formally banned, Marxist thought was quiet prevalent, and a number of prominent Iranian poets had well-known Marxist tendencies. As a result, Marxism had a tremendous appeal as the mainstream modern political ideology. Moreover, the clergy's exhortations against Marxism had the unintended consequence of intensifying its allure.

Before continuing further let me relate a couple of fleeting experiences during these college years as well. First, from the last year of high school, I entered Anjoman-e Hojatiyyeh, which was a religious organization that attempted to recruit from religious high schools in general and from ʿAlavi high school in particular. The aim of this group was to face the theological challenge of the Bahaʾi faith. In order to preserve the scientific nature of the polemic it had developed a curriculum of studies that was, on occasion, quite profound. They dealt with the historical origins and texts of the Shiʿite religion and the Bahaʾi faith. The emphasis of this group on Shiʿism in general and on some relatively obscure and esoteric aspects of this religion in particular was intriguing to me. Looking back on my intellectual development, I can trace to this involvement, the origin of my interest in the questions of sectarianism, heterodox interpretations of religious traditions, and the question of whether a particular denomination brings one closer to the truth of the faith. My involvement with this group was brief because I found its goals not entirely scientific, and I did not relish certain encounters that it required.

The second event was my exposure to groups that identified themselves as the Qur'anic Moslems which were active in various neighborhoods of Tehran. They argued that they were beyond the sectarian divisions of Shi'ite or Sunni schools and that they held a literal interpretation of the Qur'an. I used to attend their Qur'an study sessions, and as a result I became familiar with their arguments, positions, tracts, and texts. These were two relatively fleeting experiences that nevertheless left their mark on my religious and intellectual sensibilities.

Throughout these years I continued my study of and companionship with Persian literature, poetry, philosophy, and mysticism, especially the works of Rumi. It was in these years that I was introduced to three contemporary Iranian thinkers as well. The first was the aforementioned Mr. Motahhari. The first work of Motahhari that I read was his annotated interpretation of the late Mr. Tabataba'i's *The Principles of Philosophy and the Method of Realism.*[2] This book made a profound impression on me. I can even say that reading this book instilled some kind of a philosophical hubris in me. I took this book as evidence of the indisputable superiority of the Islamic philosophy. I went around believing that "the entire world is under our wings"[3] and that we can fend off any criticism and philosophical argument.

SADRI: I share this experience. I, too, remember the great exuberance that this work provoked in our minds.

SOROUSH: True [laughing], I don't know why. I was approximately twenty-one years old when I read this book. It made me feel that all the conundrums of the world have either yielded their secrets or they will upon the slightest inquiry. This book was, in a sense, my first introduction to Western philosophy as well, for until then I had not attempted a systematic and academic survey of this field. Later I read other works by Mr. Motahhari, but nothing ever rivaled the pure joy I felt from this first reading. Also, I studied the works of one of Motahhari's mentors, the late Mr. Tabataba'i, who was completing his magnum opus, *Al-Mizan*, a comprehensive exegesis of the Qur'an. During these years I systematically and exhaustively studied several interpretations of the Qur'an, both from the Shi'ite and Sunni perspectives. I am still grateful for this experience as most of my interpretive understanding of the Qur'an belongs to this period. Although I had no interpretive theory of my own, I managed to gain a fair knowledge of the interpretive positions of the Islamic scholars. What fascinated me most was the details and intricacies of the differences in interpretation. This is the same point that later on made me reflect on

6   *Reason, Freedom, & Democracy in Islam*

the mystery of the differences of opinion in the exegesis of religious texts. I can assert this sensibility constituted one of the bases of my thesis of contraction and expansion of religious knowledge in which I tried to answer the question why different interpreters disagree on the meaning of a given text.

SADRI: I detect an interesting parallel here. The idea of the meaning of various interpretations of a text occurred to you as you were studying different exegeses of the Qur'an. The hermeneutic theory in the West, too, is traceable to various interpretations of the bible. It looks like, even before coming into contact with the Western hermeneutics, you had independently arrived at a parallel position, that is, the question what causes different interpretations of a sacred text and what are the conditions for arriving at an authentic interpretation of it.

SOROUSH: This may very well be the case. I have always been interested in the nature of exegeses; not only of the Qur'an but of works of Hafez and Rumi. These three texts led me to the art of textual interpretation. What you said is entirely accurate, though. My first attempts at interpretation concerned the Qur'an and an important Sufi text, *Mathnavi*. Later on, when I combined these insights with my knowledge of the philosophy of science and philosophy of history, I arrived at a relatively comprehensive hermeneutical theory. To tell you the truth, up to the time that I composed the thesis of contraction and expansion I had not studied the hermeneutical theories of scholars such as Hans-Georg Gadamer. Indeed, I was struck by the affinity of my positions and those of Gadamer.

Historians, too, disagree on the interpretation of one historical event. So they grapple with similar issues: Why are there different interpretations of history? Is it possible to write an "ultimate" history of an event? And so on. If we combine these questions and those of textural hermeneutics, we would arrive at the intent of my thesis of contraction and expansion that proposes the fundamental openness of a text or an event to a multitude of interpretations and a plurality of readings.

The second great thinker whose ideas impressed me was the late Mehdi Bazargan. I knew him as a politician and a modern scientist with intense religious interests, but I had scant knowledge of his writings until I studied them as a university student. I remember that Bazargan's book entitled *The Infinity of the Infinitely Small*[4] had such an attraction for me that as a chemistry teacher I gave away many copies of it to my best students.

The rise of the late Dr. Shari'ati and his blockbuster lectures at the Hosseiniyyeh-e Ershad coincided with my graduation from the University of Tehran and my conscription for two year of military service. During this time I tried to attend as many of Shari'ati's lectures as possible. This continued until the Hosseiniyyeh-e was shut down by the government. After my military service I served in the southern town of Boushehr for a period of fifteen months as a supervisor in a laboratory for food and drug products. Then I returned to Tehran and engaged in pharmaceutical research for a few months while preparing to leave for England for postgraduate work.

As I have mentioned in the introduction to one of my books, I took four books along on this trip. Mulla Sadra's *Asfar al-arba'eh*, Feiz Kashani's *Mahajat al-beiza'*, Hafez's *Divan*, a compendium of his poetry, and Rumi's *Mathnavi*. This selection illustrated the major influences on my thought at the time. I forgot to mention this but during my university years I discovered Kashani's *Mahajat al-beiza'*, which is a Shi'ite restatement of Al-Ghazzali's *Ihya' al-'ulum*. This book was readily available to me in the high school's library. I came into the possession of this eight-volume set rather fortuitously. I once delivered a speech in Masjid al-Javad, a rather progressive congregation in north-central Tehran. I was then asked to name a book I would like to receive as a token of the congregation's appreciation, and I named this book. And ever since, I have never parted company with this book. It was through this book that I was exposed to the ideas of Imam Mohammad al-Ghazzali. Before this, I had only heard Al-Ghazzali's name, but I had no knowledge of his *Ihya' al-'ulum*, his *Kimiya-ye sa'adat*, or his other works. Through this work and later on, through Al-Ghazzali's own writings, I was introduced to his work more closely and seriously.

I spent a year in England working toward a postgraduate degree in analytical chemistry. Then I entered the field of philosophy and history of science. This transition marked a watershed in my intellectual carrier. My philosophical training in Iran had seldom dealt with the specific issues of modern science, such as atomic theory or the nature of induction, which clearly illustrate the rift between modern science and the Aristotelian science. Neither I nor my Iranian philosophy professors were in a position to address these problems. But the questions continued to preoccupy me. I had always wondered if there was a discipline that dealt with such questions. In England, I went to the psychology department, explained my interests, and was told to inquire at the department of philosophy of science. I had never heard of the discipline before. I immediately matriculated and found what I had been missing. Philosophy of science deals with the foundations of modern science. Our curriculum included epistemology, classical philosophy, and modern philosophy. Prior to this, I had heard of Kant, Hume, and so on and had encountered some of their opinions in the philosophical texts such as those of Motahhari and Tabataba'i. Now I realized that those treatment were, shall we say, insufficient. Philosophers like Hume and Kant were not only great thinkers in their own right, but they put their stamp on philosophies that emerged centuries later as well. Linguistic philosophy and logical positivism, for example, are based on the philosophies of Kant, Hume, and others.

The issues that the philosophy of science considers—whether science is an accumulative process or value-free, whether people's prejudgments and worldviews affect the course of science, and so on—can be viewed from the perspective of the history of science as well. This discipline explores the development and interaction of scientific ideas in such diverse disciplines as history, physics, chemistry, biology, and astronomy. The first philosopher of science I encountered was Karl Popper, who was by then retired but his students were quite influential. Professor Post of Chelsea College, who taught philosophy of science, was a close friend of Karl Popper's and an eloquent interpreter of his philosophy. The year 1974, the year I started my studies in the philosophy of science, coincided with the wider acceptance of the ideas of Thomas Kuhn as well.

SADRI: You mean Kuhn's *The Structure of Scientific Revolutions*? Was that not published a few years earlier?[5]

SOROUSH: Yes, but his book apparently did not find wide circulation until later, especially in England. I remember that the ideas of Karl Popper, Paul Feyerabend, and Imre Lakatos (whose death coincided with the first year of my studies) dominated class discussions. Among the earlier philosophers, the ideas of Pierre Duhem, who had greatly influenced Imre Lakatos, too, were discussed. Later I moved on to more contemporary philosophers. But those were extracurricular readings. Not only in the philosophy of science but also in mathematics. We were introduced to modern epistemology and logic. For instance, we studied the theories of Church and Gödel.

SADRI: How about symbolic logic? I understand that was quite popular in those years.

SOROUSH: I was exposed to mathematical logic, which was one of the main components of my education. I had to pass an examination on it before I could enter the research phase of my studies. Mathematical logic was a completely new discipline for me as well. Set theory had gradually found its way to Iranian universities, but it was mostly taught in mathematical and technical schools, and its philosophical implications remained implicit.

I did not limit myself to the philosophy of natural science, though. My specialization in University of London was in the philosophy of science, and a prerequisite of the postgraduate program in this field was an advanced degree in one of the natural sciences. I was a chemist, and my classmates were mathematicians, physicians, biologists. They came not only from disparate disciplines but also from different parts of the world. I tried to explore other avenues by applying the ideas of the philosophy of natural sciences to other areas of human knowledge. For instance, I conducted a relatively detailed survey of the philosophy of history, which I consider one of the branches of the philosophy of science. I found that most of the issues that were discussed in philosophy of science were applicable to the philosophy of history. Then I gradually explored the philosophy of social sciences and the philosophy of religion. This latter interest, however, bloomed somewhat later. Philosophy of science was a true revelation for me. It opened up new horizons and marked a significant turning point in my intellectual development. It made me question, review, and revise my previous understanding of the Aristotelian philosophy and metaphysics. I like to think of my time in England as "the period of constant contemplation." I ate, drank, slept, and walked philosophy. I was bombarded by challenging questions and stimulating insights. I was constantly at work sifting, revising, synthesizing, reconciling, and distinguishing different components of my education and knowledge. Particularly, I was grappling with the questions of the relationship between science and philosophy, that is, science and metaphysics. No single waking minute would pass, whether walking, riding on the subway, sitting at home, or working in the library, unless I was struggling with some serious and grand problem.

SADRI: Would you characterize this period more as a distressful and critical period or an exciting and exhilarating one?

SOROUSH: It was both exciting and stormy. My mind was in constant turmoil. It was also exhilarating because I felt I was making great progress achieving significant breakthroughs in my thought. I distinctly felt the advance; things were gradually falling into place. This left me at once invigorated and frustrated.

During this period, in addition to my academic duties, I was involved in two more activities. The first one was revisiting the works of Rumi. This was a critical period. Rumi had lost most of its freshness and luster for me. I was beginning to question his approach. It had become difficult for me to feel any harmony and congeniality with him. Our paths seemed to be diverging. I started to reread Rumi, but I had many questions, and it had become difficult for me to enter his world. I often would find his arguments strange, unpalatable, or incredible. But I kept struggling to reconcile the new knowledge with the old sensibilities. My other involvement had to do with developments in Iran, where the political struggle was intensifying. Hosseiniyyeh-ye Ershad had been shut down by the government, Shari'ati was under arrest, the political prisoners were on the rise, and the shah's regime was openly clashing with the demonstrators. The news of these developments reached us in continuous waves.

In the meantime, Shariʿati's books had become the fulcrum of education in the ever-expanding Islamic student associations.

SADRI: What period was this?

SOROUSH: This was around 1973 and 1974. I participated in some of these meetings. I learned from and admired the works of the late Shariʿati, but I felt they needed to be substantially fleshed out and supplemented before they could become comprehensive educational texts. Some people who were more radical, or at least more vociferous in opposition to the regime of the shah, expressed their affiliation with the Islamic guerrilla group in Iran: Mojahedin. Therefore, in some of these meetings one of the major pamphlet of this group entitled: *Shenakht* (Epistemology) was distributed. I found it rather superficial and propagandistic. My criticism of it led to a criticism of the Marxist ideology as it was introduced in Iran.[6]

As time passed, around 1977, I laid the foundation of a series of books that I completed while I was still in England. The first book in this series was entitled *What is Science, What is Philosophy?*, followed by *Philosophy of History*. My lecture series "Critical Observations on Dialectical Opposition" was later published and received with great enthusiasm in Iran. Also, the books entitled: *Science and Value* and *The Dynamic Nature of the Universe* were written in this period. The latter was my last publication on traditional metaphysics. It was, thank God, a successful undertaking. Great scholars in the field—Tabatabaʾi, Motahhari, even Khomeini—read and praised the book. In that book, I had attempted to synthesize Mulla Sadra's theory of movement in essence, in a lucid and understandable manner, with some of the insights of the modern philosophers. This was my last dialogue with Mulla Sadra. I have not terminated this meditation, but I have not revisited his work in recent years either. Of course, our paths diverged. I have found thinking along those lines increasingly difficult and cumbersome. Consequently, I turned to other methods of thought. Particularly, the historical approach. Naturally, when Iran's Islamic Revolution gained momentum, I reflected on the relationship between the revolution and religious thought while preparing to return to Iran. My return opened a new chapter in my life, as novel issues and challenges emerged on the horizon.

SADRI: What year was this?

SOROUSH: Let me see, in September 1979, a few month after the revolution, I returned to Iran. I was appointed the chair of the department of Islamic culture in Tehran's Teachers' College. After the closing of the universities, I became a member of the Advisory Council on the Cultural

Revolution where I stayed for four years. Later, I resigned from Teacher's College and became a member of the Academy of Philosophy and, finally, the Research Center for Humanities and Social Sciences, a position I still retain.[7]

But before getting further along let me clarify an important point. In the Advisory Council on Cultural Revolution our main task was reopening the universities. This is a point that is unknown to many people. Universities had been closed for political reasons. It was after this event that the council was appointed by Mr. Khomeini, who was the political leader of the government at the time. This council was composed of seven people and its mandate was to revise the curriculum and to lay down the procedures for reopening universities with the help of the professors who had been released from their routine duties. There were close to one thousand professors who were cooperating with us in different committees of the council. Others joined the Center for Academic Publications. They composed articles, books, translations, and curricula for universities and colleges. The committee, then, was charged with reopening universities, not with closing them, as some have charged. I stayed in the council for four years. I resigned as soon as it turned into the headquarters of the cultural revolution. I no longer saw a role for myself there. The council eventually succeeded in reopening the universities after a year and a half. And I went back to teaching. When I returned to Iran, my first lecture series—"In What Kind of a World Do We Live"—was broadcast from the radio. It later appeared as a book. This period coincided with the postrevolutionary turbulence that verged on political and ideological chaos. These conditions continued for a couple of years until the government gradually reasserted its control.

In this period of unlimited political and ideological freedom, people like me were constantly bombarded with inquiries and requests to engage in ideological duels. I accepted some of these challenges in order to clarify my positions to myself and others. For this reason, I consider my entire eighteen years of postrevolutionary thought as a period of unabated intellectual struggle. Throughout this period I attempted to clarify both my own relationship to religion and religiosity and the relationship of religion to social institutions. In this period, I started to teach philosophy of natural and social sciences. I included the philosophies of Winch, Habermas, and Hayek as well as those of Motahhari, Ibn Khaldoun, and others. I also taught Hegel, Herder, and Marx in the context of the philosophy of history. I have not had a chance to edit and publish my notes on this subject matter yet.

Another important subject that I explored was modern theology (kalam-e jadid). I dealt with the relationship between humanity, science, and religion. I initiated this lecture series at the divinity school of the University of Tehran. The need for a new understanding of religion drew many students to these lectures. Modern theology forced me to expand my horizons. Through these studies and reflections, I gradually ordered my thoughts.

Of the works that I regularly recommended to my students was Arthur Koestler's *Sleepwalkers*. This book had already been translated, but few actually appreciated it. Koestler, a brilliant journalist, had a secret love of religion. The book brims with wistful longing for religiosity, something he was incapable of feeling because of his Marxist upbringing. It includes excerpts from the correspondences between Galileo, Copernicus, Kepler, and others with the ecclesiastic authorities. Through studying and teaching these materials, I gradually prepared myself to tackle the problem of the conflict between religion and science in particular and the nature of religious understanding in general. I gradually gravitated toward the notions of game and competition. It is conceivable that I had taken this from both Wittgenstein and Kuhn, but in those days I was unaware of this possibility. The main idea was that the world of ideas and opinions constitutes a game, and it is the very nature of this game, rather than its outcome, that is valuable. Competition, cooperation, dialogues, and bickering among scientists advance the procession, the process of science. Therefore, although scientists seek to develop their own theories and advance their own careers, they carry science on their collective shoulders, like an independent entity. I later found that Popper, too, had come close to this approach in his three-worlds theory. This insight led me to distinguish science as a system of ideas from science as a collective and objective activity. Observing scientific debates convinced me that the world of ideas is a world of dialogue. A scientist is engaged in a dialogue even in the solitude of his contemplation. In the first years of the revolution, social sciences and humanities were under attack for being "impure" and "Western" or else insignificant and worthless. I published a series of sixteen articles in their defense. These disciplines stood accused of being responsible for the corruption of the youths and secularization of the new generation. Social sciences and humanities were considered products of corrupting Western thought and as such in need of deep cleansing or else complete purging from the universities. But I thought that the future of the country depended on people who were trained in these disciplines. These persecuted sciences needed a gallant defense. My main effort was to establish that social sciences and humanities are as important and valuable as the natural sciences. These sciences had been considered the repository of what has been dubbed "the cultural invasion of the West." In those discussions I alluded to the competitive nature of science and knowledge. My next step was to generalize this concept to religiosity. Thus I entered the domain of the philosophy of religion, armed with an understanding of the philosophy of science.

In addition to modern theology, philosophy of ethics, philosophy of history, and philosophy of experimental sciences, I started a lecture series on Rumi's *Mathnavi* at the divinity school of the University of Tehran.

This was at once a favorite subject of mine and a popular course with the students. I had the good fortune, thank God, to discuss two books of *Mathnavi*, that is, about eight thousand lines of poetry in eight consecutive semesters. I supplemented that with three more semesters at another university. These lectures were some of the most enjoyable parts of my work. I would teach these topics in a state of rapture. I felt this in my other lessons as well. I never chose a topic to teach unless I was most interested in it myself. During the teaching of these topics, I learned more than the students, because I worked harder than they did.

Let me recount the four preliminary conditions for my interest in the philosophy of religion: the first one was my self-taught knowledge of the exegeses of the Qur’an. As I mentioned before, these studies motivated me to question why various scholars arrive at different interpretations of the sacred text. Why is it, for example, that the same verse yields different interpretations at the hands of Muʿtazilite and Ashʿarite exegetes, without ever leading to a lucid and plausible solution or synthesis. The second element was my familiarity with the works of mystics and politicians. The former argued that the world is an impermanent domain to be abandoned in favor of an inner journey. Religion was understood as the methodology of such a journey. In other words, they considered the affairs of the world and those of religion as mutually exclusive. On the other hand, I witnessed the activities of politically motivated thinkers and activists who favored extracting their political doctrines from religion. Not only groups such as the Mojahedin but also individuals such as Mehdi Bazargan and ʿAli Shariʿati belonged to this category. Both the world-flight ideology of the Sufis and world-domination ideology of the politicians were extracted from the Qur’an. Bazargan and Shariʿati were particularly struck by what they saw as the Moslem abandonment of the worldly aspects of religion and the abdication of the political and social struggle. Thus they proposed a new understanding of religiosity that embraced these aspects. I was more interested in their theoretical positions than their practical and political proposals. I was trying to understand and analyze the new concepts they were using. I wondered why a certain class of interpretations of religious texts rise in a particular time and not in others. My early encounter with the so-called scientific interpretations of religion also contributed to my interest in the philosophy of religion. Finally, my understanding of the nature of science as a competitive and collective process and my subsequent application of this view of scientific knowledge to religious knowledge contributed to my interest in the philosophy of religion. Around this time, I was meeting, on a daily and later a weekly basis, with about ten colleagues who were mostly university professors. It was in one of those sessions that I first formulated twenty theses on the nature of religion and shared them with my friends. Some of these were still in embryonic form, but they gradually evolved into a philosophy of religion that emerged as my contraction and expansion thesis.

SADRI: Do you have a copy of it somewhere? I think it would be of utmost importance in retracing the evolution of your thought. By the way, do you remember any of it, offhand?

SOROUSH: I still have a copy of these twenty or so theses. I do not remember all of them to recite for you. I remember the first thesis went roughly something like this: Religiosity is people's understanding of religion just as science is their understanding of nature. This was the first step in separating religion from religious knowledge and you are right about the significance of those theses. The ideas that were first formulated in that document grew, branched out, and developed into different aspects of my present thesis. At any rate, my philosophical understanding of scientific knowledge as a collective and competitive process and my subsequent generalization of this understanding to religious knowledge opened new gates for me. Henceforth, I cast religion as a kind of human knowledge subject to the collectivity and competitiveness of the human soul. I remained mindful of the confrontations of the church with the early scientists and the disparate interpretations of religion by our philosophers, revivalists, mystics, and politicians. Thus I concentrated on the question of whether religious knowledge is susceptible to some kind of an evolution or, at any rate, change. We know that it is not for the faithful to decide whether religion, as such, evolves, particularly because we Moslems believe that Islam is the final religion. Besides, Moslems would never pretend to be *shari'*, or religious lawgivers. So change in religion itself is out of the question. But, at the same time, change is undeniable and should be recognized and explained. In this context, I applied the insights that I had gained from the philosophy of science that all phenomena, to paraphrase philosophers of science, are theory laden, that we view the world through theoretical lenses, and thus there is no such thing as a naked event or a brute fact. When we dislike one interpretation of an event, we inevitably replace it with another.

By the way, contrary to popular belief, it was not Popper's but Quine's theories on the philosophy of science that guided my explorations of the philosophy of religion. And I reveal it here for the first time. Quine is a philosopher of logic who is still alive and is the focus of much critical attention. His theory is that all science is interconnected and, as such, judged as a whole, not as a collection of individual discrete theories, in the tribunal of senses. This is the opposite of Popper's thought. Popper, in essence, believes in individual theories appearing, one by one, in the court of experimentation to be assessed by the principle of falsifiability. It was Lakatos who, with the help of Quine's ideas, developed the notion of "research programs" in science: a whole family of theories, organized in a research program, enter judgment's court. In my book *Contraction and Expansion of Religious Knowledge*, I have based one of my main arguments on this thesis. Again, when I was writing that book I was unaware that I was under the influence of Duhem and Quine's theory; only in retrospect did I perceive this connection. In any case, these were some of the preambles of my thesis of contraction and expansion, which I first taught in classes and then published as articles that were later compiled as a book. This thesis poses the question whether there is such a thing as religious knowledge with a collective nature; my answer is affirmative. The contention is, then, that this form of knowledge is, like other forms of knowledge, subject to all the attributes of knowledge. It is human, fallible, evolving, and most important of all, it is constantly in the process of exchange with other forms of knowledge. As such, its inevitable transformations mirror the transformation of science and other domains of human knowledge.

SADRI: Let me interrupt you here to ask if you remember in what year you formulated these twenty theses?

SOROUSH: It must have been around 1982 or 1983. I must still have it somewhere, and since I date all my notes, the exact date should be there. Afterward, I gradually incorporated these ideas into my courses, particularly in modern theology (*kalam*) which, as you know, deals with skeptical attacks and religious counterattacks. For instance, Marxian or Freudian premises and other ideas that emanate from the humanities and social sciences spearhead attacks on theology. This leads to a renewal of theology as it grapples with new questions and ineluctably modernizes its logical arsenal with the help of the disciplines it debates. Thus modern theology, by its very nature, is in constant renewal, a process that highlights the relationship of modern theology to other sciences as well. Their interaction resembles the craft of a locksmith who builds both keys and latches. Modern linguistics, for example, can create new problems for religion; take the question of whether religious propositions can be meaningful or not. Theologians who try to address this question of will inevitably familiarize themselves with the principles of modern philosophy. These were the step-by-step realizations that led me to the statement I quoted earlier: religion is people's understanding of divinity just as science is people's understanding of nature.

It sounds rather obvious now, but it was not so evident at the beginning. At that time it seemed farfetched to argue that religious knowledge is a variety of human knowledge, subject to change, exchange, contraction, and expansion. Once we look at the scene from above, that is, from a second-order vantage point, we will see believers with a variety of ideas, but religious knowledge as a whole would appear as a mixture of right, wrong, old, and new that floats on like a vast river. I went on articulating different aspects of these arguments in my divinity school lectures. Here again I can reveal, for the first time, that I had a colleague who was also interested in these issues. He would make appointments with me, and I would discuss certain aspect of these arguments with him. After a while he told me that my ideas were great, but that they were extremely dangerous. He reminded me of the fate of 'Abdol Razziq of Egypt (who wrote about the relationship of religion and state and whose house was set on fire). However, this same individual went ahead and published the arguments that I had shared with him under his own name.[8] This led me to expedite the publication of these articles. The first edition of the book created a wave of criticism that I included in later editions of these writings.

My continuing contemplation of Rumi made me gradually better acquainted with Sufism. The more I thought about the difference between Al-Ghazzali and Rumi, the more interested I became in the subject. For a while, Al-Ghazzali dominated my mind and soul. Truly, had it not been for Rumi, perhaps no one could have freed me from Al-Ghazzali's charm. In Al-Ghazzali, I witnessed the fear-based mysticism in its most detailed and eloquent form; in Rumi, I found love-based mysticism; in Hafez the pleasure-based mysticism (or maybe no mysticism at all). And I could not find, most unfortunately, a power-based or epic mysticism. This is what I think is lacking in our culture and literature.

Gradually I realized that these are different understandings of religiosity and divinity. Rumi, too, before reaching love-based mysticism and becoming the Rumi we know, had attained fear-based mysticism. He taught me a new kind of religiosity, and through him I discovered a wealth of insights into the nature of humanity, religion, and God that I would not have been able to glean from any other source. As I gained these insights, I discussed them with my students, and I thought they were quite moved. My first and foremost attempt to understand the essence of religion originates in the works of Rumi. Just as my inquiries of the religious canon was anchored in the works of Al-Ghazzali. Thus I learned the place of ritual and legal religiosity (fiq'h) in the context of religion as a whole. I ultimately realized that there is such a thing as an individual religion based on personal experiences, whose teacher is Rumi; just as there is such a thing as a collective religion which is what shari'ah and fiq'h teach and which is Al-Ghazzali's domain. I have other unpublished reflections on the nature of fiq'h and its uneasy relationship with the esoteric dimension of religion. These scattered reflections, published in a number of places, eventually found their way into books on Al-Ghazzali, Rumi, Hafez, and Shari'ati, which I titled *The Story of the Lords of Wisdom*. I envision other volumes in this series devoted to Sa'di, Ibn Khaldoun, and others.

The collective characteristic of religion and the strength of its influence on social life became more obvious to me after the revolution. This led me to further interrogate the thought of the late Dr. Shari'ati and his ideologization of religion, which I contrasted to the pluralism that was a requirement as well as an outcome of the thesis of contraction and expansion. As a result, I arrived at the conclusion that ideologization of religion binds it to a single interpretation and generates a class of "official" interpreters; a conclusion inimical both to Shari'ati's intent and to my own thesis of contraction and expansion. I have explicated this in my book *Loftier Than Ideology*. I will return to this issue later, but first let me mention some scattered ideas I have developed over the past few years.

My work on the philosophy of ethics culminated in the book *Fact and Value* whose argument is based on a Humean hint concerning the derivation of ought from is. Later on I expanded it with reference to the philosophies of early Mu'tazilites and Ash'arites and some contemporaries such as the late Tabataba'i. They remain unpublished. On pure metaphysics, one of my main interests, I have taught a few courses on such significant themes as causality and universals. An example of my contemplations on this subject emerges in my essay "The Sense and Essence of Secularism" [in this volume], in which I argue that secularism has an affinity with nominalism, that is, the philosophy that denies the existence of the universals. I believe that secularism is a subtle notion that can not be summarized in the principle of the separation of church and state. It has deeper philosophical implications. I have even discovered that the conflict between the mystics and Greek-influenced peripatetic philosophers in the Islamic world may have originated in this debate.

In my early years of return to Iran, I published *Masked Dogmatism* and *The World We Live*, a compilation of a few articles, including a long essay on the position of the social sciences. I also completed a number of translations. One of my favorite works in this area is my translation of Arthur Burts's *Metaphysical Foundations of Modern Science*. It is a neoclassical work written in the 1930s, but it is still accorded great significance in the philosophy and history of science. It contains a profound, eloquent, and readable analysis of the subject matter. I have added a comprehensive introduction to the book, updating it as much as possible. I translated and published another volume on the philosophy of natural sciences and two essays on the philosophy of social sciences, whose authors are Alan Rayan and Daniel Little. Along with these, I published another compilation of articles whose main contribution was the thesis of the theoretical contraction and expansion of *shari'ah*.

Recently I have had the good fortune to deliver a series of weekly lessons in a couple of the mosques over a period of six years. This was an auspicious opportunity, and I thank God for it. During these sessions, whose main audience were students, I discussed religious matters of the first order—for example, the addresses entitled "The Secret of the Success of the Prophets" and "An Exegesis of ʿAli's Address to the Virtuous from the *Nahj al-balaqeh*," which has been published and has gone through several editions. I also gave a series of talks on "The Last Testament of the Commander of the Faithful ʿAli to His Son Imam Hassan." This will soon be published and will appear in four volumes, two of which are already out. Occasionally, I have spoken about issues relating to religious occasions such as the birthday of the Prophet Mohammad or one of the Shiʿite Imams. Some of these have recently appeared in book form under the title *Story of Servitude and Love*. My last work on political philosophy, *Tolerance and Governance*, is a two-volume work that is still under review in the Ministry of Guidance. I hope that it will see the light of day after requisite editorial changes and necessary compromises. Unfortunately, this book, because of the nature of the issues it addresses has encountered difficulties in the censor's office. The censors have demanded not only that we eliminate some of the articles but also that we submit the manuscript to a reviewer of their choice to append his critical remarks. This is an unpalatable and outrageously intolerable condition, but we may have to submit to it. My articles on the *rouhaniyyat* [the clergy] were supposed to be published in that book. This book was cleared for publication by the ministry of Islamic Guidance only after a "critique" by a well-known religious fascist was imposed on the publisher as an appendix to the book. These are two articles that have created great uproar, as you know. They were originally published in *Kiyan*.

SADRI: I believe one of them is published in this volume. Is it not entitled "What the University Expects from the Hawzeh"?

SOROUSH: No, that is a different article. The articles that actually created the uproar were "Gallantry and the Clergy" and "The Roof of Livelihood on the Pillar of Religion." The article that is part of the present book was the text of a lecture delivered and published before those two. That too provoked opposition, criticism, and acrimony but not as much as the latter ones. I wrote these articles because I realized that there was a gap in my writings concerning the role of the carriers and bearers of religion—the *rouhaniyyat*, or clergy. That is why in the first of these two articles, I have stated that the clergy are not defined by their erudition or their virtue but by their dependency on religion for their livelihood. This thesis did not sit well with the clergy and was vigorously attacked. Let me add that after I published those articles on contraction and expansion in *Keyhan Farhangi*, a fascistic group took over some cultural institutions, including certain newspapers, and put an end to that journal. But fortunately some of the managers of that journal launched another one, *Kiyan*, where I continued to publish my work, even some of my poetry. The journal has met with critical acclaim and wide readership. This venue allowed me to keep up my relationship with a vast stratum of students and intellectuals throughout Iran. Their letters, phone calls, and comments are the source of great delight for me.

I also have had the good fortune to teach a group of seminary students in Qum for a period of two years. My lectures there dealt mainly with modern theology and philosophy of religion. I am delighted that these lectures are still popular, although I no longer have the opportunity and, to put it bluntly, the permission to teach in Qum. This gate, like many others, has been closed to me. However, the discussion of philosophy of religion has blossomed in the Qum seminary, and right now two or three journals are published in this area whose managers and contributors are my former students. They would not mention my name and they are not allowed to publish my works, but they pursue my ideas on the philosophy of religion, which has found many enthusiasts. A number of students have been sent from Qum to the universities around the world to study in these areas. In any event, this issue has caught the attention of the students, even professors of the Qum seminary. I find this a positive development and hope it will continue.

SADRI: Thank you for this comprehensive account. You are aware of the attempts to place you in the context of sociopolitical developments of the Islamic world. Some have even gone so far as calling you "the Luther of Islam." The idea of differentiation of spheres of life—science, religion, politics, and so on—that is the hallmark of your thought may be interpreted as a report of a colossal change in the Islamic world after a hundred years of grappling with modernity. I mean, is it fair to say that your thought grasps, in theory, what the Islamic world in general and the Iranian people in particular have experienced in the last century or so? I am invoking Hegel's allegory of the "owl of Minerva" where ideas do not precede but follow the unfolding of the reality they describe. Let me ask you, then, a two-pronged question: How do you assess the impact of the Islamic revivalism in general, and the Islamic revolution of Iran in particular, on your thought; and what affinities do you perceive between your philosophy and the ideas of other Islamic reformists and revivalists?

SOROUSH: I may not be the best person to comment on all aspects of this question, but I will state a couple of points that occur to me and leave the judgment to you. First, I have always been interested in theoretical issues. I find them engaging and rewarding. However, after the Islamic Revolution, I became interested in practical matters as well. Because I clearly realized that those who led our revolution had not thought beyond the downfall of the tyrannical regime of the shah. Thus they had no appreciation of such issues as global economy, modernity, information-driven administration, and so on. They sincerely believed that if only the rulers were just and well-meaning, society would follow its "natural" course. In the meantime, grandiose claims had been launched without a realistic method of achieving them. We had little more than enticing slogans to offer. The founders and rulers of the revolution were, and still are, mostly professional orators. To many of them success means delivering an impressive sermon, attending an elaborate ceremony, and so on. Needless to say, this does not contribute to substantive progress. Thus it was that I noticed the need not only for theoretical groundwork but also for practical problem solving.

The second point is that I always follow a single motto. It is rather easy to state but hard to practice. I believe that truths everywhere are compatible; no truth clashes with any other truth. They are all the inhabitants of the same mansion and stars of the same constellation. One truth in one corner of the world has to be harmonious and compatible with all truths elsewhere, or else it is not a truth. That is why I have never tired of my search for truth in other arenas of intellect and opinion. This truthfulness of the world is a blessing indeed, because it instigates constant search and engenders a healthy pluralism. Constantly prompted to wonder whether one's truth is a complete and comprehensive truth, one scrutinizes it thoroughly and compares it with other kinds of truth, for the condition of a principle's truthfulness is its harmony with other truths. Thus, in my search for the truth, I became oblivious to whether an idea originated in the East or West, or whether it had ancient or modern origins. Obviously, we don't possess all of the truths, and we need other places and people to help unfold different aspects of it. The Islamic Revolution created the impulse in my mind to try and gather others' truths and our truths under the same umbrella and to solve the theoretical and practical problems we were and still are confronting. My thesis of contraction and expansion indicated that for religious texts, we need other kinds of knowledge if our understanding is not to stagnate.

Third, since the Islamic Revolution of Iran was based on religious claims, I became increasingly interested in the question of the true place of religion in society. A while back someone asked me about the difference between my project and that of the late Shariʿati. I replied, without intending to draw a full comparison, "Shariʿati wanted to make religion plumper, but I want to make it leaner." The greatest pathology of religion that I have noticed after the revolution is that it has become plump, even swollen. Many claims have been made in the name of religion and many burdens are put on its shoulders. It is neither possible nor desirable for religion, given its ultimate mission, to carry such a burden. This means purifying religion, making it lighter and more buoyant, in other words, rendering religion more slender by sifting, whittling away, erasing the superfluous layers off the face of religiosity.

Every system has its own weaknesses. A religious society, too, has its own peculiar problems. One of those problems is hypocrisy. The other is ideologization of religion, which means turning it to an instrument of fanaticism and hatred. I have always stated that unity could be achieved as much through kindness as through hatred. Ideology attains this objective through hatred. These, in my view, are the plagues of the religious thought that will become epidemic if they are neglected. These problems are readily identifiable in our nascent religious society, yet our leaders are not only complacent, they unconsciously or otherwise propagate them. We confront reliance on a single source for all of society's need, in this case, the belief that all our needs can be met in the Qur'an and religious traditions; there is excessive emphasis on ritual and the legal aspects of religion (*fiq'h*) a stress on its outward manifestations. These were among the things that commanded my attention after the Islamic Revolution. I even attempted to alert the leaders of our society to the danger inherent in such a situation. Alas, our clerical leaders did not pay sufficient attention to these issues. They treated these criticisms as signs of opposition to the regime and their own power and resisted them.

These prompted me to enter the arena of social criticism. In my attempt to fight the obesity of religion, I engaged in a number of projects, including putting *fiq'h* in its properly restricted place, separating the fundamental from the tangential and accidental in religion, and distinguishing religion as an individual experience from religion as a collective institution. In all these distinctions I have tried to establish the nature and social position of religion and the nature of our relationship to God. Above all, I have tried to paint a kinder portrait of God's role in society, so that the revolutionaries can enter peaceful coexistence with him and with one another. Thus I have tried to ameliorate hatred, which some have considered the truth of religiosity. Some people in our society, under Stalinist and fascist influences, have come to believe that the essence of religion is enmity, excommunication, and punishment. They need to be admonished. I have observed that if we can reconcile Islam with revolution, why not reconcile it with human rights, democracy, and liberty? After all, revolution is an extrareligious concept as well. The reason is that our clergy are unfamiliar with these concepts, and their training has not prepared them to appreciate those traits. I have, therefore, attempted to explain that extrareligious ideas are authentic and autonomously significant and that they even affect the understanding of religion itself. Human rights is one of these important extrareligious concepts, as I have argued in one of the articles in this collection. Although this discussion needs to be settled outside religion, it has a profound influence on one's understanding of religion.

I can attribute the development of all of these ideas to the advent of the Islamic Revolution of Iran, the spread of a religious way of life and thought in our society, and the claim of our government to being Islamic. One of the discussions to which I have been very sensitive has been the idea of Islamic state and Islamic government. There is no question that clerical government is meaningless and therefore I have not even discussed it, except in my essay "Liberty and the Clergy," where I have argued that no clergy, qua clergy, should have worldly privileges, whether political or economic, over other citizens. I have also written on the meaning of religious government. All of these were results of the revolution and events in Iran. They made me think, and I tried to provide theoretical foundations for them. *why?*

I repeat, the Islamic government in our society is, unfortunately, a government without theory and doctrine. Thus in the areas of economy, politics, human rights, and international affairs, it acts in a haphazard and reactive way. It has built no foundations and principles from which to act meaningfully. Nor does it have time to do so. Even Mr. Khomeini's later edicts and pronouncements on *fiq'h* were occasioned by immediate practical concerns. He never found the time to provide theoretical foundations for them. I think we need to build theoretical foundations. If my ideas have met with some success, it is because I address and trace such issues in a theoretically impoverished environment. *if it had these, it'd be fine?*

SADRI: How about the question of the affinities between your thought and that of other revivalist and reformists? Do you think you have addressed this question adequately?

SOROUSH: Well, I might have alluded to some of these influences. And there are issues of comparison and contrast that are best left to others to develop. Of course, I can say that I have paid attention to thinkers who have harbored reformist ideas, such as Mohammad Abdoh, Seid Jamal Asad Abadi, Al-Ghazzali, Shah Valiollah Dehlavi, and other reformists and revivalists, including Mr. Khomeini. I have scrutinized their theories to find their different foci and strategies of problem solving.

SADRI: This brings us to the last question: How do you view the future of the Moslems' intellectual and social life—in other words, what major and essential problems do you find in the path of the next two or three generations of Moslems?

SOROUSH: This is a huge problem, and I am not sure if I can do justice to it. The theoretical vacuum which I bemoaned in the case of Iran stretches throughout the Islamic world. Let me point out that in one of my unpublished essays, I have distinguished between two kinds of Islam: Islam of identity and Islam of truth. In the former Islam is a guise for cultural identity and a response to what is considered the "crisis of identity." The latter refers to Islam as a repository of truths that point toward the path of worldly and otherworldly salvation. The Prophet of Islam is thus recognized as the messenger of those truths. The Prophet and other divine messengers originally invited people to a series of truths pointing toward salvation. As people accepted those truths and the religious disciplines that contained them, they gradually developed identities and built civilizations. Developing an identity or a civilization was never the intention of the prophets. The term *civilization* is a construct of the historians. Moslems, for example, were never aware that they were building or had built a "civilization" until the last century. This is a modern notion. We all know what a boundless and nebulous concept it is and how it can obfuscate judgment.

I fear that Moslems, in their confrontation with Western civilization, wish to turn to Islam as an identity. And this is encouraged by certain Moslem and non-Moslem thinkers alike. I recently reviewed Mr. Huntington's thesis and noticed that he has invoked a number of civilizations, including Islamic civilization. His notion of a "crisis of identity" in the Islamic world made me even more confident about the veracity of my own judgment. I think one of the greatest theoretical plagues of the Islamic world, in general, is that people are gradually coming to understand Islam as an identity rather than a truth. It is true that Moslems did have an Islamic identity and civilization, but they have not adopted Islam for the sake of identity or civilization. Civilizations are emergent and unintended consequences of the conscious actions of social actors. They are the sum total of material and ideal achievements of many generations. In this respect, they are like the market or language. They cannot issue from the conscious attempts of the few. As Hayek pointed out, these are spontaneous designs. Any intentional attempt would be inimical to the design. I don't argue that Moslems have no identity but that Islam should not be chosen for the sake of identity. Just as Rumi said,

> He who sews desires wheat
> Hay will fall out as a treat
> Mohammad ascended for God's visit
> On his way other angels he did meet.

So, I believe that the Islam of identity should yield to the Islam of truth. The latter can coexist with other truths; the former, however, is, by its very nature, belligerent and bellicose. It is the Islam of war, not the Islam of peace. Two identities would fight each other, while two truths would cooperate.

This was the major point, but there are more minute issues as well. There are a number of problems that can be solved only on a global scale. One example of this kind of problem is the institution of slavery. Right now it is banned not only in Islam but all over the world. There is no country that would legislate it or take slaves in the course of the wars. We know that Islam, too, assented to that institution. It was an imposition on Islam on behalf of the dominant world culture that permeated everything, and Islam was no exception. Moslems would be taken as war prisoners and turned into slaves, and they did likewise; there was no way to undermine the institution locally without abrogating it universally.

There is a certain category of phenomena that require universal participation. There is a tradition from the prophet of Islam that says: "We are
all travelers on a ship; if one person pokes a hole in it, all of us will drown." ? (Sa'di ?
This is an excellent allegory, to see all the inhabitants of the globe as
cotravelers on a ship. We Moslems have two kinds of problems, local
problems and universal problems that are the problems of humanity as
a whole. In my view, right now, problems such as peace, human rights,
and women's rights have turned into global problems. Our thinkers should
take this into consideration. Another, even more poignant example is the
environment.

Therefore, I am of the opinion that Moslems should consider certain
issues as global and tackle them at that level, so that they can reap locally what they have sewn universally. There are, of course, other issues
that are local and particular. Universal problems such as technology
demand universal solutions. Fortunately, this research-driven age offers
a far better opportunity to become familiar with other kinds of beliefs,
truths, and solutions. Christianity, Judaism, and other religions, for example, are more readily available for our scrutiny now, and vice versa.
We should seize this opportunity and try to clarify our interfaith issues.
We should become better at reconciling different truths.

SADRI: You mean an interfaith dialogue, do you not?

SOROUSH: Absolutely, an interfaith dialogue.

SADRI: Thank you very much.

SOROUSH: And thank you.

2

Islamic Revival and Reform
Theological Approaches

[Islam] demands loyalty to God, not to thrones. . . . The ultimate spiritual basis of all life, as conceived by Islam is eternal and reveals itself in variety and change. A society based on such a conception of Reality must reconcile, in its life, the categories of permanence and change.[1]

'Allameh Mohammad Iqbal Lahori

Discourse on religious revival is neither a [heretical] innovation nor a novelty;[2] nor is it an exclusive aspect of the Islamic outreach mission [da'vah]. The idea of religious reformation has a long history. Still, there is an obvious difference between the reformers of yesterday and those of today.

Revivalists of the Past: Al-Ghazzali, Feiz Kashani, Rumi, Shabestari, Amoli, Dehlavi

The sages and revivalists of the past, who were painfully aware of the necessity of religious reform and sickened by the persistent obscurity and neglect of the essence of religion, dedicated themselves to the task of pruning the superfluities, tearing asunder the veils, disclosing the superstitions, erasing the heresies, exposing the religion-mongers, and in short, wiping the dust and dirt off the face of religiosity; thus they were determined to reveal and reintroduce the true essence of religion.

Such religious scholars and sages as Al-Ghazzali and Feiz Kashani darkly wondered why religion-mongers had come to such preening prominence, leading the uneducated masses to believe that in the storefront of religiosity there is no commodity save sermons, edicts [*Fatwa*], and theology [*kalam*]. They also wondered why the outward appearance [rituals and laws] of religion [*shari'ah*] has left so little room for its true inner substance and essence; why religious legalism [*fiq'h*] is so unkind to religious ethics; why the center and the circumference of religiosity have traded places; and why not even one tenth of the enthusiasm lavished on religious law and rhetoric is devoted to spirituality (*'irfan*) and ethics. The revivalism of these earlier sages strives to distinguish essence from appearance and root from branch so that each can take its rightful place. Jalal al-Din Rumi,[3] Sheikh Mahmoud Shabestari, Seid Heidar Amoli, and a host of other sages who spoke of the *shari'ah* [rituals and laws], *tariqah* [the true path], and *haqiqah* [the inner dimension][4] of religion were, undoubtedly, treading on this domain. They did not countenance the eclipse of truth of religion behind a parade of rituals, nor did they appreciate a religion restricted to the strictures of appearance. Although they absolved, and even deemed meritorious, the laymen's fascination with the outward facets of religion, they did not regard such congregants as the most suitable subjects or bearers of the divine revelation. And even though they discouraged the chosen few from revealing the mystery of *haqiqah* [the inner dimension], they desired religion precisely because of such wondrous and inexpressible mysteries. They considered the dominion of the devotees of shallow appearances and the peddlers of facile superficialities a great injustice to the precious essence of religion and were conscientiously and enthusiastically devoted to the preservation and revival of true religion.

Those jurisconsults and sages believed that hidden in the shell of religious laws and rituals [*shari'ah*] lies an eternal and priceless pearl that is impervious to change and decline. This precious gem should be snatched from the palms of demagogues and polished.

Revivalists of Today: Seid Jamal Asad Abadi, Mohammad Iqbal Lahori, Mohammad Abdoh, Rashid Reza, 'Ali Shari'ati, Rouhollah Khomeini, Morteza Motahhari

The revivalists of our age confront a greater challenge: reconciling, to paraphrase Iqbal,[5] eternity and temporality. In the course of the past few centuries, colossal contractions and expansions have so affected the life and beliefs of humankind that even a simple understanding of the term "eternity" is difficult. Understanding and preserving the eternal message of religion in the course of such an invasive torrent of change and renewal constitutes the core of the struggles and sacrifices of the reformers of our time. The endeavors of the previous reformers were dedicated to the task of rescuing religion from the clutches of the unenlightened and the peddlers of religion. But the efforts of our contemporaries are devoted to the safe conduct of religion through the perilous path of the temporal world and to bestowing proper meaning and relevance upon it in an increasingly turbulent secular world.

Utter submission to change and renewal leaves no permanence and thus no religion worthy of the name; while insistence on permanence, and obstinate resistance to change, will render religious life in the contemporary world impossible. Therefore, reconciling the two is the great challenge of benevolent theologists of today. Ever since the Renaissance, Europe has followed the former path, and some Moslem thinkers have taken the latter. Both roads have led to the same end: The waning of religion.

Among Moslems, some superficial observers, incapable as they were of understanding the rhyme and reason of the new world, ignorant of the nature, the geography, and the geometry of religion, the history of religious culture, and the interchanges and struggles of religious thought with other ideas, assumed that religion could be rejuvenated through cosmetic changes. They disingenuously tried to extricate new scientific insights from the bowels of ancient texts, boasting of the prophecies of religion with respect to such phenomena as microbes, airplanes, electricity, vitamins, and so on. They actually hoped to scour the crust and rust of ages from the face of religion through such a ruse. It was their intention to present religion as worthy of the modern age, as acceptable to the new sensibility. The pain, however, was too excruciating to be alleviated by such clumsy and irrational schemes.

Afterward, empathetic advocates knocked at the gate of religious adjudication [ijtihad] in search of a solution. For a while, the institution of ijtihad in the Shi'ite world became a matter of self-preening pride: "We are the only ones who possess such a treasure, while others [i.e., the Sunni community] have no access to it." However, the supposed panacea compounded the pain and the claim raised a hail of severe objections: if you are, indeed, sitting by such a wellspring of life, why so many thirsty lips? Why do so many of the destitute slumber over the "treasure," forever deprived of its bounty? Why are the Shi'ite and the non-Shi'ite communities grappling with identical problems? And why are they equally incapable of solving their own problems? Furthermore, who says that all problems are legal [fiqhi] so that some form of adjudication [ijtihad] can resolve them? Who says that all the intellectual and economic transformations of the present age are summed up in legal transformations? The call for dynamic jurisprudence [fiqhi pouya] versus traditional jurisprudence [*fiqhi sonnati*] echoed in our society, and above the clamor the clear voice of Imam Khomeini was heard: "*Ijtihad* as understood and practiced by the Hawzeh (Islamic seminaries) is insufficient." This pronouncement revealed that *ijtihad* itself is in need of another *ijtihad*. And if *ijtihad* continues to be what it heretofore has been, not much hope could be pinned on it. Never mind that among the Sunni Moslems, too, as Iqbal Lahori has stated, the closure of the epoch of *ijtihad* has been all but an illusion.

Although the late martyr Motahhari[6] was looking for a "brave jurisconsult" to issue courageous edicts,[7] he knew very well that jurisconsults are the children of their time and place and thus think within the confines of their age and environment. He conceded that we Moslems have scant understanding of most Islamic issues and that the Qur'an has fallen into relative obscurity among us. Motahhari declared that replacing a certain ruling of "most likely so" [*alal aqva*] for "likely so" [*alal ah'vat*] and vice versa (which is the extent of the innovation of our jurists, themselves followers of previous jurists) will not be the cure of the contemporary predicament of the Islamic world.[8]

Seid Jamal strove to awaken Moslems, and his disciples Mohammad Abdoh and Rashid Reza attempted to revive the Qur'an. Before them the enlightened and erudite sufi, Shah Valiollah Dehlavi, in his *Hojjatollah al-Baleqeh*, called attention to the difference between the Prophet's governmental rulings (which were appropriate for the Arabia of fifteen hundred years ago and therefore inapplicable to other times and places) and the religion's eternal rules. Dehlavi urged the jurisconsults engaged in innovative adjudication to observe the subtle difference between universal religious rules on the one hand and the rites of a particular ethnic group on the other to avoid generalizing and universalizing ethnically and historically specific norms.

Tackling the newfangled problems (such as key money,[9] insurance, alcohol, prayers on the poles and on the moon,[10] and so on) based on established religious practice constituted another foray into juridical modernization and innovation. The formulation of modern scientific disciplines such as Islamic psychology and Islamic sociology, based on religious lore constituted a still more inventive endeavor. The most serious undertaking of all, though, was the effort to distinguish the constant and the variable components of religion so that it would be clear where Islam would be susceptible of change and where it would be unbending and resistant. Both Iqbal and Shari'ati[11] realized that legal and jurisprudential *(fiqhi)* problems are part of the predicament of contemporary Moslems. For instance, one cannot stand by and witness an oppressed woman from the Punjab, deprived of the right of religious divorce in order to escape a tyrannical husband, appeal to the law of apostasy.[12] However, neither thinker found the solution of such dilemmas in the institution of traditional jurisprudence and the agency of religious jurisconsults.

Shari'ati generally considered religion a cultural repository and called for a distillation and utilization of this resource. His main goal in distilling religious culture, though, was to preserve the conditions that empower the religion. Shari'ati was highly influenced by socialism's call for social justice and was thus troubled by the hegemony of the trilateral alliance of "force, fortune, and fraud" [*zoor-o-zar-o-tazvir*] over the Islamic society. He had a sociological appreciation of the interpenetration of form and substance, religious culture and ethnic culture. He, therefore, encouraged Moslems to ideologize religion and liberate it from the grips of stultifying and falsifying cultures. He advocated a restoration of the spirit of religion and a reform of its appearance. Finally, he cautioned against loss of identity and cultural retardation.

Iqbal Lahori, Shari'ati's perspicacious mentor, an ardent admirer of such great sages of the past as Rumi, was profoundly indignant about the dominance of the Greek spirit over the religious scholars' thought. He courageously declared the deliverance of religion from the hegemony of this spiritual contortion as the condition of the revival of religious thought. Iqbal attempted to revive and reconstruct the religious philosophy of Islam through a synthesis of the Islamic philosophical tradition and modern philosophy. Although he believed in the ascendant and dynamic nature of Islamic thought, he considered religious thought thoroughly compatible with the principles of constancy and stability. Indeed, he considered a certain synthesis of the above as a feasible prospect in the new age. Iqbal labored on a theoretical scheme that would help actualize this idea.

The Contribution of the Theory of the Contraction and Expansion of Religious Interpretation to the Islamic Reform and Revival

Reconciling eternity and temporality, the sacred and the profane; separating constant and variant, form and substance; reviving innovative adjudication in religion; finding courageous jurisconsults; reinvigorating religious jurisprudence; changing the appearance while preserving the spirit of religion; acquainting Islam with the contemporary age; establishing the new Islamic theology: these have been goals of the religious revivalists, but they require an epistemological theory that is absent from the revivalist literature. The theory of the contraction and expansion of religious interpretation humbly proposes such a theory. The missing link in the endeavors of the revivalists and reformers of the past is the distinction between religion and religious knowledge. They failed to recognize religious knowledge as a variety of human knowledge. This neglect caused significant inconsistencies in their judgments and allowed the desired solution to slip through their fingers.

Everywhere they turned they were haunted by agonizing questions: What is your claim and goal anyway? What is the "defect" in religion that you propose to repair? What error or ailment has befallen it that has provoked this empathy and reformist zeal? What essential subject has escaped the Prophet's mind, what good or evil has the religion left out that now demands your help in explicating or teasing out? And, anyway, if religion really does harbor such flaws and faults, why are you still committed to it? Why don't you wash your hands of it? Why have you assumed the role of the leaders rather than that of the followers? Why the ambition to complete, resuscitate, and reconstruct *shari'ah*, a responsibility worthy of prophets, rather than apostles? Furthermore, why is it that only *you* have become aware of these defects and decays while your predecessors were unaware of them? Finally, how dare you assume that a sacred, heavenly, and eternal religion would leave gaps for the "partial reason" [*aq'l-e jozvi*] and minuscule understanding of mortal human beings to fill?

The truth is that as long as one has not distinguished between religion and people's understanding of it, one will be incapable of finding an adequate answer to these intriguing questions. Yes, it is true that sacred scriptures are (in the judgment of followers) flawless; however, it is just as true that human beings' understanding of religion is flawed. Religion is sacred and heavenly, but the understanding of religion is human and earthly. That which remains constant is religion [*din*]; that which undergoes change is religious knowledge and insight [*ma'refat-e dini*]. Religion has not faltered in articulating its objectives and its explanations of good and evil; the defect is in human beings' understanding of religion's intents. Religion is in no need of reconstruction and completion. Religious knowledge and insight that is human and incomplete, however, is in constant need of reconstruction. Religion is free from cultures and unblemished by the artifacts of human minds, but religious knowledge is, without a shadow of a doubt, subject to such influences. Revivalists are not lawgivers [*shari'an*] but exegetes [*sharihan*]. Although religion has no defect or flaw, defects abound in exegeses. The prophet is guilty neither of reticence nor of neglect in his task as the messenger of divine revelation; it is the human mind that is affected by need and neglect. Reason does not come to the aid of religion to complement it; it struggles to improve its own understanding of religion. The sacred *shari'ah* never sits parallel to human opinions, so there is no possibility of agreement or disagreement between the two; it is the human understanding of religion that may be congruous or incongruous with other parts of human understanding.

It is up to God to reveal a religion, but up to us to understand and realize it. It is at this point that religious knowledge is born, entirely human and subject to all the dictates of human knowledge. Those who search for the constant and the variant in religion should know that the very distinction between the two and the determination of their embodiments belong to the domain of "religious knowledge" and, as such, they follow a particular interpretation of religion. The determination of the constant and the variant is not obtained prior to the understanding of religion but after it. Thus, everywhere we are confronted with religious knowledge that concerns and observes religion but is not religion. This verdict covers all branches of human knowledge.

To treat religious knowledge, a branch of human knowledge, as incomplete, impure, insufficient, and culture-bound; to try to mend and darn its wears and tears is, in itself, an admirable and hallowed undertaking. It is this exercise that is called religious reform and revival. We are now in a position to return to a number of questions that were raised earlier in this essay: Why is there a need for "courageous jurisconsults"? What is the relationship between courage and the production of religious edicts? And, above all, how can a jurisconsult obtain courage? Why, and in what sense, has Greek thought held sway over religious thought? What is the nature of the so-called veils that have fallen over religion, rendering it ineffectual? Where are those "unadulterated sources" that some claim exist? Why have they kept themselves out of sight for so long? What eyes, equipped with what lenses, have now brought them into view? Why have the nascent "Islamic psychology" and "Islamic sociology"[13] led such long, embryonic lives before their birth in our age; where were the adroit midwives of these ideas before? Are psychology and sociology, as such, added to religion itself or to religious knowledge? Is it the religion itself that evolves or religious knowledge? Which one actually undergoes contraction and expansion?

Only if one deigns to ask such questions will one be acquainted with the change and evolution of religious knowledge and its mechanism. If Islamic psychology has a modern birthday, if religious knowledge has remained under the tutelage of Greek thought for centuries, if the traditional style of religious adjudication [ijtihad] is deemed no longer sufficient, then must we not acknowledge the temporality of religious knowledge? Of course, only a person who is unaware of the difference between religion and religious knowledge would reach the erroneous conclusion that not religious knowledge alone, but religion itself is temporal. Not so! Divine inspiration originates in a realm beyond time and space. Revelation is not the prisoner of nature or civilization. However, what could religious knowledge, obviously the child of human comprehension, be if not temporal?

We are but a step away from acknowledging that the temporal nature of religious knowledge, a universally applicable precept, has no other meaning than the synchronization and adaptation of this branch of human knowledge with the sciences and needs of each age. A transformation in the mode of knowledge and life of humanity is the remote cause of a transformation of religious knowledge.

Now we are in a better position to answer the questions that were posed earlier: Why does religion, which is supposed to be the sovereign prince of cultures, become their bond servant? Why do revivalists call for a purification and distillation of religion? Why do the Qur'an and the Tradition [*Kitab va Sonnat*],[14] pregnant as they are with certain vital ideas, indefinitely delay the birth? Why is evolution in religious understanding inevitable? Why is the truth left for future generations to declare? Why do the religious decrees of Arab and non-Arab (Ajam) jurists betray their respective cultural temperaments?[15] Furthermore, why does the philosopher's Islam differ from that of the mystic? Finally, and above all, why do we need religious revival and reform *now*?

The theory of the contraction and expansion of religious interpretation unlocks the secret of all such questions. It separates religion and religious knowledge, considers the latter as a branch of human knowledge, and regards our understanding of religion as evolving along with other branches of human knowledge. The insights and needs of a new age embolden the jurisconsult, play midwife for the pregnant matron of *shari'ah*, and enkindle the spirit of Greek sensibility in the body of religious understanding. Further, it becomes clear that it is religious knowledge, not the scripture itself, that takes the pigments and aroma of cultures, undergoes change, and needs purification. Revivalists, who are empathetic philosophers of religion, do not replace religion with their understanding of it. They simply replace one understanding of religion with another. While accepting the eternal nature of the Qur'an and the Tradition, the revivalists refresh and complement our knowledge of them. That which remains constant is the religion; that which changes is religious understanding.

Eternity and temporality are thus reconciled; heaven and earth are reunited in a kind embrace; and constant, eternal religion begets changing and evolving religious knowledge. In this way the mystery of the inexhaustible nature of the interpretations of divine revelation, the mechanism of that interpretation, and the relationship between reason (that is, rational deliberations), human knowledge, and religion is solved. Thus a single coin realizes the common dreams of the Turk, the Roman, and the Arab.[16]

It should be clear that the historic nature of religious knowledge, in its present precise sense, is immune to harm from the vulgar demagogy that demands that instead of trying to bend religion to meet the requirements of the age, we should attempt to bend the temporal order into a religious shape. Religious practice is not temporalized at anyone's behest; it becomes temporal on its own. Temporalization is not an attribute of religion but of religious knowledge. In order to bend the temporal order into a religious shape, one should understand what religion is all about. This understanding is obtained by acquiring religious knowledge, which, in turn, is always time-bound. Therefore, forcing the temporal order into a religious mold itself is possible only through a time-bound religious knowledge. In any event, the key to understanding the theory of the contraction and expansion of religious interpretation is in comprehending two major distinctions: first, the difference between religion and our understanding of religion and, second, the difference between personal knowledge of religion and religious knowledge. Unless one scales these two monumental ramparts, one will not be able to feast one's eyes on the vast meadows and open horizons of the new theology.

Numerous are those who harbor the illusion that whatever they happen to believe is the very essence of religion and religious knowledge. Massive campaigns must be launched to tear asunder these twin veils of delusion and hubris so that one may realize that one's religious belief, however immaculate, is still one's own comprehension of religion, not religion as such. Second, it must be understood that religious knowledge is not the personal knowledge of a single individual but a branch of human knowledge that has a collective and dynamic identity and that remains viable through the constant exchange, cooperation, and competition of scholars. As such, religious knowledge is replete with error, conjecture, and conviction. Error plays as much of a role in religious knowledge as does insight. If one deems an opinion false, even though that opinion will depart from his or her personal knowledge, it does not depart from religious knowledge as such. It is in this sense that religious knowledge changes, evolves, contracts, expands, waxes, and wanes. It is temporal and in constant commerce with other realms of human culture.

The goal of the theory of the contraction and expansion of religious interpretation is not to resolve the dispute between traditional and the dynamic jurisprudence [*fiqhi sonnati va fiqhi pouya*]; nor is it the goal of this theory to modernize religion, reinterpret or complement *shari'ah*, relativize or deny the truth. Rather, the theory aims to explicate the process through which religion is understood and the manner in which this understanding undergoes change. The theory proposes that so far as the secret of the understanding of religion and the transformations of this understanding are not revealed, the endeavor to revive religion will remain incomplete.

Thus the theory of the contraction and expansion of religious interpretation, which is originally an "interpretive-epistemological"[17] theory, belongs to three other domains as well: *kalam* [Islamic theology], *usul* [applied logic in religious jurisprudence], and *irfan* [the esoteric dimension of Islam].

First, the theory belongs to *kalam* because it has to do with theology and because it reveals the extent to which our previous assumptions and *Our Expectations from Religion*[18] influence our understanding of the Qur'an and the Tradition. Second, it belongs to *usul* because it reveals precisely which sciences religious law (*fiq'h*) needs in order to accomplish the task of methodic conjecture (*istinbat*). The theory also explains the effects of the implicit and explicit assumptions of the practitioner of religious jurisprudence concerning the nature and process of the production of religious edicts and jurisprudential understanding. Furthermore, the theory clarifies the suppositions of the concept of "transparence of the text" [*zohur*] and the reason why adjudication in particulars presupposes adjudication in principles, and the extent to which religious law [*fiq'h*] is inspired by theology [*kalam*]. Third, the theory belongs to *irfan* because it defines *shari'ah*, *tariqah*, and *haqiqah* as three aspects of religion, each worthy of a particular group and heir to a unique perspective. The secret of the perennial conflict of the philosophers, jurisconsults, and mystics is thus revealed: they have clashed over discrepant interpretations of the above three dimensions of religiosity, which have emerged due to different experiences and traditions. Hence, the theory illuminates the meaning of the poem:

> The difference among Moslems, Zoroastrians, and Jews,
> Emanate, O learned one, from their various points of views.[19]

In light of this interpretive theory it is possible to understand the inevitable entry of the categories of *mohkam* [certain] and *moteshabeh* [ambivalent] not only in the Qur'an but also in the Tradition, the jurisprudence, and even in the interpretation of history. Further, it becomes evident that the categories of certainty and ambivalence themselves are subject to change. It is not as though a verse would remain certain or ambivalent forever. Also, a lucid definition of the notion of "arbitrary personal interpretation of the sacred tradition" [*tafsir be ra'y*] becomes available. In the absence of an epistemological theory, the more this issue is scrutinized, the murkier it becomes. A qualified legitimation of having a personal opinion goes a long way toward the solution of the problem. In other words, the theory explains that "interpretation without personal opinion" is utterly impossible. The argument, then, is not over the presence or absence of opinion, but over its quality and qualifications. This argument, in turn, will shed light on the further questions concerning the legitimacy of substantive interpretation [*tafsir*] and interpretive conjecture [*ta'vil*] as well.

The theory of the contraction and expansion of religious interpretation not only reconciles the categories of eternity and temporal change, tradition and modernity, heavenly and earthly, reason and revelation, but it also unites the elements of purity and potency in religious knowledge (which is the goal of revivalists and reformers) and presents a plausible interpretation of both.

There are those who, on the pretext of keeping religion pure, have rejected help from friend and foe alike. And then there are those who, in order to render religion versatile and strong have beckoned ally and alien alike. The former attempt has led to isolation and ossification of religion [*tahajjor*], the latter to opportunistic and inappropriate coalitions [*elteqat*]. The brinkmanship aimed at avoiding the twin dangers is analogous to walking a path narrower than a strand of hair and sharper than the edge of a sword. None but the nimble voyager may negotiate such a path. In addition to problem solving in the realm of theology [*kalam*], the theory of contraction and expansion [*qabz-va-bast*] engages in numerous epistemological issues. It is hoped that the seekers and enthusiasts of the latter will find the present aspect of the theory worthwhile as well.

Let us avoid some common errors. Some might expect an explication of such complex issues as the present or future relationship between the various scientific disciplines and religious jurisprudence or the future course of the evolution of the sciences. Such requests, even if not utterly unreasonable, are unfair. Is a person who claims that nature is lawful thereby obliged to know the details of the laws of visible light, planetary motion, and electrons as well? Is it incumbent upon him to discover every specific application of the general laws, and this solely because of one's belief in the lawfulness of the universe? Furthermore, who can foresee the future of knowledge? Is such a venture not tantamount to depriving knowledge of a future?

Also, there are those who ask if religion proves to be time-bound, why would we need it at all? Why not, then, immerse ourselves in the concerns of our time altogether? The root of this illusion is the belief that the secular and the sacred speak the same language. The truth, however, is that the temporal culture is no substitute for religion, only a tool for understanding its message. The two propositions are fundamentally different. Only if the Qur'an and the Tradition were receptive to just any interpretation (which is not the case) could we seek answers in any random collection of teachings.

Then there are those who have erroneously crowned experimental science as the sole measure of religion and have attributed this illusion to the theory of contraction and expansion. It is true that this theory constantly refers to human knowledge and achievements that include science, philosophy, mysticism, art, as well as human material and intellectual needs. However, all of these are influential merely in understanding and temporalizing religion. Experimental science, all its glory notwithstanding, is not the only performer on this stage.

The opening of the gates of heaven, the serendipitous descent of droplets of revelation upon the hearts of certain blessed human beings known as prophets; and the cleansing of human reason and life through the grace of such a refreshing rain is a most glorious event. The cohabitation of reason and revelation, and the former's fervor to unravel the latter's mystery is an equally beautiful sight. Religion offers many blessings to its followers and to society. For the believers, religion quickens the blaze of the sublime quest, delivers from inner attachments, grants ascent above earthly concerns, opens the heart's aperture toward the sun of the truth, and induces a sense of utter wonder in the face of the mystery of existence, so that one may hear the call of *Ho-val-Haq* (God is the Truth) from every particle of the universe. It brings within grasp the true interpretation of mystical experiences, the lessons of inner journey, and the conduct worthy of divine presence. It defies arrogance, ushers in humility, impermanence, and morality, and accelerates the pace of human emotional and intellectual evolution. For society, religion promises attenuation of avarice and injustice; mobilization for the sake of fairness, justice, benevolence, fulfillment, and enlightenment; and avoidance of the risk of experimentation with that which does not yield to experimentation, that is, the hereafter. All these are among the blessings of religion, and it would be the height of ingratitude to let this blessed bounty decay and perish in the clutches of contorted thinking, erroneous understanding, languor, and apathy. In short, a great number may perish of thirst at the wellspring of life.

We human beings are now expelled from heaven and deprived of revelation. We are profane and listless. Our life is blighted by Satan, and our understanding is fallible. To speak and act like prophets does not suit us. Apropos of our limited reason, we acquire a faint scent of the truth and act accordingly. We are *sharihan* [interpreters of religion], not *sahri'an* [initiators of religion]. We are the enticed, not the infallibles. Let them who deem their words above the mere understanding of the religion beware: their hubris may at long last tempt them to don the mantle of the prophets. The acceptance of the sovereignty of religion is far from putting one's own words in the Prophet's mouth and arrogating his seat to oneself. Rather, it means a sincere attempt to understand his message through repeated consultation with the sacred text and the Tradition. Scholars of religion have no other status or service than this. They are the compilers of religious knowledge that is neither complete nor flawless. Their worthy struggle to understand the Book and the Tradition does not yield a sacred knowledge. The prophet of Islam is the last of prophets, and his religion is the last of religions. However, no jurisprudent [*faqih*] and interpreter [*mofassir*] is the last of jurisprudents or interpreters. The last religion is already here, but the last understanding of religion has not arrived yet. There came a day when religion reached its completion,[20] but when will the understanding of religion reach its zenith? On that day not only religious knowledge but all other branches of human knowledge will have reached their apex.

None save the elect are privy to such secrets. The callous, whose hearts are untroubled by the current crisis of religion, the affliction that has left it gasping for life, are alien to this endeavor. They see nothing in the revivalists' efforts but interference, heresy, and bad religion, and reap nothing from it but loss and death. The theory of the contraction and expansion of religious understanding is, first and foremost, a theological theory. Secondarily, it is an interpretive-jurisprudential-philosophical theory.[21] It suits those who are stirred by a calling for revival and who are blessed with a fervor for understanding religion. Those who lack these motives will sustain nothing but trouble and ruin from it: "And it does not increase the wrongdoers, except in loss."[22]

For years I have beseeched God, in the words of Imam Sajjad [greetings be upon him]:[23] "Grant me an insight into Your religion, an understanding of Your rule, and a discernment of the practice that pleases You." I pray for God's benevolence and bounty on every step of this path. I knock at the gate of divine affirmation. And now let me acknowledge God's ample blessings of vindication and entreat Him to complete His magnanimity upon me.

> Allay, show the way, grant attainment
> Or quench the quest, burden us not with the assignment.[24]

3

Life and Virtue

The Relationship between
Socioeconomic Development and Ethics

(1) Values are of two kinds: those for the sake of which we live (the guiding values) and those that exist for the sake of living (the serving values.) Such guiding values as goodness, justice, generosity, and courage transcend social life, nationality, and history; they are eternal. By contrast, the serving values are life's auxiliaries: woven into the fabric of the social life and evolving with its evolution, their function is to make life easier, more desirable and pleasant. All of the rules of etiquette, pleasantries, and moral regulations belong to this category. Examples abound: sociality, affability, frugality, fairness, visiting relatives, keeping secrets, respecting the law, and so on.

A society pervaded by falsehoods, hypocrisy, swindling, cupidity, and law-breaking does not provide for good life because these social evils would undermine the security of everyone and interfere with the mutual trust that is the basis of social life. The serving values admit of exceptions because they can prove counterproductive if dogmatically applied. For instance, it is known that sometimes a white lie is preferable to revealing a damaging truth and that acquisitiveness may in certain occasions be preferable to frugality: "If the master of the faith directs me toward greed / Damn frugality; it I shall never need."[1] I believe in a metaethical value according to which a healthy society is one in which the guiding values and virtues are always the rule, not the exception. Such a society shall never allow evil to prevail under any pretext.[2]

(2) "Development" in the sense of the cultural, industrial, scientific, and economic growth of the society flexes and bends the serving values to make them follow the logic of the socioeconomic development. These crucial changes occur in two areas: first, in the primary serving values

(those that predate the socioeconomic development); second, in the secondary serving values (those that issue from the socioeconomic development).

Old habits and traditional conduct must first change before social and economic development becomes possible. Once established, a developed social system finds further opportunities to create new values. The complete supplantation of an old social system by a new one is a gradual process. It is not easy to pinpoint the order of the changing elements of the whole system. But a change in values precedes the social transformations or it is at least coterminous with it. Even when the two occur simultaneously, we are justified in ascribing causal significance to the values.[3]

(3) Three important questions are posed in the literature that deal with the values that predate social development: What are they? How can we discover them? Can they be taught to, inculcated in, or imposed on a given society? Questions about the values engendered by development are the following: What are these values? Can we separate good values from bad ones, setting a course for a "virtuous" development that would avoid the corruptions that have accompanied the progress of the West? If not, then we must resign ourselves to the fact that such separation is not possible and that Western socioeconomic development is a package deal: "Providence brought these contraries nigh / The neck comes with the butcher's choice meat of the thigh."[4]

There are those who consider the values of secularism and liberalism as the unavoidable prerequisites of development and count among its attendant values things like pornography, neo- and old-fashioned colonialism, biological and chemical weapons, and the destruction of the environment. This identification of development with repugnant prerequisites and consequences cannot help sending another chill up the spine of those weary believers who stand on the brink of the modern world, trembling before this mysterious enterprise of progress. On the opposite pole there are those who see nothing but good preceding or succeeding development: a love of knowledge as the preceding value and democracy as the succeeding value. The discussion of the relationship between development and values originates in these controversies. To prove their arguments, these adversaries turn to the marvelous and turbulent history of the West, wherein the idea of development was first conceived. They both postulate that there is only one (Western) way toward development and that surrendering to development is the only way to survive in the contemporary world. For one side, survival on the Western path is a boon; for the other, it is a march to moral disaster.

(4) Historians and sociologists agree that the values that preceded, caused, and sustained the development of the West were not the result of a conscious world-historical project of their authors. Bacon, Luther, and Machiavelli did not set out to create the contemporary civilization

of the West, nor were they aware of their crucial role as the architects of a monumental change in the history of the world. Yet, the empirical science of Bacon, the secular religion of Luther, and the amoral politics of Machiavelli combined with other relevant ideas and events to create the edifice of the modern world.

The dilemma of developing nations is that they want to engineer this change consciously. Thus they missed important historical opportunities because they provoked forms of resistance that did not inhibit the West. The result is the creation of half-industrial/half-traditional hybrid systems that are incapable of managing their own affairs in the cultural, political, and world-historical arenas. For this reason it is better to keep the issue of development as a preoccupation of the elites rather than allowing it to turn into a chain fettering the movements of the masses.

(5) Probably the most important transformation in the area of ethics and values prior to the Western development, the one that unleashed the modernist and bourgeois juggernauts, was the secularization of ethics. This process had two distinct characteristics that arose simultaneously with modernism and grew along with it: the first was to steer ethics from the empyrean of spiritual perfection and the afterlife toward the terra firma of happiness and felicity in this world. The other was harnessing traditional "sins" such as cupidity, ambition, and materialism as fuel for engines of progress. Bentham, the father of utilitarianism and one of the forerunners of this transformation, made morality into an inner-worldly calculus; Mandeville turned the ethics of everyday life on its head; likewise, Machiavelli reversed the foundations of political ethics.

(6) We translate the word *happiness* (which is related to *happening*, *mishap*, *perhaps*) and *heureux* or *bonheure* into the Persian *khoshbakhti*, or *khoshvaqti*. The element of luck[5] is salient in all these terms. This indicates that happiness for our predecessors depended more on chance or the favor of heavens than on one's own effort. In Hafez's words: "Though the beloved's embrace is not granted to those who strive / To your utmost, my poor heart, you must drive," and "As the final felicity depends not on the ascetic or cunning labor / It is better to leave ones affairs to heavens' favor." And Rumi says:

Destiny has a playful mind of its own, your steed, not steadfast.
Drop your cunning; the matter depends on how the fortune is cast.
One favor from heavens is better than a hundred efforts.
A hundred corruptions lurk in each one of our efforts.[6]

But modern utilitarianism turned this wild beast of accidental and irrational happiness (which was at the core of the old ethics and around which a whole constellation of habits, conventions, expectations, and behavioral patterns had formed) into an obedient, domesticated animal. Ethical axioms were evaluated in terms of their ability to ensure public happiness, pleasure, and welfare. Rational calculation dispelled the chaos, insecurity, and lack of causality that dominated the world of ethics and happiness and kept the world in confusion and sorrows.[7] Although the word happiness and its synonyms retained the vestiges of chance, their meaning had changed: this new wine in the old semantic chalice kept the revelers of modernity in good cheer.

(7) It is believed that Bentham, Hume, Adam Smith, and other architects of the modern era were all influenced by Dr. Bernard Mandeville, a Dutch physician. Although not widely known, he was one of the founders of the modern world. His book, *The Fable of the Bees*, first published in 1705 and republished in two volumes in 1728, caused a violent tempest. The gist of his thesis is that a society consists of two groups, not unlike a beehive. On one side stand the hardworking, righteous, noble, and productive members. On the other side lay the pompous, idle, and slothful nobility, the class of gluttony and deception. In his story, one day the idle nobility decides to become truly noble by emulating the good workers, and this causes the downfall of that society. No longer did art find enthusiasts or artists patrons. Mandeville concludes that there is an affinity between "private vices and public goods." The subtitle of his book reads: *An Enquiry into the Origin of Moral Virtue*. The contemporary economist F. Hayek says that Mandeville unwittingly discovered the spontaneous nature of social and economic law. These systems do not need designers and planners.[8] Mandeville was an undeniably prescient observer of profound social transformations who encouraged traits that had always been censured by the ethical philosophers: selfishness, profiteering, ostentation, and boasting. According to Mandeville, these private vices contribute to the social equilibrium. If everyone were to follow the traditional maxims of frugality and asceticism, the whole society would fall apart. It is thanks to selfish profit seekers that business is lively. Those who hunger for power and ostentation stoke the fire of politics and the seekers of vanity and fame keep the flame of the academy and library aglow. It is the efforts of those who have a love of the worldly pleasures that enrich and improve this world.

(8) Such revered philosophers as Al-Ghazzali, Rumi, and Thomas Aquinas were aware of this paradox. The transgressors and the sinners carry half of the weight of public affairs by entering into a genuine but undeclared contract with the upright and righteous members of the society: "In the enterprise of existence disbelief is inevitable." But this intuition was never allowed to form the basis of a new ethical system wherein the wicked are relieved of their shame because of their function in ensuring the equilibrium of economy and society. This is the gist of Al-Ghazzali's theory of obliviousness (*ghaflat*).[9] Rumi, who was annoyed by the various ranks of police functionaries, considered them as the manifestation of God's anger and fury and thus as necessary evils.[10]

The virtue and wickedness of human beings in this world is based on their ignorance of what they engage in. This ignorance is the principal pillar of this world. Thomas Aquinas stated: "Multae utilitates impedirenture si omnia peccata districte prohiberenture" (If no one commits a sin, many useful things will disappear). In Marx's adroit hands this "obliviousness" was later molded into the concept of "ideology," which was given the character of an opiate that induces oblivion.[11]

(9) Rumi rightly observed that "awareness is the blight of this world." The wicked used to sin in shame without realizing the salutary implications of their actions on the society as a whole. Here the mere realization caused a fundamental change: the old world receded, gave way to a new, vital expanding one. With private vices regarded as public goods the next step was inevitable: if they are deemed public goods, why are they not private goods as well? Thus did a new morality displace the official books on ethics: a transformation of values.

This was the total human (*l'homme total*) of modernity, emerging from the shadows to embrace ambition openly, to haggle and to unabashedly strive for the worldly glory of high corporate and political office. Freed from internal constraints of traditional piety, the new humanity kept order (political and legal) through the natural play of checks and balances.

(10) The modern world is the ethical inverse of the old world. The ancient apocalyptic prophecies came true: reason is enslaved to desire, the external governs the internal, and vices have supplanted virtues. It required a great deal of courage to declare that the life blood of modern life is the traditional vices not virtues. The scale of vice and virtue is now held upside down as former vices are valued as necessary fuel for the furnace of the world. This appreciation is in direct contradiction to Rumi's view that the wealthy are the carriers of the dung that is to be burned at the bathhouse of the world.[12]

Now let us consider the change of values in relation to the search for knowledge. Such ethical thinkers as Al-Ghazzali have censured those who would seek knowledge out of hubris, pretension, contention, ostentation, greed, or lust for power, fame, and office, especially at the royal courts. He is disappointed that many scholars are affected by these traits that are indeed the blight of knowledge.[13] But, had one studied the majority of students even in those days,[14] one would have concluded that the popularity of scholarship and the favor lavished on knowledge and learning were rooted in love of fame, vanity, and wealth. Thus, those who feel such emotions in themselves must not be ashamed nor feel guilty for the exhilaration they feel when their audiences grow.[15] They must not heed the Sufi teaching that worldly wealth is a punishment for sins inflicted on the sinner before his death.[16] This transformation in values removed the fetters from the hands and feet of humanity and prepared it to enter into the fields of development.

The secularization of ethics, the rationalization of happiness, the centrality of humanity, and the transposition of vices and virtues constitute the serving values that preceded the birth of socioeconomic development and continue to propel it. Some have chosen such daunting terms as "egoism" (or ego-worship) and "individualism" to describe these transformations. But despite their somber tones, these terms fail to express the central ideas of the modern era. It is better to characterize what occurred as a lowering and rearranging of the system of values.

(11) Let us once more evoke Rumi in describing the values that precede social and economic development:

> First, man hungers for bread.
> As food is life's main thread.
> When at long last he reaches satiety,
> He seeks fame, the praise of poets and notoriety.
> So his nobility would be lauded.
> And from podiums his virtues applauded.[17]

Development brings in its wake leisure and occasionally pride, obliviousness, and disdain for traditional values. But some have neglected the fact that it also provides the opportunity for cultivating the higher and more spiritual needs. The distress of acquiring one's daily bread, shelter, and clothing would hardly allow for engagement in arts and the pursuit of worldly knowledge and mystical gnosis. But once mankind is liberated from the arduous and worrisome tasks of the mundane world, it can take wing and fly in the sphere of the higher concerns. Once the needs of the body are met, the hunger of the soul may be more apparent.

Socioeconomic development fulfills the primary needs, not the higher values. Such values as justice, freedom, wisdom, and so on are invariant, but humans, still in the clutches of physical want, have no chance to aspire to them. The God of those struggling for subsistence is the God of the oppressed, not that of the mystics. He is a God that vanquishes the oppressors, facilitates survival, pays off debts, and grants wishes. As soon as the veil of these primary needs is removed, the sun of divine beauty will reflect in the mirror of the higher and more refined spiritual yearnings. Only then is the religion of pure contemplation realized. God will finally shed the garbs of the savior and the benefactor to assume that of the beloved.

This general development in values and spiritual needs follows material and technological development. Yet this very spiritual awareness can hamper material development precisely by disparaging the lower needs and awakening the desire for higher aspirations. It also mitigates the effects of recklessness, acquisitiveness, loss of identity, overmechanization and one-dimensionality that erupted at the outset of the age of modernity. Society not only crossed the threshold of the modernization and socioeconomic development, but also raised a ladder to ascend to the heights of religious and ethical ideals. In this sense, socioeconomic development must be considered as an important stage in the evolution of humanity and, as such, even ethically sanctioned.

The profound scientific, humanist, and philosophical critiques of development that are current in the West are all the by-products of material development. Technology and development have run their course, revealing their own nature and assuming higher forms. This has allowed human beings to also experience and advance beyond technological and socioeconomic limitations where they can behold higher horizons and learn new lessons. The advent of postmodernism is a case in point. It evinces all the signs of having been chastened by the tyranny of the arrogant knight of modern rationality. It marks a turning away from this rationality and a desire to rise above it. This implies the search for other sources of knowledge, a search similar to that launched by Romanticism two centuries earlier. This is why André Malraux said that the twenty-first century will be a religious one or nothing at all.

(12) There is a plethora of values, emphases, and beliefs associated with development in the modern world: tolerance, freedom of speech, fine arts, enhanced order and stability in life, the meaning of life, the essential unity of religions, defiance of technological dominance, preservation of the ecosystem, popularity of science and research, women's rights, amusing and edifying leisure activities, heightened participation in the political life, and so on.

The most salient among these values, however, is democracy with its multifarious definitions and foundations. However, the primary condition for the realization of democracy is the liberation of human beings from the elementary needs and necessities of life. It is true that human beings have always opposed inequity and demanded justice (democracy being a modern manifestation of this perennial human quest), but justice can prevail only where its seekers are not weighed down by poverty and insecurity. It is available to those who have already escaped other forms of slavery. Democracy is desirable for all, but in practice it is not available to all. It requires a certain level of normative, political, and governmental development that is contingent upon economic development.

Only those who have forged new human relationships among themselves will take democracy seriously and demand it earnestly. The greatest dictatorship is that of poverty and ignorance. It is in their shadows that tyrannical rule rises and prospers, extinguishing the torch of liberty and justice in hearts. Thus certain levels of prosperity and security are not only the preambles of development, they are necessary for its continued existence. Only then would they reveal their subtle and spiritual charms, winning admirers and lovers everywhere.

Freedom of speech is desirable for those who have something to say, those who have the time, leisure, and security to think, learn, read, and inquire. All of this becomes possible when people's energies are not drained in dealing with the elementary needs and where the seeds of ideas are allowed to germinate in the fertile communal soil. Freedom of speech is not meant only for protesting injustices (that is only one aspect of democracy), nor is it meant only for avoiding the excommunicators' curse. First and foremost, it is meant to let us learn what others know and to let us teach them what we know. This capability is both a prerequisite of development and a result of it.

Democracy is a method of governing a developed society brimming with new values and facts. Furthermore, for a developed society, democracy is a necessity, not merely a hobby or a luxury. In other words, tyranny is not a viable option for a developed society that hinges on science, because science operates in a matrix of freedom of research and adversarial dialogue of ideas, a practice incompatible with political repression.

In a developed society, where decisive operations are more cerebral than manual, and where innovation turns into a requirement of progress, the institutions that cultivate innovative minds gain more power and become harder to dominate. Ruling over minds is not as easy as enslaving bodies.

Subtle and spiritual values (such as the love of liberty and of knowledge) are more prevalent in developed societies because human beings are less enslaved by elementary needs. Still, ideology, the instrument of intellectual enslavement that imposes subjective schemes on objective realities, has not lost its holds on such societies. Therefore it is necessary to bolster the role and the service of the free media. Democratization of the spread of knowledge and the establishment of popular control over the flow of information (in addition to that of wealth and power) is among the most significant promoters and properties of democracy in developed societies. It is not true (as some have argued) that the bourgeois mentality and the ethos of haggling alone have primed people's minds for democratic dialogue; a more significant factor in this process is the rational thought and rational management that is the very lifeblood of a democratic social system.

(13) There is no doubt that the mores of development and prosperity, although not antagonistic to the ideals of ethics, are different from the mores of asceticism and mysticism, which prescribe austerity and world abnegation. What is virtue if not the proper etiquette for a given situation? The ethicists have stated, for example, that the proper appreciation of wealth is gratitude, just as the proper etiquette of poverty is patience. The affluent and thankful person is by no means ethically inferior to the patient poor one.[18] It is, therefore, imprudent to hold poverty as superior to wealth.

Choosing poverty and deprivation instead of wealth and conviviality is a well-meaning and well-worn Sufi [ascetic] prescription for redemption. However, it has little weight on the scale of sober analysis. This is one of those contested issues that has produced more confusion than clarity among the ethicists. Only a sociological and psychological analysis can shed light on this quandary. Two great thinkers from the Shi'ite and Sunni schools of thought; Al-Ghazzali and Feiz Kashani, have, after extensive inquiry, reached the same verdict concerning this issue: "It should be generally admitted that poverty is better and safer than affluence because the poor have less of an interest in the worldly affairs and to that extent, they will be more inclined to prayer and pious reflection."[19]

These great thinkers confess that the poor and the rich are both infatuated and captivated by the world, albeit in different ways. "The world is the object of adoration of the perplexed. Those who are deprived of it are obsessed with seeking it, and those who are endowed with it are preoccupied with preserving it." Still, these ethicists argue that "in the majority of cases the danger of poverty is less than that of affluence, because the temptations of wealth are greater than those of poverty. This seems to be the nature of human beings, with very few exceptions."[20] This verdict originates in the belief that "weakness brings about security"; that the amputee is, of necessity, less likely to sin. To paraphrase Rumi, "Poverty is a better guard for the righteous." This fear culminates in the macabre poetic image:

> I will craft a dagger, steel-plated,
> Slashing my eyes, so the heart is liberated.

This is the same virtue of world flight (as opposed to world mastery) that has inspired the righteous flight into wilderness:

> He said the city is the abode of the handsome,
> Slipping on mud, even elephants are overcome.[21]

This is the morality that mocks worldliness. Sa'di tells us of a merchant who "one night in the island of Kish was boasting of his trade plans to take Persian sulphur to China, Chinese ceramics to Rome, Roman silk to India, Indian steel to Syria, Syrian mirrors to Yemen, Yemenite swords to Persia, and . . ." Sa'di interrupted him with this taunt:

> The narrow eyes of the man of the world
> are plugged, with either frugality or the grave's mold.

All of these attitudes are based on the erroneous assumption that poverty is preferable to wealth and that the rich are farther removed from salvation and more susceptible to a host of afflictions, from greed and penury to neglect and pride. It has been a rare voice like that of Hafez who courageously challenged the popular morality of asceticism.[22]

It is curious that Al-Ghazzali and Feiz Kashani, who deem ingratitude as the pitfall of wealth and impatience as the pitfall of poverty, propagated patient destitute instead of grateful affluence. They placed the security of the faithful on the shores of poverty and warned them against seeking the ocean's pearls:

> In the sea there are treasures aplenty,
> Stay on the shore if you seek safety.

There seems to be no other reason for this preference for poverty over affluence than the highly visible social inequalities that have made the affluent more rebellious, indulgent, and sinful. Otherwise, what could have been the reason for preferring one moral virtue, patience, over another, gratitude, and for fearing the pitfalls of wealth more than those of poverty?

Saʿdi, as an admirer and an indebted student of Al-Ghazzali's school of thought, nevertheless refused to accept the premise of the superiority of poverty over wealth. He believed that "the financially insecure is spiritually insecure." He debated the "bold Dervish" on this issue: "The power of generosity, of worship, of unblemished property and clothes, of secure life, and of unburdened heart" all belong to the affluent. He argued that "leisure can not be combined with poverty, nor security amidst destitute." He proposed that the virtues such as "donations, devotional offerings, friendly gatherings, and the varieties of alms-giving" are all good deeds, indeed forms of worship, that are available only to the affluent. He notes, on the other hand, "many an innocent soul who has fallen victim to sin and corruption because of poverty, bidding farewell to good reputation forever." Saʿdi conceded that among the rich there are those who are "short on ambition, and gratitude, who would sooner acquire and accumulate than spend and donate . . . would not bother about the hardship of the poor, and who have no fear of the almighty." But he is still convinced that this world and the next one belong to "the affluent who at once enjoy their wealth and bestow it generously; those who have joyous hearts and generous hands."[23] All this rhetoric is meant as a response to Al-Ghazzali's preference for the "patient poor over the grateful rich" and his belief that "at worship . . . the rich will never attain the elation of the poor . . ." and that even if they are equally parsimonious, the poor would be superior because "parsimony is no virtue for the rich who are supposed to give alms and be generous."[24]

In any event, the above debate shows that superiority of poverty over affluence is by no means a foregone conclusion. Although the world of our ancestors is awash in poverty and the world of our contemporaries is brimming with affluence and happiness, neither situation is morally superior to the other. On the contrary, if the virtues of poverty and those of wealth are properly observed, they would be morally equivalent. If the modern way of life is somehow flawed, it is not because it fails to be poor and patient, but because it fails to be rich and grateful. Only a fatalist would find affluence and gratitude mutually exclusive.[25]

(14) Science, the actually existing nature-searching and nature-challenging science, is nowadays the axis, the focus, and engine of development. Societies, to the extent that they possess it, are possessors of progress and modernity. The weaknesses and strengths of science mirror those of development. In other words, science and development share the same trajectory and destiny. A different kind of science, if possible, will yield a different world, history, and social development. The discoveries of science and achievements of civilization make a return to the past impossible.

This view has, and has always had, certain opponents. The most important and recent of these are represented in schools of thought that perceive an indissoluble nexus between knowledge and power (Foucault) or find an undeniable connection between science and human biases and interests (Habermas). There are others who, while accepting the validity of science, find it influenced by social determinations and forces (the Edinburgh school, Barnes and Bloor.) Others define science as an unconscious ideology of a community of practitioners (Kuhn.) Finally, there are those (Feyerabend) who equate science with some kind of magic and superstition.[26] Thus they all challenge the objectivity and realism of science and seek to reduce it to something of a social custom or norm, comparable to individual and collective tastes. It was a combination of such ideas that led to the onslaught of postmodernism against reason and science. Although these ideas are beginning to show signs of decline, they are still attractive to some intellectual thrill-seekers.

Some of our own "science-busters," too, have excitedly adopted this new handiwork of Western thought as a new weapon to protect their narrow-minded claims and beliefs. However, they should be aware that the aforementioned ideas, assuming they are valid, do not include the experimental sciences alone. They infect all domains of human knowledge. It is not as if modern sociology, for example, would be awash in power, human biases, and social forces that render it devoid of objectivity and validity, while Islamic philosophy and the like would go unscathed. This epistemological morsel obstructs not only the throat of science but of all human knowledge. It consigns *all* knowledge and belief to relativity.

Second, dethroning science is one thing, invalidating it quiet another. Postmodernism, which has issued the verdict of the relativity of truth (which is tantamount to denying it) is now, according to its own verdict, either devoid of the truth or else invites the charge of self-contradiction. In either case, it lacks the decisiveness and the power to function as a weapon against science. It is true that science is no longer considered as the only possible form of knowledge and the sole valid method for the discovery of the truth. But this refutes only a positivistic notion of science. Refutation of positivism is not the same thing as the refutation of science.

Third, the prevailing method of all of the above schools of thought in establishing epistemological antiscientific ideas about science has been one of historical induction. The works of the likes of Foucault, Kuhn, and Feyerabend are replete with extensive analyses and logical extrapolations of certain historical instances. Now how is it possible to deny the fundamental validity of such inductive-experimental methods while relying on them to advance these very ideas?

Fourth, the turbulent history of the philosophy of science, and particularly the advent of immense epistemological twists and turns in the conception of science, along with the profound, hair-splitting observations of the analytical philosophers of the twentieth century, indicates the extent of the damage the philosophers of science have inflicted on positivism and its extravagant and arrogant claims. It is in the historical context of antiscientism that the hostility of the above thinkers to science can be understood. The hasty and the uneducated should not neglect the situational and intellectual context of other people's ideas and judge a phenomenon before learning about its causes.

Positivism was rooted in two tenets: the denial of the historicity of science and reason and the belief in the possibility of unmediated, that is, non-theory-laden and naked observation. Accordingly, the entire effort of the antipositivist schools of thought was to demonstrate that observation prior to and unaffected by theory[27] would be a chimera.[28] The meaning and mystery of the objectivity of science, for the positivists, was nothing but the liberation from presuppositions. Similarly, the refutation of objectivity for the later thinkers was nothing but a refutation of the positivist presuppositions. If induction is so denigrated nowadays, it is not only due to its logical sterility, nor is it a result of the principle of philosophical indeterminacy. Rather, it is due to the discovery of a crowded empirical world that has lured the nature of things from their recondite lairs and released them into a blinding and bewildering storm of forces and fields. The resultant dizzying confluence of phenomena render the task of scientific induction terrifyingly complex.

In any case, postmodernism, which could do no more than debunk positivistic reason, has reached a point where it has to decide whether to espouse relativism or appeal to some other method of immediate realization of the truth. Positivism should be defeated, but not at the expense of overthrowing science and reason.

Fifth, the complex and illuminating conflict of realism and antirealism in the philosophy of science should be sustained. There are wondrous epistemological benefits to the resolution of this question.

If we accept that science has been successful in the task of manipulation of nature, then how could we possibly interpret this success in rational terms except by admitting that it reflects reality? Is not every step of success with nature indicative of a step in the establishment of the realism of science? Can a totally subjective and instrumental pseudo-epistemology (as some of the followers of the Frankfurt school accuse science of harboring) be so successful in practice? Even an instrument, in order to be effective, has to be appropriate to the medium in which it operates. Science, even if it is nothing but a tool (the instrumental view of science), is, thanks to its successes, not alien from reality and has, in that capacity, a general comparability and compatibility with it.[29]

One should not exaggerate criticism of science. The antipositivist attacks on science should not be interpreted as attacks on the rational value and worth of science per se. Nor should humanity neglect such an extraordinarily effective tool in understanding its history. Most importantly, one should beware of a misinterpretation of the fateful convergence of science and development and of thus impugning development by attacking science. Truth-seeking entails science-seeking. Science is at once the repository and the guide to the secrets of nature. Human beings are deliberative actors. They act within the radius of their knowledge. It is modern knowledge that has splashed novel colors over the worn-out mat of our existence. The new color will not fade. If there is any controversy here, it is not about science but about discovering the proper relationship between knowledge and justice and forging a desirable connection between them.

Rejection of science betrays new narrow-mindedness reminiscent of the dark ages. This attack on science has become prevalent in our society in various disguises: positivism, humanism, materialism, occidentalism, existentialism, phenomenology, or hermeneutics. All of these have but one root cause: uncertainty about the veracity of the new science and neglect of the truth. No truth-seeking human being can afford to be oblivious, neutral, and cold toward this steadfast new guest of humanity. Those who spread nonsense about development do so because they have no clear view of science and cannot separate the realm of epistemology from the other aspects of Western civilization. Thus, they have a contradictory and duplicitous encounter with development. On the one hand, they fail to reconcile themselves with it because of their anti-Western hollow pretensions. On the other hand, they fail to run away from it because of their historicistic views about the historic destiny of the West.

One needs to clarify one's relationship to science. The scientists and the truth-seekers have, of course, clarified their relationship to it. Science is different from customs, morality, art, and the habits of Westerners and "infidels." Customs and mores are noncognitive phenomena (although some argue that they inform epistemology). Science, however, is a cognitive phenomenon. Customs are themselves realities that may become subject to scientific inquiry. Science, on the other hand, is a handiwork of reason and a creature of criticism. It is the mirror of reality and a guide to action. It is exactly this reflective, criticizable, and rational nature of science that sets it apart from other Western phenomena. Yes, science is not utterly impartial, but what could be more impartial than science?[30] If a path has to be beaten to take us forward, it has to originate in science.[31]

We should make room for science because the values that encourage science are the same values that encourage development. Nature-conquering, ambitious, truth-seeking science does not enter just any realm and does not obtain under just any condition. Science, while conjectural, is, in practice, very effective. From this point of view, science has given skepticism a higher status than the ancients' certitude. This science is mutinous and ambitious. Above all, because of its alliance with technology, it has become self-augmenting and self-developing, so that it can not survive except through the medium of highly competitive and cooperative communities that are not only truth-seeking but skeptical, ambitious, and arrogant. There are scientists who sell their expertise for material gain and reputation. Although such ambitions have always been the very blood coursing in the veins of science, they are now being soberly offered as the oil that keeps the lamp of science burning brighter than ever. Take a cursory look at the role of academic credentials, scientific prizes, and social positions accorded to the contemporary scientists to catch a glimpse of the picture of science in the mirror of the modern age. Skepticism, tolerance, competition, and ambition should be revered as the four heavenly streams that keep the meadows of science and the orchards of development alive and green.

(15) Now it becomes clear that the principles of development are composed of two sets of principles: the ethics of science and ethics of prosperity. The mores of modern times have, for the first time, underlined, endorsed, and articulated these virtues. Thus yesterday's grotesque secret has become today's preening beauty.

This explanation is offered so no one would conclude that development legitimizes vice and that, conversely, more deceit, subterfuge, injustice, fraud, and sloth stimulate further development; that an increase in social displays of lust and corruption (just as it is seen in the Western societies) signals the onset of development. These assumptions are seriously flawed and utterly superficial. Deceit and subterfuge, for example, are compatible neither with the mores of science nor with those of prosperity. They destroy the mutual trust that is the very foundation of social solidarity and human coexistence.

On the other hand, such phenomena as sexual excess found in the developed countries is one of the vices attending prosperity. Just as poverty is vulnerable to one set of vices, prosperity is susceptible to another. All the wealthy are not grateful, nor are all the poor patient. An abundance of knowledge and wealth can provide the requisite profundity and leisure to make the experience of subtle spirituality possible. On the other hand, once the fetters of primary needs are lifted, the human soul is more tempted to rebel, indulge, and neglect. That is why a developed society needs a sovereign morality even more than an undeveloped one because the observance of the morality of power is far more complex and necessary than the practice of the morality of paralysis and poverty.

Arresting development, attacking science, and glorifying poverty is not the answer to the vices that attend prosperity. Development opens up the space for criticism. One should seize the opportunity to launch a critique of development and to apply self-correcting measures (morally, practically, and theoretically). What the sober Western critics are doing now is, indeed, a manifestation of their appreciation of this opportunity.

On the path of development we should draw on our traditions. However, traditions may prove to be both fetters and fulcrums. They should be, at once, sought as shelters and avoided as prisons. The mores of science and prosperity are two groups of useful traditions that we need now more than ever before.

4

The Sense and Essence of Secularism

1. The Fundamental Rift between Tradition and Modernity

Modern humankind is profoundly and fundamentally different from its forebears. The difference is evident in the realm of ideas and worldviews as well as in action and life. Humankind has acquired different perspectives, altered expectations, and new patterns of behavior in every respect. As a result, the contemporary world seems to retain its past qualities only in the most superficial sense. Such notions as economy, morality, government, and money are analogous to jars filled with new wine.

Here, I would like to outline some of these transformations. Modern humankind is no longer satisfied with an interpretation of the world. It has become an active subject instead of a passive object. It rejects the status quo and believes it should use all its abilities to transform the world. It considers nothing as final, ineluctable, and immutable. In contrast, traditional humanity regarded everything as settled and predetermined and deemed it neither possible nor desirable to change the world. Instead, it was satisfied with minor adjustments of behaviors and relationships. It believed that the "natural" order of the world (both in society and in nature) should not be disturbed. This belief is evident in allegories in which society was compared to a body with the rulers as the head and the workers as the feet; or metaphors in which politics is likened to medicine for the social body. Health was defined as preservation of every humor in its natural place. The philosophers of antiquity taught that anything that is removed from its natural position has a tendency to return to it. That is how they explained movement itself. Thus it was assumed that if everything in the universe were left in its natural place, all movement would cease. The concept of "natural place" was of utmost importance to the ancient philosophers. In the modern world, however, there is no room for "natural places" in nature or in society. No modern thinker would argue that fire, for example, "tends" to move upward because, as an element, its natural place is in the "ethereal sphere"; or that royalty are naturally placed at the top of their society. Monarchies have survived only as formalities. They have lost their claim to a natural place and their continued ritual survival is entirely in the hands of republican governments. But this has not always been the case. In the premodern past, the institution of monarchy was never challenged even if a particular unjust monarch could be deposed.

The world of medicine provides us with another vivid example of the versatility of the modern perspective. Modern surgery not only removes and replaces organs, but it stands ready to discuss a better design and order for the human body. The intervention is no longer purely medical but architectural. Modern medicine doesn't always take the human organism to be the epitome of an ideal design. In the past, by contrast, the goal of medicine was to return patients back to their natural state. The natural state was considered as the ideal state. "Health" was identified with this "natural" state just as "disease" was equated with deviation from it. This paradigm has long since been abandoned, at least in its strict and traditional form. Today's physicians and surgeons will not hesitate to replace an organ with an artificial substitute that would work longer and better than the original organ, thus extending and improving the quality of life. The naturally given form and function of human body is no longer considered inviolate and sacrosanct.

This change of attitude is not limited only to politics and medicine. It is ubiquitous. Modern humankind has assumed the role of an aggressive and active agent in the world, whereas traditional humankind perceived itself as a guest in a ready-made house, in which the occupant had no opportunity or right to object or to change anything. Human beings were content to their "share" of life and cherished the maxim: "we were allotted no more than these few scraps from the destiny's table."[1]

The advent of the scientific worldview, along with modern philosophical anthropology, has gradually relegated this attitude to obscurity and replaced it with an active and ambitious outlook. Our aim here is not to evaluate but to merely describe this process. Modern humanity aims to create the world in its own image rather than accepting it as it is. Nothing is deemed indisputably "given." Ours is, to paraphrase Marx,[2] the epoch of transforming—not merely understanding—the world. Some have confused the traditional concept of "determination" with the lack of free will. The former denotes the measured and balanced nature of reality while the latter means fatalistic submission. The former is what Sheikh Shabestari intended by this poem:

> This world is like features of a beautiful face.
> Each feature is just fine in its proper place.[3]

Without a doubt, the deterministic approach to life required a peculiar understanding of religion. In the past, religion seldom encouraged energetic, radical, and ambitious transformation and exploitation of the world. Ethicists and religious sages of yore were unlikely to encourage momentous, dynamic, and useful utilization of the world's resources. Some believe they actively discouraged such an attitude. Traditional morality and religious temperament required humility before the creator. One of the attributes of such a humility was acquiescence in and gratitude for one's lot in life; in other words, the virtuous individual was expected to accept his lot, justly use and share it, and generally lead a tranquil life.

Modern humanity, due to its new worldview, has forged a novel relationship with religion. If we are mired in theoretical and practical difficulties today, it is because we have gradually and materially advanced toward the modern epoch, while our thoughts have lagged behind. Most of our perceptions of ourselves and of the world are relics of the past. Everything about the modern world invites us to abandon this perspective. Our acute anxieties are born out of this conflict.

The contrast between modernity and tradition does not end here: a modern person is critical and demanding (not placid and inert), in search of change (not merely of understanding), in favor of revolution (not just reform), active (not passive), at home with skepticism and anxiety (not certitude), interested in clarity and causality (not bewilderment and enchantment), prone to pride and joy (not sorrow of separation), mindful of life (not death), in pursuit of rights (not only duties), sponsor of creative (not imitative) art, oriented to the external (not just the internal) world, a lover (not a despiser) of life, an intervener in (not merely a user of) the world, a user of reason in the service of criticism (not just for understanding). Modern humanity is, in a word, oblivious to its limits and proud of its creative possibilities. It is, therefore, far from Rumi's description:

> Since we are the created, rather than the creator,
> We are meant to be meek and demure.

2. Secularism and Religion

The above reflections lead us to the analysis of secularism and its relationship to religiosity. Secularism has been understood as a deliberate effort to exclude religion from worldly affairs. But the truth is that secular governments are not opposed to religion; they accept it but not as a basis for their legitimacy or as a foundation for their actions. Every government, in order to survive and endure, needs two things: a source of legitimation and a normative framework. There was a time when governments borrowed these requirements from religion. However, in our era (roughly the last three hundred years) this practice has become obsolete. Nowadays governments derive their legitimacy from the consent of the governed. The norms of governance too, are determined, in theory at least, by laws established by institutions representing the people.

One may think of two possible motivations for secularism's insistence on the separation of religion and government: the belief in the fundamental falsehood of religion, coupled with the fear of its deleterious effects on politics, or the belief in the fundamental truth of religion coupled with concern over its contamination and profanation by political concerns. In any case, secularism succeeded in banishing religion from the realm of politics and placing the right of legislation and government exclusively in people's hands.

Secularism arose from two sources: the growth of modern scientific thought and rationality and the profound changes in the meaning and relationship of rights and duties. Here I will try to further elaborate on these issues.

3. Secularism and Modern Worldview

In my view, the proper analysis of modern history entails an understanding of modern knowledge.[4] The analysis of the history of humankind, too, depends on understanding the history of knowledge. Humanity would have lingered in the traditional world had it not been for the advent of modern scientific knowledge and its metaphysical foundations. Even the shift from the emphasis on duties to emphasis on rights is a result of this newly acquired insight. The modern scientific knowledge has transformed not only humanity's view of the world, but also its view of its own abilities and place in it. Thus a revolution analogous to the one in natural science has overtaken the social sciences such as anthropology, sociology, economics, and political science. Secularism, in this sense, is nothing but the "scientification" and rationalization of social and political thought and deliberation.[5]

The scientific treatment of society mirrors the scientific treatment of nature. It is rare that a discovery in modern natural science has not found its way into social science. Modern knowledge has established its hegemony in the world in a way that allows no exceptions. The first postulate of epistemologists and scientists is that once an effective tool is found, it should be used as widely as possible.

With the passage of centuries, the change in the metaphysical-philosophical view of nature affected the social and psychological realm. As a result, our understanding of society and economy was revolutionized as well. It is impossible to combine a nonscientific view of natural phenomena with a scientific-empirical social policy and method of management. The scientific treatment of social affairs and the scientific-empirical control of political and moral issues was preceded by scientific understanding and control in the natural domain. As the modern scientific attitude supplanted the metaphysical-philosophical attitude, the search for material and efficient causes substituted the search for final causes; the question shifted from "why" to "how"; the inquiry focused on laws of nature rather than on effects of natures; the investigation of natural inclinations superseded the search for violent aberrations, and skepticism displaced certitude. The eventual application of these intellectual trends to society dispelled its aura of mystery and subjected it to the blade of empirical research. Society became a scientific subject matter, an independent domain of research. The search for its "laws" became a scientific undertaking. Gone were the days when humankind infused all affairs with occult qualities and recoiled from investigating their innermost secrets. Shorn of their sacred, fear-inspiring, and daunting qualities, the worlds of nature and society were no longer unknown and unknowable conundrums. In their encounters with nature, the philosophers of yore had been lured by the temptation of discovering invariant "natures" and essences of things. For them, science was nothing but the discovery of the substantial forms and their occult qualities seen from a dogmatic philosophical-metaphysical vantage point. The modern science of nature was born when scientists abandoned such inquiries and concentrated on the observable regularities of phenomena, thereby making possible the great leap in scientific intervention in the world of nature we call modern technology.[6]

The ancients' natural philosophy was also in harmony with their social theory and politics. The two categories have proved complementary throughout the modern scientific developments. Although the change in the latter lagged behind the change in the former in the modern times, it was inevitable. The bold intervention in the world of nature inspired similar strategies in the world of politics; the same scientific, rational, and objectifying attitude toward the world of nature permeated social and political thought as well. Just as the discovery of empirical laws rendered metaphysical speculation obsolete, the focus on realpolitik relegated the meditations on the politics of all logically possible societies to obscurity and concentrated, instead, on the discovery of the moral and legal processes of actually existing societies (à la Machiavelli and his intellectual progeny).

This was the dawn of secularism. From an epistemological point of view, the presecular age is marked by the hegemony of metaphysical thought in political, economic, and social realms. In this era human beings lacked the courage to intervene in social affairs. For them society and politics remained unexplored, in need of conceptual independence and a clear definition. Thus, a lack of clarity about the nature and concept of society and politics reduced people to passivity instead of active mediation and improvement of their social environment.

There is a difference between riding a vehicle and constructing it. The institution of monarchy, for example, was like a ready horse, not a deliberately designed vehicle of transportation. Let's not forget that human beings at this stage were still more inclined to use than to invent. Society was still a "natural," God-given, and predestined phenomenon. One did not intervene in "nature." Social design and engineering was inconceivable. It was only the bold interventions in nature through industry and technology that rendered the idea of resisting traditions and habits conceivable in society as well, thus launching the scientific social theory and scientific intervention in social policy. Harnessing natural forces, discovering natural secrets, and the inventing of new instruments changed the face of the earth, gave people the courage to revise social conventions and to initiate deliberate reforms in the world of politics. Thus, the sciences of morality, politics, and economics were born.

There was, of course, an additional dimension to this change. The very definitions and connotations of human morality and happiness were transformed. Because the temperament of a creative, active, and intervening humanity is different from that of a passive one. Human notions of autonomy and morality have changed apace. Science and power have created a new morality.[7] In a word, society, morality, and politics have all become the handiwork of man. There is nothing that is accepted as preordained and inviolate anymore. In our world not only television, the computer, and the airplane are man-made, but the morality, the polity, and ideology as well. There is no inviolable point of departure save the concept of the "truth" itself. But even truth, according to some postmodernists, is humanly constituted; we fashion the truth rather than discover it.

It is true that some modern economists such as Adam Smith have argued that society needs to remain unaltered and that the state should exert minimal intervention in the economy so that the "invisible hand" can maintain the market in equilibrium, but this in no way conflicts with scientific management and systematic economics. It does not constitute a mystification of the market. On the contrary, it is meant as an effort to demystify it: to understand how prices are adjusted, how inflation occurs, and how depression sets in. Socialist governments that advocate active intervention in the market, too, are far from metaphysical. The clash of these two positions occurs within the scientific approach, not between science and metaphysics. They are, and have always been, scientific in aspiration regardless of their truth value.

The span of human intervention in the world has widened along with the increased radius of human knowledge. History bears clear testimony to this relationship. An expansion of knowledge has led to an expansion of power, and further demystification of nature, society, and economy. If we consider this whole process evolutionary (which is not inconceivable), if we regard all truths commensurable and convergent (which is unavoidable), and if we further deem humanity more or less successful in the discovery of the truth (again, a plausible assumption), then we will have to declare the odyssey of human knowledge, as a whole, conducive to the happiness and well-being of humankind and ultimately instrumental in comprehending the true message of divine revelation.

Scientific thought and rational management mean subjecting everything to critique and rational questioning in order to prevent leaders and followers from acting blindly and irrationally. That is why a secular government should be defined not only by what it is not, that is, a nonreligious government, but by what it is, a government susceptible to criticism, checks, and balances. Thus we may define secularism as a regime in whose polity no values and rules are beyond human appraisal and verification and in which no protocol, status, position, or ordinance is above public scrutiny. Everything is open to critique, from the head of state to the manner of government and the direction of policy determination. This is the meaning of secularism. Naturally, when politics is desacralized (that is, when it becomes rational and scientific) while religion remains sacred, the two are separated. This is the meaning of and the reason for the separation of religion and state in secular societies.

Like the separation of religion and science, this need not be an antagonistic breach. Religion is not identical with science, nor is it a progenitor, an arbiter, or a guide for it. Still less does it follow the objectives of science. At the same time, religion need not deny or oppose science. Everything that dons the garb of science (be it government or management) enters a similar relationship with religion. Religious management or religious science is as conceivable as religious thermodynamics or religious geometry. The truth is that politics can be mixed with religion only if a nonsacral understanding of religion is juxtaposed with a nonsacral method of administration. Otherwise, blending sacred religion with the secular politics would be absurd.[8] My theory of contraction and expansion introduces the only natural way to attain that goal.[9]

In order to better understand the causes of the prevalence and popularity of secularism, one needs to remember the presecular days. The fact is that the behavior of the religious hierarchy was a major cause of the antireligious and antichurch movement. The rebellion was not against God but against those who ruled and committed atrocities in the name of God. Those who were subjected to such inequities, intimidations, deceptions, and crimes, even if they were religious, rose against the regime or else acquiesced in an alternative secular rule. In presecular times, religion was a sponsor of political regimes. It lent politics both legitimacy and legality. But the transgressions, injustices, conflagrations, inequities, and deifications that resulted from this alliance proved intolerable. The insightful among the subjects started asking themselves: how can human beings, while remaining human, lead divine (that is, infallible) governments?

Human rule is just that, and no element of it can be attributed to divinity. What transpires among us humans, whether in the name of God or otherwise, is, of necessity, human and fallible. It should thus be open to rational supervision and scrutiny. The social and political domain admits of no irrational or supernational displays commanding passive witness and submission. Everything that enters nature, including religion and revelation, bends to its ways. Everything that enters human society becomes social and human. This means that in the realm of nature and human society, there is no such thing as supernatural and meta-social phenomena. Even the ethereal spirits don corporeal clothes upon entering the domain of nature. Viewing human nature and human affairs as natural has become an instrument for rectifying the injurious errors of the past.

In any event, if the scientific approach to nature is said to be antithetical to religion, then the scientific approach to politics would also conflict with religion. However, this does not have to be the case. Human beings can remain spiritual and religious while enjoying the benefits of rational administration of their affairs. Those who consider modern science blasphemous or try to break its majesty with a thousand ifs and buts have no appreciation of the truths that have been uncovered by science. They are naive.

The notion that the new world gradually rids itself of religion is only half true. It is true in so far as the modern world condemns ignorant and vulgar religiosity to extinction. However, it also allows a different kind of religiosity, a learned and examined religion, to prosper on a higher level. Scientific treatment of political and economic affairs does in no sense preclude a well-defined role for God and religion in political, social, and natural affairs. Determining the limits of that role and the exact form of that relationship remains to be worked out by scholars. The least we can say in this respect is that religiosity or lack thereof do not enter the essence of government. However, as an external reality, government is subordinate to society and constitutes one of its forms of realization. If a society is religious, its government too will take a religious hue. This will become clearer later on.

4. The Modern Primacy of Rights over Duties

Secularism received a further boost from the changes in the relationship between rights and duties. It pleases us to speak of human rights in the modern world, where rights are honored above duties. One of the markers of the modern—in contradistinction to the traditional—world is the emergence of the "rights-carrier" as opposed to the "duty-bound" human being.

The language of religion can shed light on this issue. By "the language of religion" we mean the specific categories used by religion for the purpose of exhortation and communication which are quite distinct from those used in the languages of science and philosophy. The language of religion (especially that of Islam as exemplified by the Qur'an and the Tradition) is the language of duties, not rights. In these texts, human beings are given commandments by a supremely sovereign authority. The language of shari'ah is that of commanding, as the picture of humanity in the mirror of religion is that of a duty-bound creature. Human beings are required to believe, pray, give alms, and conduct themselves in such matters as matrimony and inheritance in accordance with traditional guidelines. They are constantly warned not to overstep the boundaries set by God lest they be held responsible and have to suffer the consequences of such trespass. Of course the religious texts do occasionally address the rights of humans, but such passages are very rare and exceptional. For instance, in the Qur'an we read: "Whoever is slain unjustly, We have appointed to his next-of-kin authority; but let him not exceed in slaying; he shall be helped."[10]

On occasions like this the rights are emphasized but, besides being rare, these passages often derive the rights from duties; rights are in a clearly subordinate position. Often even the word right [haq] is used as a synonym for duty. For instance, in "The Treatise on Rights" ["Resale-ye Hoqouq"] attributed to Imam Sajjad,[11] we read about the right of the father over his son or daughter, the right of neighbor over neighbor, the right of God over the people, and so on. In fact, these are not rights but duties that imply respecting the rights of others at the expense of oneself. What is at issue here is not my rights which are to be respected by my neighbors, but their rights, which I am supposed to respect.

In this treatise and others like it, there is no trace of human rights (e.g., the right to freedom of speech, marriage, and religion) in the modern sense of the word. According to the experts, the subject matter of religious law (shari'ah) is the action oriented to performing duties. Here they first imagine humans as duty-bound subjects and then describe their duties. No one has ever suggested that shari'ah deals with the subject who has certain rights. Observing the difference between what is taught under the rubric of rights in our universities and the field of shari'ah, which deals with duties, illustrates the depth of the rift between the modern and the traditional views.[12] The knowledge of duties is as marginal to modern law as that of rights is to traditional religious law.

Humankind's subjective mastery of nature allowed this newly creative and dominant race to radically transform the world and its view of itself. This radically different picture would be responsible for the transposition of rights and duties. Humans, having been promoted from the status of guests to that of hosts (and then to architects of the house) now saw themselves more as bearers of rights rather than bondsmen of duties.

The concept of human rights itself changes in two main stages. At the outset, "rights" meant "liberty," "leave," or "permission." In this sense, the right to learn meant that if people wished to gain knowledge they might do so and no one would have the right to interfere with the liberty of learning. But gradually these rights evolved into demands. People demanded their rights and governments were accordingly charged with new tasks and responsibilities.

The theoreticians of the past used to say; "Sovereigns are mirrors of the sovereignty of God." The authority of kings was an expression of divine authority. In theology [kalam] God was portrayed as an absolute bearer of rights and free of all duties toward human beings. Accordingly, kings were viewed in the same light, assuming a minimum of responsibility and carrying a full measure of rights. But now even those states that are based on the principle of minimal government intervention in public affairs are burdened with heavy duties toward the people who have assumed the role of creditors demanding their rights from the government. Of course the duties of the government and the demands of the people are predicated on primary rights won by humanity in modern times.

In my judgment, this is one of the main reasons behind the failure of the modern world to comprehend the principles of "the guardianship of the jurisconsult" [velayat-e faqih] and "the Islamic government" [hokoumat-e Islami] that prevail in postrevolutionary Iran. The government founded on the guardianship of the jurisconsult as based on duties as it is, conflicts with the mentality of modern humanity as well as with most of the modern political philosophies that base the idea of the state on the principles of the rights of human beings. In the latter system the people, who are endowed with rights, exert them by electing their leaders to a government that guarantees to protect the public good. In this sense government serves and manages more than it rules. By contrast the government based on the guardianship of the jurisconsult is based on duties. Because the religious law (fiq'h) views human beings as duty-bound, everything starts with obligations: people are obliged to vote, obey the leader, and form a government because they have already accepted a series of religious principles and injunctions.

We can observe the modern transformation of duties into rights in the sphere of religion as well. In the modern world people have the right (not the duty) to have a religion; they are free to be religious or nonreligious. By contrast, idea of duties prescribes an obligation to be religious and deems both the government and the people as guardians of faith. The difference between these two ideas is clear. The guiding principle of the former view is *performing* (as in performing prayers), while the latter case is based on the prospect of *realizing* (as in realizing profits.) With the assumption of duties the society is seen as a temple whose purpose is to please its creator. The viewpoint of rights envisions society as a marketplace where the aim is satisfying the members. The former pursues the satisfaction of the creator, the latter that of the people.

Society will not encounter any problems as long as the government and the people share the same view of obligations. This has been the customary practice for centuries, and no difficulties have ensued. Conversely, if social relations are based on rights, again no problems will occur. The difficulties arise when the following question is posed: does one's religious duty toward the government supersede one's rights? Any asymmetry in the perceptions of the people and the government will lead to problems. Also, the blurring of the lines by the leaders of the religious governments is a source of confusion. They may speak the language of rights one day and switch to that of duties in the next, undoing their own efforts, making sound judgment impossible, and confounding the mind.

One of the most important problems of all religious governments lies in whether they recognize the rights of people on a basis that is independent from the religious law. The issue of the choice between guardianship [*velayat*] and representation [*vekalat*] belongs to this general area. To regard the ruler as the guardian is consistent with the view of a duty-bound society, while considering the leader as a representative implies a society based on rights. All of our problems stem from attempts to combine these two attitudes. Now let us take a closer look at the religious implications of these two views.

Religion forbids us from assuming a God-like character.[13] Religion also commits us to serving God. So, the place of the believer falls somewhere between negating the former and engaging in the latter. But, what is the position of the modern humanity? Of course, it reserves for itself the right to serve God—as opposed to the traditional obligation to do so. On the positive side, however, modern humanity does not tolerate the presumption of God-like character. This is especially true in politics and government where limiting the power of the state, division of powers, and the doctrine of checks and balances are established in order to prevent accumulation of power that might lead to such Godly claims. Therefore, while lightening the burden of duties, the modern world has also undermined a right that has always been a source of evil and corruption: that is, the right to act as a God-like potentate with unlimited powers.[14] Secularism rejects God-like pretensions because it does not consider government to be an extension of the divine power within human society. Management skills require merely human, not God-like powers.[15] In the modern world the government and the rulers are the most responsible agents. They are, by no means, embodiments of the truth. The subjects do not await their high-handed generosity but rather demand their rights and participate in political affairs.

5. The Roots of the Secularization of the Human Mind

The above reasons for the secularization of the world are proximate causes. Now we must seek the remote as well as the primary causes of secularization. The main cause of secularization cannot be traced to political motivations that sought to restrict the powers of tyrants by denying religious legitimation to the government through separating religion from politics. This was one of the consequences of secularism, not its cause. Secularism was the progeny of rational metaphysics. The gateways leading to secularism and separating God and his designs from the world and its explanation were thrown open once the philosophers (primarily the Greek ones) embarked on the project of philosophizing the world order and subsuming it under nonreligious metaphysical categories.

By abandoning the idea of just deserts [esteh'qaq] and bringing forth the concepts of nature and essence, they inspired humanity to accept a rational explanation of the world in absence of God and helped give rise to democracy and technocracy. Aristotle rightly defined the philosophers as those who described "natures," in contradistinction to earlier sages, who spoke of gods.[16] The discussion of objective good and bad ushered in the era of ethics in absence of Gods; values referred to the inherent nature of deeds rather than to divine sanctions. The notion of "nature," and therefore natural rights, opened the gate to the laws of causality and natural rights at the expense of duties. In the words of Leo Strauss, the word *nature* does not occur in the Torah.[17] This is true of all religions because the discovery of nature and natural rights was an independent philosophical breakthrough with grave consequences for religious life. Gradually the essences of things gained autonomy from God, whose job was restricted to fleshing out the essences, rather than making them what they are. God was no longer the creator of essences but the agent of their realization.[18]

Thus, philosophical musings about nature, essences, and substances gave the world and the things in it an autonomy that could not be imagined by the pre-Platonic religious mind. The controversies between the sages ('arifan) and philosophers refers to this very problem. The sages wished a kind of rebirth for humanity that would erase causality from the mind and put an end to the obsession with particular, proximate, and ultimate causal chains with respect to God's existence as the "Prime Mover:"

> When mankind is a second time born
> The chain of causes it shall scorn.
> The "Prime Mover" will not be part of his belief
> The "Proximate Cause" will cause him naught but grief.[19]

Why? because putting God at the end of the chain of causes and making Him subject to causal and philosophical regulations offends the faithful. It does not befit the religious outlook to limit God's absolute freedom within the framework of the laws of causality or to force such divine attributes as justice, benevolence, beneficence, and compassion (as well as His freedom to answer prayers or change a previously determined course of events) into the tight strictures of causal relationships. Such an outlook not only affronts the heart of the believers, but it also creates such difficulties that even Greek philosophy would despair of solving.

One must not underestimate the disenchantment that follows from the introduction of such concepts as "essence" and "nature" into the world-view of believers. If we assume an essence for something, we can not help but remove it from the universe of religion since it can not have two essences at once. Water, for instance, has a given essence. Thus we can not have a religious water (or wine, for that matter) and an irreligious one. The same would apply to justice, government, science, philosophy, and so on. It is as impossible to imagine an Islamic or Christian philosophy or sociology, as it is to conceive of an essentially religious government.[20] This difficulty will also spread to such concepts as laws and essentially divine and religious ethics and law [fiq'h].

Let us recapitulate what we have learned so far:

A. We can grasp the depth of animosity expressed by such religious leaders as Al-Ghazzali[21] and Sohrevardi[22] toward the Greek philosophy. The problem is not only with such marginal issues as the difficulty of imagining a physical hereafter or reconciling divine knowledge with philosophical thinking. The philosophical intrusion threatens the entire edifice of religious worldview.

B. We can appreciate the bitter disagreement between the Mu'tazilite and Ash'arite thinkers over whether the philosophizing, that is, Hellenizing, of religion would lead to unconditional surrender of religion to Greek philosophy.

C. We can perceive why Greek philosophy and religion are, by and large, mutually exclusive and why the efforts to reconcile Hellenic reason and revelation have failed.

D. We can see the subtle and cunning methods by which secular thinking penetrates the mind. This is why some have likened the religious philosophers (their protestations against irreligion notwithstanding) to the enemy's Trojan horse within the fortress of religion.

E. We can observe—to the astonishment of many of those who have dabbled in philosophy—that modern philosophies may be considerably closer to religious views than the "Islamicized" essentialist philosophies. We also discover the futility of the efforts of some Islamic neo-Aristoteleans to Islamicize sociology, economics, and law.

6. The Social and Political Implications of Secularism

It is clear that the assumption of autonomous essences ties the hands of the earthly tyrants who wish to mold human beings to their desires. The possessor of an innate form does not accede to external manipulations. Before submitting humans to the tyrants' arbitrary will, certain philosophies—namely Hegelianism and Marxism, its direct scion—must first denature humanity in a torrent of historicism. Marx's dictum regarding the need to "change the world" referred to his fundamental desire to revamp human nature and create a new history. Like God, he set out to invent everything over and originate new essences. Such philosophies deem humanity to be pure potentiality, completely determined by the social environment. These dangerous assumptions pave the way for the harshest forms of despotism. Conversely, belief in autonomous essences, even in apolitical or religious guise, preserves the autonomy of the individual and his resistance in the face of oppression. It protects, human dignity and honor and restrains the powerful. Independent essences define the limits of power.

The attack against the doctrine of "just deserts," transforming it into a matter of the laws of causality, fits the philosophers' penchant for naturalism and is an integral part of their attempts to secularize the sphere of thought.[23] Some theologians have used the laws of causality in order to rationalize the problem of sanctions in the hereafter. They have argued that the allotment of sanctions in the hereafter, unlike the procedural penalties meted out by the criminal justice systems of this world, are nothing more than direct causal relationships. For instance, the divine punishment for uttering a falsehood is actually the direct result, or the flip side, of the evil deed itself. It is not a punishment that is determined and meted out because the perpetrator has deserved it, rather the torment is the direct effect of lying. The liar has not "deserved" but merely generated the punishment. The same could be said of becoming sick as a result of not observing the rules of hygiene, a rise of prices as a result of an increase in demand, or the ebb and flow of the sea caused by the moon's gravitational pull. The ebb and flow of the sea is not a positive or a negative sanction for the moon but merely the natural consequences of it.

Reducing the system of good and evil deeds and their punishment and reward in the hereafter to a causal chain eliminates the principle of "just deserts" and overturns God's entire ethical and judicial system. The triumph of the law of causality over that of just deserts removes the good and evil and, thus, virtue and vice from the realm of human action. Sin, repugnance, and crime would lose their meanings, so would asceticism, virtue, and moderation, paving the way for a secular ethics whereby people are likely to consider the consequences of their actions rather than contemplate their obligations. Replacing a system of obligations with a calculus of gain and loss is consistent with secular ethics. It leads to a kind of utilitarianism where ethics proceeds without the assumption of God and crime is viewed not as good or bad but as deviant behavior. Thus secular thought was born to explain nature and ethics in the absence of God. The secular design for the society that was realized in modern times is the last stage of this process.

In societies where secular thought is not prevalent such social ills as inflation and famine are regarded as a sort of divine punishment. But modern society does not use the language of just deserts or that of rights and duties in explaining such problems. Instead, following the Greek tradition, it follows the rules of causes and effects. This would preclude the use of religious concepts. For instance, in the religious outlook water is considered a bounty [ne'mat]. Seeing water in this light evokes a number of related concepts such as "the benefactor," "giving thanks for the blessings," "reward for good deeds," "punishment for evil acts" and so on. In the words of Whitehead, when professors replaced the prophets, everything changed. If we refuse to consider water as a blessing, none of the related concepts will apply either. The system used by the prophets to explain the world was deeply imbued with the concepts of duties and obligations of human beings toward a God who alone had rights. No one was the owner of one's own existence. By contrast, the philosophers and professors erected an autonomous, self-reliant, and causally integrated system that lacked the concept of just deserts. The experts of social, political, and economic sciences inherited this philosophical system. Thus the concepts of rights and duties were abandoned. We have inherited this latter system. The mainstream social sciences advise against using the ethical systems in the management of social affairs, relegating them to the sphere of conscience. Thus the concepts of rights and obligations were reduced to matters of trial and error and restitutive concerns.

This was the story of the secularization of humankind which started with Greek philosophy and ended with European science. Then European science paved the way for intervening first in the natural and then in the social and political worlds, without the slightest help from God. The embryo of nonreligion was nurtured in this womb. The story of secularism is the story of nonreligious reason; a reason which is neither religious nor antireligious. The veil that separates this reason from religion is none other than the metaphysical reason. Tearing this veil asunder, if it could be torn at all, points toward the way out of the sphere of secularism.

5

Doctrine and Justification

The New Challenges
of the Philosophy of Religion

Fortunately, the philosophy of religion has received some attention since the revolution and has turned into a relatively familiar subject matter.

For those who are unfamiliar with the issue, let me just state that the philosophy of religion means "religiology." It is concerned both with the inner and the outer domains of religion. Both are likely to become problematic for a philosopher of religion: on the one hand, extrareligious schools of thought project new patterns of thought and propose new insights, questions, and doubts that guide believers and thinkers in particular directions and plant new images of religion in their minds. On the other hand, every religion has its own principles and teachings that form a constellation of methodologically and epistemologically coherent and interlocking beliefs that have practical implications.

Issues such as the nature of miracles, prayers, revelation, Satan, religious values, and faith are among intrareligious issues, while the questions of free will, human rights, meaningfulness of religions propositions, and practical verification of religion are extrareligious problems. Thus it is not surprising that the introduction of Aristotelian philosophy to the Islamic world has presented the Islamic philosophers with certain religious problems. Nor is it unusual that the twentieth-century world and its new philosophies such as existentialism and analytic philosophy have posed new problems for the philosophers of religion. Religious philosophy in this sense is connected to and nourished by, an inexhaustible source of new problems and insights such as the language of religion, its relation to reality, and the verifiability of religious claims.

Some of these are old questions that have acquired new formulations and methods of exploration. In the wake of the arguments advanced by modern critical philosophy and new epistemological schools, the limits of human understanding came under close scrutiny. This discussion was gradually extended from understanding to language; so the question became not just what human beings can and cannot understand but also what they can and cannot articulate. The question, in other words, shifted from the limitations of the mind to the limitations of language. (We may call the former problem Kantian and the latter Wittgensteinian.) As such, epistemology and linguistics posed two significant types of questions for the philosophers of religion and invited them to contemplate and to respond.

Some of the modern analytical philosophers considered any unscientific language meaningless and nonsensical. They thus forced philosophers of religion to defend the meaningfulness of religious propositions. As the philosophers of science launched the arguments concerning the verification and falsification of the scientific propositions, philosophers of religion found themselves confronted by the same questions. Are religious claims objectively verifiable? Do the faithful and the devout ever put the object of their faith and devotion to the test? Can history be considered an arena for investigation and verification of the truth of religions? Is the history of a religion related to its core beliefs (or its ideology) in any way? Is an unverifiable doctrine rationally acceptable?

These examples demonstrate the way in which ideas that originate and evolve outside of the context of religion pervade the philosophy of religion and provide religion and the faithful with new questions. The question concerning the meaningfulness of religious propositions, for example, is unprecedented in traditional Islamic theology [kalam]. We know of no traditional philosopher who has addressed this issue. The traditional theologians agreed, their particular disagreements notwithstanding, that they all understood one another's language of religion and that their propositions were meaningful. What was important for them was to prove their claims and to refute those of their opponents. When modern philosophy raised the suspicion that some of the discussions that philosophers have spent centuries elaborating may be altogether meaningless, devoid of any substance, the philosophers of religion wondered whether religious debates might belong to this category.

These questions gradually let to another: What is the language of religion? The ideal model of the positivists for a meaningful language was the language of science. For them "unscientific" meant "meaningless." Therefore, the question of the unity or multiplicity of languages, and the unity or multiplicity of criteria of meaningfulness of propositions became serious issues. The question was: Is there only one language, the language of science, to be used by all thinkers and students of religion, so they may communicate more "scientifically" and sound more plausible and rational? Or, are there different classes of independent languages, each with its own inner life and legitimate domain, each one as rational as any other? If this is the case, then, what kind of a language is the religious language? Is it the language of poetry? The language of myth? The language of propositions? A conventional language? Or a technical language? It is clear that all these questions are the results of novel epistemologies and new schools of thought.

The challenges to religious epistemology are of utmost significance for the cultural history of religion, alerting philosophers of religion to new issues and encouraging them to tackle new problems. To paraphrase the late Iqbal Lahori, religion has now found two new rivals: human science and history. In other words, there are three sources of discovery of the truth now available to human beings. The difficult task for contemporary humanity is to reconcile these three sources.

Kant's own investigation of the limits of human understanding, his questioning (and according to him, refutation) of all theological and metaphysical arguments concerning God's existence, became a fountainhead of Western theology and philosophy. It may be stated with certainty that now, in the second part of the twentieth century, there is hardly a philosopher or theologian who would confidently assert that it is possible to adduce an irrefutable argument for the existence of God.

What the theologians argue nowadays is not the proof but the "rationality" of religious beliefs. They aim to establish that being religious and believing in God, revelation, the invisible world, the hereafter, and the angels is reasonable; that those who have such beliefs are normal and rational human beings; that becoming religious is not tantamount to abandoning reason; and that rationality and faith are not mutually exclusive.

Arguing that faith, revelation, miracles, prayers, the hereafter, and so on, are reasonable, does not establish whether they are right or wrong. One may as well commit a "reasonable" mistake. But such a mistake, far from lunacy, is a sign of the proper use of one's rational faculties. Theologians, under the bombardment of Kantian philosophy, have retreated to such humble tasks as demonstrating that the religious experience is as acceptable as the sensual or rational experience and that while as liable to error, it is, nevertheless, as respectable and reasonable as any other form of experience; and that religious knowledge is revision in light of religious experience but that it is, nevertheless, a respectable, meritorious, and plausible form of knowledge. Only a handful of theologians are left who still deem irreligion irrational.

This is the focus of the investigations of such contemporary philosophers as Plantinga and Alston.[1] They have proposed novel ideas, indeed, emphasizing justification of religious thought in their epistemological treatises." Justification is attained, primarily, through two methods: the inductive method (which means depending upon reasons) and causal method (which means depending upon reliable channels of perception). They argue that the former is an unreliable method that has been traditionally used in sciences. The latter depends on reliable (but not infallible) sources of knowledge. To be reliable, knowledge has to be somehow related to the reality. It is in this sense that we rely upon reason and sensory perception, because they are supposed to have access to reality. It is in this sense that these philosophers justify religious experience, revelation, and inspiration. That is, they authenticate the religious knowledge and its fruits, which they consider dependable and worthy of serious and rational consideration.

Let me briefly consider a modern Christian theological controversy concerning the salvation and felicity of mankind at this point. The theological question is the following: Is there a single path toward salvation in any given age, or are there multiple paths? Does a Christian, a Moslem, or a Zoroastrian have the right to believe that all those outside his or her religious practice suffer in vain and will never attain salvation? Are they deceived by an illusion of salvation and felicity? Are they subjects of God's abandonment and wrath? Have they inadvertently gone astray? Are they thus bereft of God's love and eternal bliss? Is the path of divine guidance and salvation so narrow as to admit only one's co-religionists? Has God surrendered all human beings, save adherents of one faith, to Satan? Are the majority of people on this earth banished from God's redemption and hopelessly lost? What is the judgment of reason and the verdict of religion on this issue? These questions are valid for denominations and sects within a religion as well. Protestant, Catholic, and Orthodox Christians, as well as Shi'ite and Sunni Moslems, are confronted with the same problem. On the one hand, faith and certitude mean belief in a certain doctrine, that presumably excludes others as infidels and misguided. On the other hand, the vast scope of insoluble religious differences compounded by the self-assurance of everyone involved gives rise to the suspicion that God may favor this pluralism and that each group partakes of an aspect of the truth (and therefore, of guidance and salvation). Is the truth not one, and all the differences, to paraphrase Rumi, "differences of perspective"? Are we not all like that shepherd who realized the limits of his conception of God only after Moses came along?[2] Is the difference among religions in kind or in degree? Do all religions have a single essence? These questions and others like them set one group of theologians such as Barth and Brunner against the others including Kung, Hick, Smart, and Toynbee. Hick defends pluralism and inclusivism while Barth, who is an "exclusivist," advocates neoorthodoxy and recognizes no revelation outside Christianity.

Since 1964 the Catholic Church has recognized paths of salvation for those outside the church, including Moslems. But because not all theo-

logians are Catholic and because the pope's edict is not binding on Protestant and Orthodox theologians, this controversy continues to rage
within Christianity. The lesson of this discussion for us Moslems is to
reconsider our intrareligious differences, that is, the Shi'ite-Sunni controversy, and to establish the desirable unity on something more substantial than short-term political contingencies. All of the foregoing has been
but a preamble to an exposition of the philosophy of religion especially
the issue of justifiability of religion claims.

The Question of Justifiability
of Religious Doctrines

Theological discussions about the nature and attributes of God, in particular, have been the focus of this inquiry. It has been asked, for example,
whether or not God's absence would make a discernible difference in the
world or whether God's justice can be demonstrated in the external world.
Justifiability, of course, means different things in different schools of
thought in philosophy of science and epistemology. For some, a claim may
be justified by adducing positive examples and for others by adducing
negative examples. If neither positive nor negative examples can be
shown, then one has to conclude that the claim in question is empirically unjustifiable. Therefore, justifiability is contingent upon showing
positive and negative instances; in other words, verifications and falsifi-
cations. If we proceed from this vantage point, we will face curious questions. Some have tried to establish that religious ideas—particularly those
having to do with the nature of the Almighty—are all empirically unjustifiable, because for every positive instance one can cite a negative
and falsifying one. These philosophers maintain that those who argue
that God is just and compassionate resort only to positive instances in
which justice is done: the needy receive what they truly need, the in-
fant who has no teeth will receive the mother's milk that is so providently
prepared in advance and so on. These philosophers adduce a plethora of
negative instances that contradict the positive ones. The hungry and the
starving, the oppressed, the ailing, the deprived, and the miserable suffer in great numbers, and no one comes to their rescue.

The other side has responded with a salvo of rhetorical arguments such
as the following: Afflictions and evils have latent blessings; they are
necessary counterparts of the blessed endowments; they are "nonexistent" or negative in nature;[3] goods outnumber the evils; evil is a result of
human free will; and so forth. None of these arguments have satisfied
the opponents who have asked what would the world look like if it were
unjust? They argue that all the putative justifications lead to the conclusion that no matter what the world is like, it is just; thus there is
no practical way to distinguish just and unjust. This is exactly what

unverifiability means. One is, then, compelled to assume God's justice (and, analogously, his other attributes) as qualities beyond empirical justification. In other words, the claims concerning God's existence and attributes are metaphysical propositions, not experimental ones.

But the debate does not end here. Believers want to be able to witness God's handiwork in this world. When they state that God is compassionate, merciful, responsive, just, or vengeful, they don't mean this in an unobservable, incomprehensible, and inscrutable way. They want to savor God's compassion and justice. Therefore, either the meaning of divine justice and compassion should be altered, or the premise of God's presence in the world should be revised so that the question of empirical justifiability is properly addressed.

The First Proposition:
Unjustifiability of the Doctrine

If we follow this proposition and rule that religious ideas (particularly those concerning God's attributes) are empirically unjustifiable, we can assume we are safe from the attack of contradictory evidence. We can assert God is just in a peculiar sense even if he creates thousands of deformed babies, tyrannical rulers, fatal diseases, and if he fails to save millions of people suffering from inequity, poverty, and other afflictions. None of these contradict God's justice. The belief in the unverifiability and unfalsifiablity of religious propositions has this benefit: it will immunize belief against all that transpires on the turbulent surface of the world by keeping it suspended above worldly events at all times, like an airplane that is undisturbed by agitations of land and sea. The trouble starts when this airplane attempts to land. Then it can no longer be oblivious to mountains and oceans. Do those who believe in a compassionate, just, or vengeful God believe in a shrouded compassion, justice, or vengeance that is utterly absent from the reality and for which no instances can be furnished? Would they not want to witness evidence of God's presence in all contours of reality? Is this "testimony" an objective, demonstrable, generally shared, and intersubjective phenomenon? Or is it only in the believers' eyes?

Some theologians have tried to point to God's provident hand in human perception, while others have attempted to interpret both positive and negative instances as verifications of the premise of God's compassion and justice. Thus they argue: the positive instances confirm God's compassion and justice, and negative instances, too, are cloaked positive instances whose secret will be revealed on the day of judgment. Then it will become clear that they have not been contrary to God's justice. These theologians, then, argue that religious claims are testable if the test of the hereafter is taken into account. In other words, and to paraphrase a poem,

Don't tell me a heart makes no sound when it breaks,
In the hereafter all can hear the sound it makes.

If we assume that there is another world and that God's presence and sovereignty transcend the concrete natural world; if we assume that the world history constitutes but a short span of the life of humanity and of the entire creation; then we can expand the arena of verification to include the day of judgment, where God's expansive justice and mercy will be manifest. God will then display himself, not only in the limited mirror of this world, but in the infinitely vast mirror of existence.

Some of our theologians, too, have employed this line of reasoning to prove the existence of the hereafter. But this manner of reasoning is tantamount to making the claim unverifiable. For what would you conclude if you were charged with examining a substance and then told that the required laboratory cannot be found in this world? Would you not conclude that the substance in question cannot be examined in this world? This unverifiability of metaphysical propositions means that they are not testable. We need another method for ascertaining their truth or falsehood. This implication is clear: it is never easy to assert that such and such an event was a divine blessing or a damnation. Similarly, one cannot attribute acquired wealth or the defeat of an enemy to divine grace or curse. Such designations are the exclusive domain of God and his appointed ones.

Another group of theologians have proposed that the external world shows that God is, to say the least, neither unjust nor ignorant, and that is all we can know about God's justice, knowledge, and so on. Beyond this, we cannot know the truth about the nature of God's attributes and the way they apply to the external events of the world. This assertion, too, denies the verifiability of justice and knowledge by obscuring their meaning.

Let us now consider the justifiability of religion as a worldly system; that is, whether the success or failure of a religious system is a test of its truth or falsehood. Here religion is treated as an externally realized and sociohistorically developed doctrine, capable of concrete developments that can lead either to success or to failure. The question is to what extent does the success or failure of a religious civilization, administration, or organization reveal its truth or falsehood? Let me illustrate this with an example: the breakdown of Soviet Marxism is one of the most important events of the latter part of the twentieth century. There is a plethora of interpretations concerning this momentous event. While the foes of Marxism can hardly conceal their euphoria beneath the awe, Marxists, despondent, disturbed, and baffled, have attempted desperate justifications of these events. Of course, the fair-minded and the wise among them are simply trying to learn the lessons of this colossal collapse.

One of the lessons the opponents draw from this event is the fundamental flaws of the Marxist ideology. Behold the irony of history: instead of Marxists witnessing the demise of capitalism, the capitalists watched the death throes of Marxism. A "Marxist" explanation of this event is that Marxism, having reached the point of its historical disintegration, dug its own grave. (This is the interpretation Marxists would have given of the demise of capitalism.) The non-Marxist interpretation of the event is that the inner defects of the ideology (for example, its antiscientific and tyrannical nature) precipitated its demise. A sympathetic interpretation would hold neither the historical necessity nor the inherent defects of the doctrine responsible. Instead, it would blame the conspiracy of the enemies or the incompetence of administrators.

The question is, first, whether such an analysis can be extended to religious organization and second, whether social and historical success and failure can be grounds for judging the truth or falsehood of an ideology. A positive response would mean the ideology is justifiable and a negative response would mean that it is not. Which leads to this question: How can an unverifiable ideology, placed above the events of this world and deemed immune to confirmation and refutation, actually bolster an externally established system? How would such a system relate and connect itself with its respective ideology? The judgment of untestability implies severing bonds that neither a secular regime like Marxism nor a religious system like the Islamic civilization can afford to lose; for they owe their very identity to such bonds.

Let us ask ourselves how we would and should have judged the results had the tables been turned. Would we not come to believe that the prevailing system is in the right because it is successful, and that the vanquished regime is in the wrong because it is unsuccessful? Would the Marxists themselves not have made the same judgement? So why do they now refuse to concede and resort to pretexts and excuses? The debate is about the relationship between a doctrine and the system based on it. Is this relationship acceptable only in the case of the success of the system? Or does it hold in all cases? In other words, is there a connection between a theory and its historical and practical unfolding? To what extend could we argue that the defects of the administrators and followers, and not those of the doctrine itself, are the source of the problem? If we are going to maintain that an actual system springing from an idea has no relationship to the idea whatsoever, why then identify that system with that idea at all? Why should we call it a Marxist regime or an Islamic civilization? In order to purge an idea from the evil deeds done in its name, are we liable to use the sharp blade of judgment to clip all of the good resulting from that idea as well? Do we not thus sever a school of thought from all its positive and negative consequences?

It is truly difficult to pass such a judgment: to witness generations of dedicated followers fighting, sacrificing, creating, writing, and investing all their energies and faculties in the realization of a doctrine, and then, once the idea is realized and proven undesirable, to assert that the fault is theirs and not the doctrine's; and to further claim that the doctrine, as such, is unjustifiable and that all its practical requirements and consequences are to be ignored. Such an excuse may be accepted once or twice, but forever?

Such a position, is not only hard to digest from a rational point of view, but it also renders all the endeavors of the followers of a doctrine meaningless. It not only sets the idea loose from the grip of verification, but it also dissolves its connection to the society and history. It washes off the blemishes, but it also washes away the merits. It makes the doctrine analogous to a poor person incapable of exploitation by the thieves but also incapable of generosity to friends. Furthermore, those who absolve an idea from its negative practical consequences are usually inclined to take credit for the positive results. This shows that they believe in the connection of theory and practice in their hearts even if they deny it with their tongue.

The more important point is that untestability is tantamount to unrealizibility. If an idea is actualized, the arena of its actualization is the realm of its trial; but when we consider an idea above testability, we deny it reality—in which case what is the point in trying to actualize it? In what sense can we say that an idea worthy of the dedication of followers and devotees is actualized? So much for the first proposition.

The Second Proposition:
Partial Justifiability of Ideas,
Positive Evidence

There is a second proposition that suggests we attribute only the accomplishments and positive results to the original idea while attributing all the difficulties and disappointments to alien and invidious elements.

The proponents of this position argue that there is always a possibility that an idea is misunderstood, inappropriately applied or actually subverted by opponents and enemies. This is how some Marxists justify the collapse of the Soviet system in Russia. They argue that either global capitalism or its fifth column inside the Soviet Union engineered its demise, they blame it on an incompetent administration or a lack of democracy; or they may resort to geographical, climactic, geopolitical, and other similar causal explanations. (Mr. Kianoori has resorted to these arguments in his interview with *Keyhan-e Havai* concerning the fate of the Soviet Union.)[4]

Let us examine the merits of this argument. It is true that one can not discount external conspiracies and enmities or the impact of geographical and global factors. All of these, however, constitute what philosophers

call the efficient causes or triggering factors; if there were no "suscepti-
bility," they would have no impact. For example, if Marxism had not been
susceptible to dictatorship, Stalin could not have engaged in all that cruelty, brutality, and tyranny in its name. If a doctrine does not have a
propensity and an aptitude for the abuse of power, it will not be easily
manipulated to that end. A doctrine that does not offer a lucid theory
for the restriction of powers would allow a dictator such as Stalin to bru-
tally and pervasively "socialize," eliminate his friends, enter a pact with
Hitler, harass Finland, conduct bloody purges in the military, and still
orchestrate the masses to sing his praises: "O the man of Georgia who
bring us the springtime." Misunderstanding and misapplication may be
the work of the antagonists, the fools, and the enemies, but a doctrine
cannot be absolved from the responsibility of allowing such abuses. It
may well be so unrefined, vague, and ambivalent as to be open to numerous partisan readings. Such a doctrine would fall to conspirators far
more easily than a stable and well-founded doctrine that closes the gates
of conspiracy to antagonistic opponents and the gaps of misunderstanding to ignorant proponents.

If a doctrine continues to yield disastrous results, should these consequences not be finally attributed to the doctrine rather than to an un-
ending string of misunderstandings and conspiracies? The truth is that
the taking account of the desirable and the undesirable consequences is
the spirit of verification. A doctrine is verifiable if it is advanced by the
positive instances and held back by the negative ones. To claim gain and
to disown loss is to pass the test of "shrewdness," not verifiability. Inter-
estingly enough, the opponents of a doctrine exaggerate in the other
direction, that is, they minimize the external factors and blame all failures on the doctrine itself. For instance, the opponents of Marxism blame
its collapse solely on the impracticality of Marxism.

There is another strategy for avoiding negative results while claiming positive ones. It is often argued that only a fully implemented doctrine could be held responsible for desirable as well as undesirable
results. Therefore, where external and internal hostile elements interfere with the full realization and establishment of a doctrine, criticism
of negative consequences is unwarranted. This too leads to untestability.
Why should we count the positive results and discount the negative
ones in the event of incomplete implementation of a doctrine? Why
not the other way around? Why not discount both? It is clear that such
a rhetorical strategy leads to arbitrarily including or excluding un-
favorable results, or, to put it more philosophically, to the violation of
principle of sufficient reason and finally to the unverifiability of the
doctrine.

Nor is it plausible to claim that laws are just and humane while people
are vicious, immoral, and ungrateful, attributing the faults to people and
the merits to the doctrine. Laws are written for the people. The law should

take into account people's faults, immorality, sloth, corruption, greed, and deviousness. The law is not written for the angels or for rehearsal's sake. It is absurd to claim that the law is perfect and the people imperfect. A law that does not take into account people's imperfections is itself imperfect. If a lawgiver does not understand what kinds of creatures human beings are, what they will do with his laws, and how they would use his proposed liberties and limitations, he is bound to introduce an inconsistent and unstable doctrine. *He*, then, will be responsible for the practical distortions of the doctrine not the people. This is analogous to the case of an author who writes a complex and turgid book and then complains that the readers are ignorant and unworthy of his prose. Such an author should be reminded: books are for the readers, not the other way around. An incomprehensible book is no book.

It is clear that neither the first theory nor the second is defensible. It is not possible to place a doctrine above verification and realization; nor is it feasible to cunningly attribute the accomplishments to the doctrine and the failures to its enemies and opponents.

Now in the absence of a "reason" one should look for the "cause" of such unreasonable maneuvers. Why do some people appeal to such flimsy and false arguments? The cause is, inevitably and exclusively, loving dedication. The devotees of a doctrine cannot be the best critics and examiners of it. Examination requires a kind of impartiality and rational disinterestedness that is very rare among the staunch followers of a doctrine. Rumi sets reason and passion against each other. He reveals the affinity of reason to examination and calculation on the one hand and the proclivity of passion to recklessness and scandal on the other. The radical abandon of passion leaves no room for the sober calculations of reason:

> It's Passion that knows abandon, not reason,
> Reason aims only to gain and to attain.
> Passion is riotous, selfless, audacious,
> In trials, like a millstone; tenacious
> Passion neither scrutinizes God's will
> Nor does it consider profit or peril.[5]

Devotees of any belief system are too preoccupied with their faith and too assured of the truth, beauty, and perfection of their belief to notice the need to examine it. They cannot find the courage and the confidence to engage in such an enterprise. Nor do they see a need to renew, reinforce, or revise their covenant with their beloved faith. Thus they leave verification to others. No wonder they are incapable of seeing the mole of imperfection on the face of their beloved.

However, belief is too important to be left to lovers alone. The zealot cannot be trusted with sober reflection. Hafez was right:

What business does the infatuated lover have engaging in prudent deliberations?
It is worldly affairs that require reflections and meditations.

Where the affairs of the state are concerned, the heat of love is disruptive and the chill of reason conducive. Ideological societies are susceptible to various afflictions that are discernible with the analytical eye of reason rather than the indulgent eye of passion. When we proclaim, out of love, that a doctrine is untestable, we sever the connection of the doctrine with social reality; we then tie our own hands in dealing with all those afflictions even when we can see them coming. Ideological societies foster traits such as dogmatism, illusion of perfection, duplicity, sacralization of mundane affairs, and triumph of imitation over exploration. In such societies easy and cheap dogmatism substitutes for the rare and expensive certitude. Love is well compensated, but reason is not. There is praise and glorification of the leaders aplenty but few criticisms of their words and deeds. There is a plethora of external conspiracy theories but a dearth of self-criticism or the candid discussion of internal shortcomings and errors. The subservient agents are valued above the critical individuals. The imitators, those who parrot and praise the words of the leaders, are favored over independent investigators. These afflictions are not the handiwork of the alien conspirators. They are the immediate results of ideological systems. If they are not rationally and deliberately harnessed, they will be made even more piercing and scalding by the inherent fervor of love and commitment. The Soviet Marxist system was as susceptible of such afflictions as is the Iranian Islamic system. The secular identity of the former or the sacred nature of the latter is irrelevant in this respect. Marxists, too, condemned the duplicity, hypocrisy, and dogmatism in which they were wallowing. The doctrine, whether heavenly or earthly, will have to be comprehended by the minds of earthlings; further, it is to be implemented by earthly hands. It is this secular nature of the implementation of any doctrine that renders the doctrine so vulnerable.[6]

The Third Proposition:
Partial Justifiability of Ideas,
Negative Evidence

The third proposition, too, belongs to the same genus. It, too, has risen out of emotions (hatred, in this case) and leads, in the last analysis, to untestability. This proposition holds that only negative results should be attributed to a doctrine. Bertrand Russell, for example, saw only one advantage to religiosity: that attention to the heavens in times of prayer helped promote the science of astronomy. In the same vein, Andrew

White, in his *Warfare between Science and Theology*, singles out the church as the most bloodthirsty institution on the face of the earth. This is a hostile and repudiating glance. It is critical but unfair. The same kind of criticism is found in our society toward Marxism and liberalism. We tend to see absolutely nothing positive in them, but we seem all too eager to put even their adversaries' faults on their bill.

The Fourth Proposition: Conditional Justifiability of Ideas

This proposition is more complex and requires closer scrutiny of the issue of testability. It suggests that we first examine the internal stability and coherence of a system in a theoretical vein. If this investigation reveals a gap in its ramparts, then we are justified in attributing to it the actual ensuing faults and setbacks. A doctrine that, upon close scrutiny, does not reveal any theoretical weaknesses and defects should not be blamed for practical failures and defeats. The culprit, in this case, would be the extrinsic and hostile elements. The calamitous faults of Marxism had been identified by its critics years ago, so its collapse was far from improbable or unexpected. That is why the breakdown of the system can be attributed to the internal flaws of the doctrine that undergirded the system. The same is true of liberalism. It is possible to deduce logically what kind of external effects it will produce. When those effects (whether good or bad) materialize, there is no room for hesitation; they must be attributed to the doctrine. A superficial observation of the results, without a close investigation of the theory allows the proponents to exonerate the doctrine of any responsibility for the results, attributing faults to the misunderstanding and misuse of the proponents or to the conspiracies of the enemies. It also allows the opponents to put the full weight of the blame and guilt on the shoulders of the doctrine thus disregarding the role of its adversaries. Observation and verification preceded by the analysis of the doctrine will preclude such improper judgments.

Besides, how could we hold ideologies responsible for everything that is done in their name? The history of Islam is full of the likes of Yazid and Hajjaj, who have committed acts that violate the spirit of Islam. Should their deeds be attributed to the doctrine? Is the history of a doctrine identical with the doctrine? And, in any case, what is the gauge that measures the full realization of a discipline?

Based on this proposition, the decline of the Islamic civilization and the fact that it lags behind the modern world cannot be attributed to the history of Islam but to the history of un-Islamic deeds of Moslems. Thus, if we heed the intrinsically Islamic teachings concerning the value of education, science, research, wise use of natural resources, and so on, we shall confess that the historical trajectory of Islam was not rooted in the religious doctrine but rather resulted from misunderstanding, malice, and colonial oppression. Al-Ghazzali's attempt to establish that religious canon [*shariʿah*] is only part of the religion, Sadr al Din Shirazi's labors to make reason and religion commensurable, Iqbal Lahori's declaration that nature is not regarded by Islam with contempt, and Shariʿati's crusade against the tradition of turning the blood of Imam Hussein into a pacifying opiate, all exemplify the belief that Moslems have strayed from the true teachings of their religion and have been duly punished for these departures.

This proposition, while not devoid of merit, errs on two accounts: first, it ignores the fact that it is always a certain interpretation of the doctrine that prevails and creates its own requisite apparatus and effects. Emphasis on the content of the doctrine is identical with regarding one's own interpretation of the doctrine as the criterion by which others' interpretations are to be judged. This is a theological position, not a historical analysis (although the source of history does not exclude theological presuppositions). It amounts to writing history according to one's own beliefs. Surely, it is implausible to study the history of Moslems as if it were the history of non-Moslems or to ignore issues that violate our beliefs. The actual history of Moslems cannot be divorced from the tenets of Islam. The same goes for other ideologies, such as Marxism and Christianity. If Shiʿites and Sunnis refuse to recognize each other's histories as the history of Islam, then we could be left with neither Islam nor a history of Islam (mutual conflict of two different concepts leads to their mutual annulment).[7]

The truth is that the history of Islam is the history of the Shiʿites as well as the Sunnis. From a historical point of view, they equally partake of Islam (even if theologically they might not.) Each has an interpretation of Islam. It is these interpretations that are embodied in history. The history of religion is the arena of practical and external manifestations of these divergent interpretations. Judgments and disagreements concerning the correct interpretation of religion are theological debates and intrareligious matters of the history of religion, not extrareligious determinants.

The second problem with this proposition is that it considers elucidating the ideational origins of a doctrine as the best way of understanding it. This is a mistake, for often the historical manifestations of an idea lead the investigator to subtle discoveries unattainable through any other method. Ideas and doctrines entail certain consequences that unfold only in practical application. The reason is that doctrines, in the process of actualization, blend with people's individual and collective characters and beget results undetectable in the theoretical origins of the doctrine alone. Thus, an examination of lofty values and abstract claims of a doctrine do not necessarily guarantee its practical success. It is entirely conceivable, for example, for a doctrine to condemn usury but to foster such social and economic circumstances that make it virtually inevitable. A religion might forbid sin, but it might also engender it in practice. A doctrine might proscribe flattery but concentrate power in certain places or in certain hands to such an extent that flattery would become a well-rewarded trait.

None but the astute few could have surmised that Marxism would turn into a tyranny, that the governments based on it would become absolutist, that the revolutionary party would transform itself into a new privileged class, and that the proletariat would become the first victims of the regime that promised to cherish and exalt them. All this occurred at the practical phase of the realization of the doctrine that had proposed to inaugurate a new phase of the history of humanity.

Science, philosophy, and language, all manifest themselves in history much better than they do in logic and in theory. Detailed a posteriori knowledge completes abstract a priori understanding. It is impossible to surmise, in advance and in full, what social and psychosocial consequences and relations of domination will proceed from doctrines and belief systems as diverse as secularism, predestination, Hegelian dialectics, or historical materialism. Understanding, unfolding, and manifestation of these doctrines are all contingent upon the passage of time. The same goes for religious knowledge. It is never complete. Different historical circumstances and the interplay of religious knowledge with other kinds of knowledge further illuminate its depths and bring it closer to perfection.

Finally, not all the ingredients of a doctrine are purely philosophical and rational. Certain aspects of it are purely practical and experimental (such as legal, jurisprudential, penal, and economic rules). Only a practical trial can determine their relative strengths. We can, then, conclude that the fourth proposition which invites us to a theoretical analysis of the doctrine prior to the observation of results, does contain a valid claim. But if the above reservations are ignored, if theological analysis is allowed to mix with historical interpretation, if we make our own interpretation of a doctrine the arbiter of the history of that doctrine and thus allow the doctrine to obscure our view of certain patches of history, we will reach only bitter, harmful, and irrational results. Close scrutiny reveals that this denies universality to verification and multiplies the views of doctrine and history by the number of arbitrary discernments, tastes, and attachments brought to bear upon it. Personalizing verification is tantamount to making it untenable.

Fifth Proposition: Full Verifiability of Ideas

This brings us to the fifth preposition, which holds that doctrines are entirely testable and that history is the arena of their trial and error. The success or failure of systems built upon doctrines are those doctrines' direct responsibility. That is, the history of every doctrine is, more or less, its mirror. It reveals as much about a doctrine as does the study of its philosophical and moral foundations. Furthermore, the philosophy and history of the doctrine are interlocutors whose dialogue yields a far better account of the doctrine than either alone. If we temporarily suspend our emotional attachments and accept that between the history of a doctrine and the doctrine itself there can exist only a link or a break, and if we rule that a break (with whatever justification) is unreasonable, then only one choice remains: confirming the existence of a link. Reason dictates that if a system grows in the shade of a doctrine, then it owes its fame and shame, rise and fall, effects and defects to that doctrine.

In one case, and one case alone, may we find an exception to this rule, and that is when we find the doctrinal rules (in the case of religions) purely ritual and devoid of any social significance. This entails asserting, in the case of Islam, that religious tithe [zakat] has nothing to do with redistribution of wealth but with reducing psychic attachment to property; that the rule concerning amputating burglars' fingers does not aim to curb burglary but to punish the burglars; that the goal of the religious war of defense [jihad] is not to fight off the enemy and to protect the Islamic domain but to attain martyrdom and its attending rewards; and so forth. If, on the other hand, we consider these as methods of solving practical problems of life, then only by reference to the history of Islam can we assess their efficacy in solving those problems.

This theory looks easy enough at first but is not devoid of subsequent difficulties. It is hard, for example, to regard the rule of Umayyad and Abbasid dynasties as part of the history of Islam (from the Shi'ite point of view) or to consider colonialism and fascism as part and parcel of the history of liberalism (from the liberal point of view) or to count the history of China or Yugoslavia as part of the history of Marxism (from the orthodox Marxist point of view.)

The problem is that we tend to juxtapose an uninterpreted history with an uninterpreted doctrine. No doctrine can give itself a historical reality. It is always a particular interpretation of the doctrine that is actualized and becomes a historical force. Therefore, the history of Islam or Marxism are the histories of various interpretations of these doctrines. As actualized and practically verified, they have become subjects of amendments, reinterpretations, and factional skirmishes. All of these are part and parcel of the history of a doctrine and should enter its final evaluation. All should be viewed as admonitory evidence. False interpretations and improper conclusions, however sincerely drawn, are still, indubitably, fruits of the doctrine. They, too, demonstrate the capabilities and limitations of the doctrine. Engels, Bloch, Bernstein, Lukács, Mandel, Althusser, Mao, and Lenin represent different spots on the spectrum of the Marxist thought; just as Shi'ites, Kharejites, Ash'arites, Mu'tazilites, Umayyads, Abbasids, and so on, represent various manifestations of Islam. No one interpretation colors the doctrine as a whole; contraries occur on the same continuum. Historical analysis relies on all these conflicts and yet is distinct from them. It attempts to present the general spirit and sweep of history. This history is the subject to judgment and verification. That is why its relationship to the prevailing interpretations is undeniable.

We should resist the idea that Christianity, Marxism, or Islam would have yielded totally different histories had they occurred under different circumstance or had they been entrusted to different hands. This assumption ignores the capabilities and inner proclivities of these doctrines and leaves the reins of transformation and circumspection entirely in the hands of fortuitous events, adventitious factors, or external malevolence. This is not to deny the role of malice or historical accidents, but merely to deprive them of omnipotence. Factional conflicts and abuses of principles in Islam and Christianity owe as much to human volition as to the teachings of these religions. If the history of Islam disappears altogether, the same Qur'an and Tradition would generate other similar factional controversies concerning interpretation. These debates would then engender political tensions. In the heat of the strife, foes, impostors, and opportunists would roam free; and soon enough all manner of purities, impurities, virtues, sins, rebellions, adulterations, deceptions, and false religiosities would reign again. In short, another Islamic civilization similar to this one would arise. History will not exactly repeat itself, but if the Qur'an and the Tradition remain constant and if the nature of human beings does not change, it would be futile to expect a history radically different from the one that has already unfolded; unless we hope that human nature will be different this time around and that the world will assume an entirely different character.

The formula of "doctrine plus people" has an immutable natural process of evolution. If it gets a chance to repeat itself, it will take the same general course. The key here is viewing history as "natural." Controversies, conflicts, misunderstandings, and errors are not imposed on the history of a doctrine but are inherent in it. One should not consider all or most of the followers of a doctrine to be gullible or knavish, innocently deceived or cunningly deceiving. That would amount to a false and conspiratorial vision of history, contrary to the religious belief in God's mercy, leaving revelation open to adulteration, abandoning the faithful to confusion, and letting the multitudes perish of thirst at the water's edge.

Ideology, like language, provides a special space where both good and evil find an opportunity to grow. The Persian language fostered both the pithy poetry of Rumi and Hafez and the obscenities of Souzani Samarqandi and Iraj Mirza. Money facilitates charity, munificence, and economic exchange as well as theft, fraud, and bribery. Islam made possible both the vices of the Umayyad dynasty and the virtues of the Shi'ite Imams. It allowed both false righteousness and true virtue. It nurtured

Yazid as well as Bayazid, the villainous Hajjaj as well as the righteous Omar Ibn Abdol Aziz.[8] It would be useless to assert that if all human beings were endowed with virtue and good taste, obscene and insulting language would disappear. The trick is how to realize that "if". Language is not always at the disposal of the virtuous, foul-mouthed rogues partake of it as well. That is why the works of Hafez and Souzani both belong to the history of the Persian language. Both are requisites of human language. If history is repeated, and if the same language is made available to the same people, it will yield, more or less, the same results. Language is that which manifests itself in the history of language. The same is true of money, philosophy, religion, humanity, and so on. People like Mo'avieh always abuse religion; thieves will always prey on legitimate wealth; apostates will always manipulate philosophy; devils will always ensnare the innocent.

Here we are not concerned with the definition of religion, man, money, or philosophy but with their external and historical reality. When we assert that religion is that which the history of religion reveals, we don't mean to imply that the essence of religion condones apostasy, duplicity, and self-righteousness. What we mean is that such pestilence always infects the harvest of religion and such thorns always accompany the flower. The seed of religion resists contamination, but the plant that grows out of that seed opens a canopy for the virtuous and villainous alike. Religion is not sent for angels but for human beings, subject to envy, frailty, avarice, and impatience; these are the creatures who adopt religion, understand it, and use it, out of natural inclination, not force, intent, or animosity.[9] They endow religion with particular forms and characters, theoretically and practically. The interpretations of Islam, Christianity, Marxism, and liberalism have undergone historical trials and have revealed their respective historical contours. If these interpretations are repeated a hundred times over, they will not assume different forms or contents nor will they inaugurate a radically new history.

The question then arises, what do the religious reformers want from reform? Why don't they acquiesce to aberrations and monstrosities? Why don't they accept the history of religion as it is? Reformers should not, of course, expect religion to yield more than it is capable of offering. And this capability is revealed, more or less, by the history of religion. However, such traits as rehabilitating religious thought; correcting misreadings; exposing impious, malevolent, and duplicitous adversaries; redirecting religion toward its essence; rectifying misunderstandings; and tearing asunder the veils of ignorance and ill will are among the duties of the faithful and, as such, they are part of the history of religion. Ideology and religion are susceptible to all the above-mentioned afflictions when they are sound, effective, and properly understood, much less when they are twisted and mangled in thought and practice. Reformers have experienced and accepted not only the doctrine but the mundane history of religion. Although they have detected the gathering of the flies, they have not forsaken their taste for the sweetness of the truth. They have realized that the grove of history does not yield flowers without thorns, and that religion is no exception. They try to proclaim a new understanding and a new history.

The portrait of religion is to be seen not only in the mirror of reasoned principles but in the mirror of history as well. The testimony of history on human and divine doctrines should be heeded. Ideologues are in the habit of making many promises and delivering few. History bears witness that most of their promises remain unfulfilled and that their testimonies have proved false. Historical verification will put an end to such hyperboles and lies. History and theology need each other's company, now more than ever before.

6

Reason and Freedom

In the name of God the Beneficent, the Merciful.
There is no might or power save that which flows from the
most high, the most expansive.

It is heartening as well as liberating to freely attend a meeting of the free-dom-seeking brothers and sisters of the university community in order to address the noble and worthy topic of freedom. We have all at least reflected on this important problem. Some of us have gone beyond think-ing to fight in the cause of freedom in the course of the revolution.

We are not the first to join this issue. Nor can we ever say or think enough about freedom. What Rumi said about love is true of freedom as well:

> As much as I enlarge on love,
> I am ashamed when I come to Love.
> Renditions of tongue reveal the core,
> But silent love reveals more.

No matter how well we articulate this theme, upon reaching the truth, the essence and the worth of freedom for the spiritual life of humanity, we shall find that words fail us. I hope we can reach a height in which we may advance beyond the explanation of freedom and its essence.

The title of my discussion is the relationship between reason and free-dom. Our sages have found a number of binary divisions in reason. They have divided reason into the pure [*nazari*] and practical [*amali*], the innate [*fetri*] and acquired [*kasbi*], and the particular [*jozvi*] and universal [*kolli*]. They have counterposed reason to madness, idiocy, love, and wrath. They have alternately applied the concept of reason to the faculty of reasoning or to its contents. The latter has meant the apprehension of either self-evident or the acquired truths. The neo-Platonists consider reason an external entity rather than an internal faculty. In the west "rationality" used to be associated with metaphysics, but now it is more or less connected to experiment and quantity. It is also somehow related to the analytical and logical qualities of thought. It used to defy relativity, but today it has become relative. Any of these intricacies is deserving of investigation.

The same is true of the concept of freedom. It has been divided into civil and philosophical, external and internal. Some have observed the differences between the social and spiritual varieties of freedoms, between "freedom from" and "freedom to" or "negative" and "positive" liberties. Freedom is contrasted to submission to the divine will, human bondage, or the law. There is even a distinction between freedom and the feeling of freedom. Freedom is compared and contrasted to such opposing concepts as tyranny and democracy; at other times it is used as a synonym of democracy. Some have looked at it as a right, others as a reality. Hegel viewed it as the goal toward which the absolute spirit is advancing. Some have tried to reconcile freedom with equality and justice; others have despaired of achieving this aim. Freedom has been equated with rebellion as well as subordination. Existentialists identify it as the essence of humanity. Suggestive as these leads are, it is not possible to follow all of them in a single lecture.

My speech is about the kind of reason that serves as a dynamic faculty for thinking and seeking the truth; it is about the kind of freedom that is required by reason qua reason. Therefore we will seek to clarify the relationship between reason and freedom. We will ask whether reason and freedom help or hinder each other. We shall thus talk about the freedom for exercising the faculty of reason, that is the freedom of thinking.

(1) We are sympathetic to freedom and demand it because we are rational. Freedom and unfreedom are a matter of indifference to creatures deprived of reason. We cannot speak of freedom in the case of either the superhuman angels or the subhuman beasts. We are impassioned about freedom and consider it the sine qua non of humanity because reason and freedom are inextricably intertwined. The absence of one would vitiate the existence of the other. Freedom belongs to the rational human beings. Reason requires the company of its close kindred spirit: freedom.

(2) We can have two visions of reason: reason as destination and reason as path. The first sees reason as the source and repository of truths. The second sees it as a critical, dynamic, yet forbearing force that me-

ticulously *seeks* the truth by negotiating tortuous paths of trial and error. Now, if we identify reason only by its dynamic movement and sifting quality, we will be obligated to provide the requisite environment for its existence and growth. Considering it as a mere repository of truth will require a different treatment.

(3) The vision of reason as a treasure trove of truths is not conducive to thinking about the origin and the manner of arriving at the truths. But viewing reason as a truth-seeking, sifting, and appraising agent entails as much respect to the method of achieving the truth as it does to the truth itself. Here it is not enough to attain the truth; the manner of its attainment is equally important. While the former is indifferent to freedom, the latter depends on it.

Reason as storehouse entails a notion of enforced truth; the dynamic view of reason would prefer the methodically acquired error for it contains the kind of flow that is the only guarantor of the life and longevity of reason. The advocates of administered truth need no room for questioning and doubt; dynamic reason would see such an environment as stifling and stupefying. Realizing the difference between the two views of reason may help us to understand the motives of those who feign interest in freedom but end up castigating and denouncing it, ostensibly out of concern for peace and humanity, but actually out of fear that errors might contaminate the stock of truths stored in the warehouse of reason.

Here we are not talking about those who praise violence; who have never spent any time on ideas, thinking, and its requirements. These use opposition to freedom as a front for opposing reason itself. Rather, we are talking about those who are truly concerned about the people and sincerely care about the truth while advocating limits on freedom, arguing that if we allow freedom of thought, false opinions might gain currency. Obviously this view is only compatible with the warehouse—or fortress—view of reason. But for those who prefer methodically adduced errors to imposed truths, truth must be chosen from among competing false opinions. Our mission as rational human beings is to search actively for the truth. This view attaches more value to earning a modest living in a small trade than to finding a treasure in the wilderness. The second version of reason employs a method that can be exercised by everyone, while the first version depends on luck and fate, thus benefiting only the elite. Systems that have sought to dictate the truth have abused humanity more than those open to the possibility, indeed the necessity, of making errors as a precondition.

Some scholars have argued that freedom must be denied to those who indulge in philosophical questions concerning human nature, happiness, and destiny because of the attendant confusing multiplicity of views that arise from such speculation. They have suggested a screening process for filtering out harmful ideas. Yet these same scholars have sanctioned unconditional freedom of thought in the natural and empirical sciences, presumably because these sciences are based on solid foundations that preclude such controversies. What a preposterous distinction this is! We need more freedom where there is darkness and conflict of views, not less. Where the issue is in doubt, we are more in need of others' views. Freedom is there not only for people to say their piece and blow off steam. It is there because they need each others' help against darkness and falsehood. The initial darkness is the pathway for reaching the final light. History teaches us that the conditions of freedom have prevailed wherever problems have been resolved. Truths that are taken for granted today have not been acquired easily; they, too, have passed through the crucible of criticism, appraisal, and controversy.

If we choose the dynamic vision of reason as our guiding light, we shall not fear errors as a menace to freedom. Nor will we condemn freedom of thinking or the clash of ideas. We shall gain a new respect for the blend of tastes and colors and learn to search for the sweet truth in the midst of the bitter errors: "All the sweetness in this world and beyond / Do shrouds of bitterness ever surround."[1] We prefer the fecund hardships of the dynamic reason that benefits everyone to the drowsy clutch of the static reason.

(4) Those who shun freedom as the enemy of truth and as a possible breeding ground for wrong ideas do not realize that freedom is itself a truth (*haq*).[2] It is as though these people do not consider freedom as a blessing, a truth or virtue. They act as if it is so much hot air, an illusion or a myth, failing to recognize that the realization of freedom leads to the strengthening of the truth and the weakening of the falsehood. The world is the marketplace for the exchange of ideas. We give and take, and we trust that the ascendence of the nobler truths is worth the sacrifice of an occasional minor truth: "As the barrel of wine shall last, let the occasional chalice break."

Only those who are in love with their own feeble ideas will fear freedom while the lovers of truth can not help but love freedom as much. Freedom might upset personal convictions, but it cannot possibly offend the truth except for those who presume to personify the absolute truth. Barring those who suffer from self-adulation and megalomania, no one will be harmed by freedom.

(5) According to the Commander of the Faithful[3]: "Justice is spacious. One who feels confined by justice shall find injustice even more confining."[4] Flight from justice leads only to injustice, where there is even less in the way of liberty, rights, and growth. Just as there is no happy medium between justice and injustice so there is none for reason, logic, and their opposites. Reason has a certain expansiveness, the alternative to which is the narrowness and the darkness of ignorance. And the same is true of freedom: anyone who finds it frustrating will find the alternative even more so. Some well-wishers of humanity (I am not talking about

the malicious, the ignorant, and those who glorify violence and wage war against reason) may make the mistake of resenting freedom because it may allow the forces of darkness and corruption to surround righteousness. This group must realize that denouncing freedom is itself an evil worse than any they might wish to fight. No one who is blessed with foresight and wisdom would rely on evil in order to establish the reign of the good. Such an endeavor is based on the misguided idea that the ends justify the means. No end is completely detached from the means. Means are constitutive of the end as much as the premises determine the final conclusions. Besides, reaching the truth in an open environment is essentially different from attaining it in a closed one. In fact, these are two different species of truth that are acquired in two different ways. If truth is fragile in an open environment, it is even more so in a closed one. Freedom provides a range and dynamism for the truth that is absent in unfreedom. It is true that freedom can make falsehoods bolder. But this lesser evil may be condoned in view of the greater good that freedom makes possible.

(6) If the naked truth were to reveal itself easily to us, we would not spurn it and would prefer even imposed truth to methodically derived errors. But the entire experience of mankind shows us that truth is never naked but is often concealed a hundredfold. If truth were naked and easy, the word discovery would not arise or acquire so much veneration. *Discovery* means uncovering the truth, which is a public, prolonged, and difficult task.

The fact is that freedom in not a currency with which we bribe people so they may feel better, but a necessary tool they need to uncover the truth. Only those who consider themselves to be directly inspired by God, who profess to possess the absolute truth, and who find their reason above benefiting from the assistance and consultation of others, will refuse the gifts of freedom. Others will find themselves in serious need of the freedom that allows public participation and discourse. Freedom is the slogan of the humble and the needy; it is the catchword of those who are aware of the penury of their own reason. Human beings still need the light of a star even if they have reached the sun; they can not afford to turn down a jar of water even in the midst of the sea:

> In the midst of the ocean I settle
> Craving still the water in the kettle.
> Like David, possessing calves, ninety
> I covet the rival's calf to increase my bounty.

(7) Emotionalism breeds devotees, while reason fosters autonomous individuals. The lightning of emotions dazzles the eye of reason. In emotional upheavals, when reason is paralyzed, rational analysis is replaced

with the urge to act out of blind devotion, which often leads to remorse. Of course, we cannot advance without leaning on the staff of emotions, but without seeing through the eyes of reason we might stumble into the gutter of fanaticism. Those emotions that slay reason just as easily slaughter freedom. Rational discourse among human beings must not be replaced by emotional harangues. Emotionalism alone cannot support a social system save one based on blind devotion to a master. Emotions dim or douse the light of reason and dissolve human autonomy. It is true that reason causes conflict, but its main product is autonomy. By fostering independence of the mind, reason prevents the dissolution of the individual personality, which is essential for preservation of freedom. Emotional subservience is even more tragic and devastating when it is manipulated by a corrupt authority. Such affective states as anger and lust, which shackle reason from within, also limit one's external freedom. We are indebted to those philosophers and theologians who have fed the fire of reason, even if they have indulged in speculative controversies, focusing people's attention on trivial and often misleading problems. Otherwise the world would have been enveloped by darkness, bereft of love, reason, and order. It is hardly surprising that hatred of reason rises under tyranny and dictatorship. Fascists found a friend in the passions of youth and a foe in the rationality of the mature. Nazis despised democracy and public deliberation because they carried the aroma of reason; worshipping Hitler was encouraged because it was based on blind and brutish obedience. The death or degradation of rational discourse might give rise to ultrarational states of mind or mystic love-sickness among the rarified elites. It is, however, much more likely that in such a situation utter idiocy and competition over devotees[5] will prevail, precluding the use of the small allotment of practical reason that is available to the people.

I shudder every time I evoke the impassioned poetry of Rumi and Hafez in my lectures, lest their ecstatic odes to love and their contempt for reason be used as a weapon by the enemies of reason and freedom. I am afraid this will lead us to spurn the small measure of reason that we have been granted at the sight of a mirage. The august words of these sages are to be revered, but I ask you: how many of their audience have ascended to the peak of spiritual heights? Humanity takes pride in the few who have reached those lofty peaks. Indeed we love humanity for the sake of these few exemplars. But the rest of us who are not so blessed must use our God-given gift of reason and engage in rational discourse. Freedom is liberating, but it also implies responsibility. The idle, who are content to live a life without the trouble of freedom and responsibility, are delighted to jettison them, using the pretext of mystic intoxication. Let us not ignore our divine gifts. Let us not direct the blessed instructions of our sages to support base intentions by indolently parroting:

> One should trade reason for innocence,
> Insanity is the path to the lofty trance.
> I have explored the ways of providence in reason.
> I have resolved to choose the path of unreason.[6]

Let us remember that reason has two rivals: love and stupidity. Love is the share of the virtuosi. The rest must know what is left for them. Eric Fromm, in his explanation of the success of fascism in Nazi Germany, argues that those who sing the praises of freedom shun it in practice because it is a heavy burden to carry. They would sooner prostrate themselves to the authority of another human being than face the responsibilities of being free. Reason elevates us, diminishes the fires of anger and lust, and creates the serenity needed for internal freedom. In Rumi's words:

> He said I shall die where two roads are crossed,
> The path of anger and that of lust.
> Who can resist the forces of lust and anger?
> In search of such a man I ever meander.[7]

And this cannot be accomplished except by strengthening reason. So much for internal freedom. Let me tell you that the same obtains in the case of external freedom: strengthening reason rids us of all kinds of bondage and oppression. As Rumi says: "There is no blight worse than lack of knowledge." It is not possible to strengthen reason without creating a free environment for reasoning. Individual reason can, in Rumi's words, secrete passions and be enthralled by emotions. But collective reason is free from such enslavement. Individual desires and prejudices nearly vanish when reason is made universal. "Oh gallant man, passion is the contrary of reason / What unleashes passions, can not be called reason."[8]

(8) Can reason be enslaved by ideology? Here the word *ideology* is not used in its common usage to imply a school of thought (e.g., "Islamic ideology" or "Marxist ideology"). Rather *ideology* in the present context denotes its exact and precise meaning: those ideas that have causes but no reasons. In this sense ideology is the veil of reason; it is the enemy of rationality and clarity. It contradicts objectivity and forces one to see the world through a single narrow aperture even if the result is a distorted view of the world. Idealism and dogmatism often accompany an ideology, but its core is the quality that conceals its falseness by placing it above rational discourse. One can only dote on an ideology or be infatuated by it; one can never rationally evaluate it.

No reasons can be properly adduced for a false idea. If we try to find rational grounds or reasons for ideologies, they too must be flawed. The only thing to do at this juncture is to look for the causes and the origins of the idea in question. Here we can trace the interests and advantages of various groups in so far as they constitute the causes of certain ideas. This points to the ideological nature of ideas or, in Marxist parlance, to their "class origins." With this definition the fight against ideology cannot be a rational one because ideology is by definition antirational. To fight an ideology, then, becomes an actual and concrete struggle. Because ideology has no rational grounds, any effort to eliminate its causes must be extrarational and ideational.

The view of freedom espoused by a school of thought hinges on whether it considers human reason a prisoner of ideologies. The history of Marxism is a case in point. If you share the Marxist belief that people's views are distorted and that their rationality is flawed (as eyes that may be myopic) by objective causes (not subjective reasons), then you would not waste time on convincing the believers of the error of their ways. In order to set them straight, you would have to perform like a surgeon not a teacher. Everything depends on you, the sole possessor of the right reason. For communists, giving free rein to public reasoning is a laughable idea. Instead, they favor building an infirmary for the sick, ideology-addled minds. They blame the prevalence of ideology on the class system.

Ideology consists of the systematically generated errors of mind, the basic malfunctioning of the scales of reason. But it does not follow that freedom from ideology is the same as immunity to error. In the latter case making a mistake is not a systematic result but a random occurrence. The extent to which freedom and reason require each other must be apparent from the preceding. To view reason as a permanent slave of ideology entails hostility to freedom, while accepting error as an accidental yet correctable byproduct of reason generates respect for free and public discourse which is the only way errors may be eliminated.

(9) I started out by emphasizing that we pursue freedom with such unfailing devotion because we possess a precious gem: reason. A spirit from a different world; in the words of Rumi, a "totally other."[9] Reason is by nature a free zone. Some philosophers have used the chain of causality to make a case for determinism. They say the feeling of freedom is but an illusion because we are confined by causality: we are born into a particular family, among the followers of a specific religion, and under the domination of a given government. Everything is inculcated in us during childhood. We are indebted to others for everything. How can we begin to talk about freedom when we are the products of genetics or environment? Consider the position of Bertrand Russell: "Newtonian physics and scientific laws have left no elbowroom for human agency, volition and freedom. Only the recent introduction of quantum mechanics has broken certain links in the chain of causality and opened up some space for freedom." The following is an example of how these philosophers contrast causality to freedom and human volition. Russell asks:

How can I claim to be free when the very movements of my lips are already determined?

But I would like to argue that even if we accept these arguments (despite many reservations), the realm of reason remains free. If causality does amount to an ineluctable chain, reason is free from this chain; if it does not, reason is free in every direction. Reason is not an "essential nature"; it is not bound by the chain of causality. It can be penetrated only by "reasons." Our emotions are bound to the chain of causality, and thus they can bring us difficulties and even bondage. Reason is by definition impervious to force. Thus the intrusion of any nonrational elements (such as ideology, passion, or anger) disturbs its purity and impairs its liberty. The freedom of pure reason does not imply freedom from logic, which is the very nature of reason. To remain free and pure, reason needs a free range. By providing external freedom, we help individual reasons to join forces, lose all traits of their isolation, and become even more pure and radiant. Another condition for the purification of reason is resisting the temptations of the flesh, mastering the passions, and taming the wild beast of anger:

> Hide from the strangers, not friends of the inner ring
> Coats are made for the winter, not the bloom of spring.
> If reason joins forces with reason seeking delight,
> Light shall prevail and the Path will be bright.
> Should desire couple with desire and trade,
> Darkness will descend and the Path shall fade.[10]

> Reinforce reason with the help of reason.
> Invoke the 'consultation verse' for every season.[11]

(10) Freedom feeds only on freedom, as reason feeds only on reason. This is one of the pleasant points of convergence of these two blessings (the other being the expansiveness provided by reason and freedom, compared to the narrowness resulting from their absence). This feedback serves us in two areas: self-correction and proficiency. In order to become proficient in reasoning, we must reason; in order to catch the mistakes of reason, we must seek the assistance of reason. The same is true of freedom. In order to discover and correct the problems of freedom, we need freedom. In order to better utilize freedom, we need to be free and exercise our freedom. We can not prepare for public freedom by practicing in private. This is a machine that is fueled by its own products.

(11) Some of our orators have made disparaging comments about "those who have elevated freedom to a principle." Of course. Why should it not be the main principle? Freedom is essential. Even those who adopt the path of religion and submission are valued because they have chosen this path freely. True submission is predicated upon the principle of freedom; indeed, they are one and the same. Is there any merit in an

imposed religion or forced prayers? Have we forgotten the Qur'anic verse: "Let there be no compulsion in faith"?[12] Have we not read the following statement by Noah in the Holy Qur'an: "Shall we compel you to accept it when ye are averse to it"?[13] Did not Pharaoh taunt his repentant sorcerers thus: "Believe ye in Him before I give you permission?"[14] Who would want to emulate Pharaoh and make people's beliefs contingent upon his decree? Religion is, by definition, incompatible with coercion. Freedom has two virtues: it endows life and the choices we make in it with meaning.

(12) No seeker of justice can be indifferent to the question of freedom. If we define justice as the realization of all rights, it would be an affront to justice to neglect the right to be free. The antinomy some have supposed between freedom and justice (under the guise of the contrast between democracy and socialism) is a false one. Freedom is one of the components of justice. The seeker of freedom is partly in pursuit of justice, and the seeker of justice cannot help pursue freedom as well. Without freedom, justice is incomplete. Why, then, should we shy away from choosing freedom as a principle, especially when it is freedom that complements justice and constitutes the very meaning and soul of laws? The value of freedom is so fundamental that even the enemies of freedom need it to express their opposition. Why should we not embrace freedom as our principle when it, like God, does not begrudge its benefits even to its enemies? The right to liberty is a component of justice and is included in it. At the same time, the discussion and illumination of justice requires freedom, which is, in this sense, the forerunner of justice.

(13) Freedom and reason have yet another similarity: they can both be dismissed because of their imperfections or accepted in spite of them. We see both of these attitudes in our society. Some use the slightest excuse to squelch freedom, while others do everything possible to expand its reign. To be sure, freedom has its undesirable consequences, and the same is true of reason. The question is whether you are a friend or foe of freedom and reason at heart. As a friend, you will forgive the faults of freedom and strive to correct its errors. As a foe, you will use a single shortcoming to abandon freedom altogether. "He is a false lover of flowers who deigns / not to bear its thorns' pains."[15] Anyone who speaks about freedom must answer this question: are freedom, human dignity, and reason worth their occasional failings? Is the flower of freedom to be trampled because it has a few thorns?

The same holds for reason. Has reason been always the harbinger of righteousness, commonweal, and bliss for mankind? Even the advocates of reason accept that many are misled by their own reason. Have we not heard of the demonic as well as divine reason?[16] Doesn't our reason often find itself at the mercy of temptations? Does it not stumble and err? As in the case of freedom, we have two possible approaches. There are sophists (and occasionally the Sufis) who argue that for exactly these reasons we must jettison reason to avoid being beguiled and deceived by it. And there are rationalists who say that as lovers of reason we must find a way to "de-thorn" this flower. The Sophists reject reason because of its rare lapses. Those who oppose freedom because of its occasional faults and afflictions are the sophists of the world of politics. We must understand that nothing can replace reason and freedom. We need freedom and reason even if we intend to reform and rectify them. How can we spurn such generous healers? To indulge in sophistic rejection of freedom and reason will bring us certain harm and condign punishment for refusing our divine legacy. The beauty, enchantment, and bliss of freedom and reason impel us to retain them at any cost.

The defenders of freedom are well aware of its problems, but they do not think that these problems could be remedied by turning their backs on freedom. The supporters of reason do not assume that all false religions are valid or that the temptations and the squabbles of the disbelievers are acceptable. Defending freedom is not the same as defending any obscenity, falsehood, or iniquity. Rather it is like defending a sun that shines on everything—even the waste—or a holy fire that may consume even the sacred pages of *Mathnavi*.[17] Freedom is a noble fortune that may bring an occasional loss, a method and a tool that may be occasionally wielded by the corrupt and the wicked. Defending the flower is not the same as defending the thorn; but what can we do if flowers grow on thorny branches? After all, we are not entrusted with the administration of the world: we were neither allowed to invent this world nor consulted about its ways. Thus, we must develop a systematic and comprehensive point of view. The sages have held a similar view on the problem of evil in the world: if fire decides to abide our will and burn only the bad and spare the good, it will no longer be fire. Fire will then become "un-fire." Fire is what it is; it cannot change its nature in order to accommodate our wishes.

It is true that the emergence of any deception or corruption stabs at the heart of lovers of freedom, but even this is beneficial. In the parlance of the metaphysicians, the intrusion of evil and corruption into the scheme of divine ordination or into the realm of freedom is accidental: they are the unintended by-products of reason and freedom. These unsavory elements can be best repelled in the light of freedom and reason. If you allow reason to remain free, someone like Ibn Kamouneh will emerge to introduce doubt about the oneness of God[18] and garner the title of "the pride of the devils" from Mulla Sadra[19] as if all the disciples of Satan glorify him for throwing such a stumbling block in the path of the faithful. This is the nature of reason. Rumi did not overstate the case when he said: "The trustworthy and blissful soul has perceived / That cunning in Satan, and love in Man were conceived." The prevalence of cunning will bring forth the likes of "the pride of the devils" to insinuate a Satanic doubt and cause a great Shi'a scholar (the late Aqa Hossein

Khansari) to say "if the Lord of Time[20] should appear, my first request to him would be to settle this question." This is one of the consequences of the cunning of reason. But is it true that defending reason amounts to defending every doubt and scandal? The defender of reason is well aware that all of the consequences of rational discourse will not conform to one's wishes. But the antagonistic consequences of reason must also be resolved by reason: "I escape to you, from you." The question of Ibn Kamouneh must be examined and rebuffed by reason. This was done by Sadr al-Din Shirazi. The same is true of freedom. As we said earlier, freedom and reason feed on each other: we can not help freedom by tyranny nor save reason by ignorance. Reforming freedom and reason can not be accomplished by shutting them down.

(14) Freedom is a contest. Internal freedom is achieved by liberating oneself from the rein of passion and anger. External freedom consists in emancipating oneself from the yoke of potentates, despot, charlatans, and exploiters. The prerequisite for achieving external freedom is participation in the contest of freedom, which is a public process based on rules and regulations. Some people think that freedom means throwing caution to the winds and instigating anarchy, insanity, and disorder. But freedom is far from a synonym for irresponsibility and anomie. To remain free and to protect freedom is a duty of the free-minded. "One must tolerate the enemies, except the enemies of tolerance." An ignorant critic of this wise maxim has said that this constitutes an unwarranted exception to the maxim of freedom. Indeed, this is not an exception but the main rule of the game. This judgment is a consequence of refusing to view freedom as a contest. The contest of freedom eliminates the masters of mediocrity, the pompous windbags, and the incompetent overlords. It honors responsibility and courage. In a closed and oppressive system, there is no contest between the people, so the government arbitrarily promotes some to the positions of leadership. People do not get to compete, and truths do not get a chance to shine against falsehoods. Rather the distribution of rewards is determined by the dominant will of one group: the same "masters of mediocrity" who would surely lose in a fair contest. But there is no victory without the competition. Those who wish to rest on their laurels without participating in the game use any excuse to disrupt the game and would not hesitate to use force to do so. The law contradicts neither a rule-governed contest nor freedom. It is the disruption of the rules of the game that contradicts freedom. Violence must be applied only to those who refuse to play according to the rules.

As I said, the game is restricting, because it has set and constraining rules. But if you leave the game you would be more restricted because lawlessness, or what Durkheim termed "anomie," is still more undesirable. The violation of freedom and law will turn justice to injustice and promote the incompetent. Conversely, to view freedom as a game allows all to participate and accept responsibility for it. If some violate the rules of the game or withdraw from it, they can no longer complain of the proliferation of problems. Freedom is not there to accommodate the particular interests of a particular group.[21] Freedom must be revered for its own sake. The game of freedom must be spirited and continual if its benefits are to spread to all.

(15) This game, like any other, improves with practice. There is no doubt that in the beginning there will be a great deal of loss and waste, but there is no shorter or better way to learn the game. It is impossible to become a good player without actually playing. This is the meaning of our earlier assumption that "freedom only feeds on itself." A soccer player becomes a champion only by playing the game. The game of freedom is no less demanding.

(16) Is truth more powerful than falsehood? In my estimation those who (in good faith, not for self-serving reasons) hold freedom in contempt and reject it, fearing that falsehoods may find a foothold, harbor two misgivings. For one thing, they suspect that human reason is weak and servile. For another, they do not have much faith in the stamina of the truth; they fear it will falter in an open clash with mendacity.

I am not sure about the origins of these two misgivings, but there is no doubt about their implications. Where both reason and the truth are held to be weak, freedom cannot be cultivated. But we find a different story in the holy Qur'an. When Moses was fearful that the pharaoh's sorcerers would put a spell on the rational faculties of the people and turn them away from the right path, God firmly admonished him: "Fear not, for thou hast indeed the upper hand"[22] This is not addressed only to Moses, but to all Moses-like noble souls throughout the ages: they must not fear but rest assured that they are superior to the legions of the pharaoh.

I am not arguing that because of our confidence in the strength of the truth, we must deliberately promote falsehoods. Rather I am saying that we must not exaggerate the power of those who peddle lies and worry that they may vanquish the truth. We must perform our duties, struggle and wage *jihad* against falsehoods, and put our trust in God. We must know that fraud will not succeed nor the iniquitous prevail. This is the meaning of *tavakkol* [trust in God].

(17) In addressing the relationship between truth and freedom, I have already rejected the assumption that pursuit of truth and freedom are mutually exclusive. Only when all opinions have been aired can one recognize the truth. This is the meaning of "hearing all and choosing the best."[23] So seeking the truth does not exclude loving freedom; the two depend on each other.

The fact is that what is opposed to the truth is not freedom but power. It is a mistake to think that repressing falsehoods would promote truths. Has it not occurred to us that the corruptive consequences of power are far more harmful than those of any falsehood? Those who rhapsodize about the dangers of freedom choose not to speak about the dangers of despotic power. This is the result of complacency, lack of historical vision, disregard for the blessings of reason and its requisite climate, craving for power, and, last but not least, a political culture deeply influenced by centuries of tyranny.

What about the blights of power? Would an oppressive regime abide the propagation of truths that are not conducive to its reign? Would it not attempt to monopolize the sphere of ideas in order to establish its own legitimacy? A dominant regime considers itself to be the measure of all truths. Even if we assume that such a regime acts in good faith, there is evidence to suggest that it will not always be successful in discriminating between truth and falsehood. Is it not true that tyrannies attract a considerable retinue of corrupt panegyrists and sycophants? What is this but moral and social corruption? Is it a wonder that those who miss few occasions to deliver a litany against the evils of freedom refuse to put two words together about the evil of absolute power? "Eyes and ears open, and intellect in such a bind? / Lord be praised who allows the closing of the mind."[24] What is inconsistent with the search for freedom is the hunger for power, even the power that arrogates to itself the right to seek the truth and vanquish all falsehoods. It is not enough to have good intentions. Method is essential here. The Holy Qurʾan states: "That House of the Hereafter we shall give to those who intend not high-handedness or mischief on earth: and the end is (best) for the righteous."[25]

It is amusing to listen to the reasoning of those who say "freedom allowed someone like Marx to propagate atheism. Then someone else cultivated this seed in Russia, whose people suffered for more than seventy years before repenting in disgrace." What unctuous sophistry! What caused Marx's ideas to take root in the foreign soil of Russia, the truth of his theory notwithstanding? Was it freedom or power, right or might? Would his ideas have lasted so long if freedom of conscience, expression, and the press prevailed there? Would the buds of truth blossom in a climate where all intellectual and political dissent were suppressed or confined to mental hospitals, prisons, and work camps? Is this regime not the very quintessence of falsehood and the most harrowing form of depravity? The wrong must be challenged, but only with the methods that are themselves right. The right must be propagated, but never with the machinations of the wrong. The method of the wrong consists in suppression of freedom. Marx deserves the castigation implied in the following question: Would he be allowed to express himself in an ideal society of his own design as well as he did in London?

The problem of the enemies of freedom is that they think that power has caused corruption only because it has been wielded by others. They think that power in their hands would magically retain its charms but lose its blemishes. They do not seem to realize that "absolute power has only one logic: to subdue the truth; to turn it into its handmaiden." They do not seem to realize that power controls the man, not the other way around. They do not know that when they attain absolute power, they will no longer be what they used to be. This is a steed that transforms its rider. They do not seem to realize that power greatly magnifies human frailties. They do not understand that striving to curb absolute power is the most exalted of all good deeds, or that a political order without a system of checks and balances is nothing more than an ineffective and ruthless order. One of the most important shortcomings of Marxism was its lack of a system of harnessing power. The Marxists thought that the state would wither away. In reality, however, it gained in power and stature and increased its repression, injustice, and tyranny. So the loss of Marxism must be billed to the ledger of absolute power, not that of freedom of conscience. With freedom of conscience, autonomy of truth, and respect for reason few of these moral and social corruptions would have taken root.

Therefore, it should not be said that if we guaranteed freedom of expression, another Marx will appear and lead humanity astray. While such a society may permit a Marx-like figure to emerge, it will surely allow his opponents to confront and defeat him. Do not assume that only your enemies err and wallow in falsehoods while your minds are the overflowing fountainheads of pure, unadulterated truth. Allow your own errors to be exposed as well. Do not assume that the truth and falsehood are so clearly delineated in absence of a free sphere. What caused all that corruption was the intellectual guardianship of Marx and Engels, and the same will ensue wherever such guardianship exists.[26]

(18) The dull-witted, the sluggish, the crooked, and the indigent are afraid of entering a marketplace rife with bright and brisk merchants. In the words of Rumi: "Hatred of the light is the pretenders' blight / The pure gold adores the daylight."[27] Only those who lack in ideas need fear the marketplace of ideas. Because of their own penury, they curse the marketplace and view the wealthy merchants with bitterness. Here I engage in a forthright genetic and motivational analysis because most of the enemies of freedom do not argue in good faith or according to the rules of rational discourse. In order to hide the fact that their coffers are empty, some elevate themselves above the truth and would sooner sacrifice it than confess their own bankruptcy. Their defense of the truth and religion is only an excuse. Their threadbare mantles merely cloak their flaws; their seclusion is due to lack of proper garments.

These people must acquire worth and wealth instead of shutting down the market. They must gain enlightenment and allow the lights to remain lit: "Do not burn the rug to spite a flea / Do not waste your day on a fly's plea."[28] Why choose the illicit course of deception, character assassination, intimidation, cant, calumny, and destruction when acquiring virtue is a lot easier and more legitimate? Is it not better to adopt scholarly modesty, bow at the alter of truth, and humble oneself to God, the creator of all truths? Instead of abolishing the contest, is it not easier to train and prepare to win it? Why close the mosque when it is better to join the ranks of its worshippers?

(19) No blessing is more precious for mankind than the free choice of the way of the prophets. Nothing is better for humanity than submission based on free will. Blessed are those who are guided in this manner who freely choose the way of the prophets and are awash in a cascade of divine grace: "For those who believe and work righteousness is (every) blessedness and a beautiful place of (final) return."[29] But in the absence of this state of grace, nothing is better for humankind than the possession of freedom. All free societies, whether they are religious or nonreligious, are humane. But totalitarian societies abide neither divinity nor humanity. All that remains is ruthlessness and brutishness. The free societies are closer to the prophets than the totalitarian ones. Our thinkers have so far been more afraid of falsehood than of power. It is high time we put excessive power at the top of the list of falsehoods and reflect on its enormous potential to breed corruptions.

(20) We need both internal and external freedom. Our wise predecessors were more concerned with internal freedom. Rumi said:

> Oh honorable ones, we have slain the external foe,
> A more forbidding enemy lurks down below.
> Dislodging it, intellect and reason would not dare;
> The inner lion is not the play-thing of a hare.
> It is a common lion who breaks the legion's rows.
> The true lion is he who breaks the inner foes.[30]

This is all true, except for the part about slaying the external foe. Our sages had not slain the external foe nor were they concerned with real foes. They did not care who ruled them—the Mongols, the Abbasid caliphs or the Saldjuqid dynasty. This venerable sage and many others like him are only concerned with inner challenges. This is a worthy but incomplete enterprise because the external enemy can easily divert our attention from the internal battle. The inner battle is contingent upon overcoming the external enemy; sometimes the two conflicts are one and the same. Living under tyranny plunges the whole society into such iniquity and causes such legitimation and institutionalization of corruption that fighting the internal enemy becomes impossible.

Conversely, the contemporary Westerners have entirely forsaken the internal battle. The battle against desires has vanished from their discourse. Their concern in words and deeds revolve around the external enemy. "Liberty, Equality and Fraternity" was the slogan of the French Revolution, which sought liberation from the king, the church, the nobility, and unfair taxation. Liberation from passions and ambitions were not at issue. The truth is that if the internal and external freedom are not combined, both will suffer. In Rumi's exultant parlance, those who have not tasted internal justice and moderation will never appreciate external justice. Those who are not free from internal tyrants shall, at the slightest provocation, sell out the external freedom as well. Those who have not beheaded their own tyrannical desires are unable to recognize the external tyrants: "The art of separating the unjust from the just he will acquire / Who beheads the inner tyrannical desire."[31]

Thus, in the Western world we see injustice, colonialism, and arrogance toward other countries alongside the pursuit of liberty. There is external freedom, but no one is interested in internal freedom. Internal freedom can be achieved only by the light of submission and through following the guidance of the divine messengers. Those who are deprived from this beacon of guidance can not fully embrace either kind of freedom.

What we desperately need today is to take our cue from the seekers of freedom and from our own religious and mystic culture, to combine external and internal freedoms: the freedom predicated on submission and the submission predicated on freedom. We must tie these two together and desire them at once. We must not elevate one at the expense of the other. The bird that has been flying on one wing must be blessed with two wings in order to reach the nest of bliss.[32] And peace be upon you.

7

The Ethics of the Gods

I have always enjoyed writing about ethics. Why should a subject that is at once the groundwork of religion and of life not be delightful? It is, indeed, a daunting subject. There is a kind of sanctity in ethics that places it above analysis, experimentation, and reduction. Behavioral sociology and psychology have been unable to supplant it.

Yet among the rarest wonders that has emerged from the fountainhead of the history of ideas is the belief that there is nothing more variable, relative, context-dependent, and exception-ridden than morality. The problem concerns not only historically conditioned ethical behavior but the principles of morality as well. In other words, the issue is not only whether the principles of right or wrong are embedded in human nature, but also whether there is a conflict between reason and passion, whether there is such a thing as moral conscience, whether "ought" can be derived from "is," and whether human beings have a free will. The more difficult problem is the lamentable inability of the science of ethics to offer a set of lucid definitions and standards.

In the wake of centuries of debate, we still don't have a set of universal guidelines. As a result, moral instruction remains weak and dim. Truthfulness has a clear meaning and definition, but no ethicist has yet been able to rule that it is universally advisable. Breaking a promise is a relatively clear notion, but no one has suggested that it is evil under all circumstances. On the other hand, although all thinkers have agreed on the goodness of justice and the evil of inequity, no one has proposed a clear definition of justice and injustice. Ethics seems to entail its own "indeterminacy" theorem. As the accuracy of one side of the equation increases, the generality of the other decreases. This lack of determinacy is the enigma of enigmas. It reveals not only that ethics is not a precise and axiomatic science but also that it will never be. Even if we follow the lead of the Mu'tazilite school of thought in designating good and evil as natural and objective categories, deriving *ought* from *is*,[1] and establishing commonsensical moral maxims as self-evident, a priori precepts[2] devoid of cultural relativity and contingency, we still will have failed to shed even a sliver of light on the problem of the "indeterminacy" of morality or on the nature of rights, justice, fairness, power, and freedom.

* * *

This essay is burdened with no such preposterous ambitions. The author is aware that such questions are complex, if not irresolvable. The aim of this essay, then, is modest: it seeks to demarcate the line between two kinds of morality: morality fit for gods and morality fit for servants of God. The hope is that such a delineation will facilitate a precise formulation of certain moral issues.

Let's start from the question why ethicists have deemed such virtues as truthfulness, integrity, kindness, humility, and so on as sound, even though they know that all of these virtues admit of exceptions? There are three major responses to this question.

The first response is that these precepts are, in truth, without exception. If all the conditions and stipulations are specified, we will realize that the virtue of truthfulness, for example, stated along with all of its prerequisites and conditions, is truly universal. The same holds for the vice of deceitfulness. This is true of all the other injunctions in the science of ethics; they seem riddled with exceptions only because they are formulated in a summary fashion, not because they are truly exceptionable. Let us consider the criticisms of the above proposition:

A. One cannot decide whether a virtue such as modesty, for example, is always good or bad. Rather, one needs to wait until all of the necessary and sufficient conditions of its universality are discovered so that a final verdict on its goodness or evil can be passed down. This amounts to an indefinite suspension of the science of ethics.

B. It is not clear how long one need wait for such an accumulation of conditions or what method should be used to arrive at all of the prerequisites. Nor is it clear whether these methods are rational or experimental. This uncertainty leads us to despair of ever attaining a science of ethics.

C. How do we know that when we reach the totality of conditions for a comprehensive definition of moral virtue, say integrity or courage, we can still rule that they are universally good? The advocates of the first proposition must logically admit that the value of a simple moral precept, in the absence of its attending circumstances remains inadequate and uncertain. Thus, it cannot be overruled that after sufficient inves-

tigation integrity may be found to be universally evil, while recklessness is enthroned as universally good!

D. Contrary to the belief of the proponents of the first proposition, moral
precepts do not become more precise and expressive through enumera-
tion of all their attending conditions. They only get murkier and dim-
mer. All those stipulations and conditions simply muddy the waters of
judgment. They draw moral notions and injunctions into a quagmire
of ifs, buts, and other amendments that make it impossible to find a
morsel of unadulterated good and evil. This form of obfuscation avoids
any conclusive account of the presumed conditions or the method of
their discovery. There has never existed a clear formula and method
for offering an exhaustive definition of any notion, including ethics.
Thus it becomes impossible to define anything of value with this
method.

E. Since no one has ever proved that all moral virtues will be consistent
with one another (and, indeed, no moral philosopher has ever formulated such an argument), those who want to offer exhaustive definitions of moral precepts need to demonstrate that they will not conflict
with one another. In other words, they will have to define each virtue
in such a way that it would implicitly dovetail with the other virtues.
Since one cannot claim that all the virtues and vices are discovered and
enumerated, it would be impossible and implausible to state the final
formulae of any of the notions in question (and, by implication, it will
be impossible to rule on their goodness or evil).

Based on the above criticisms, the first proposition appears to belong to
the category of "self-destructive cleverness." It is a cure that compounds
the pain and exacerbates the illness.[3] It leaves the science of ethics forever suspended. We abandoned our diluted empirical ethics in the hope
of reaching a pure ethics that proved to be a mirage. It is as if the science
of ethics cannot be anything but an imperfect jumble and that any attempt
to improve it will only pile new uncertainties atop the prevailing ones.

The second response proposes that the ethical rules and regulations
are neither permanent nor necessary, but merely normal and frequent.
The evil of deceit or the merit of truthfulness, for example, are not matters of necessity, nature, or permanence but of habit and frequency. It is
thus said that the former is habitually and more frequently undesirable
and the latter desirable without denying exceptions to the rule.[4]

The exceptions are so rare that they do not inhibit us from generalizing (in most situations), nor do they prohibit people from applying them.
It appears that this proposition is a discreet and rational resolution whose
minimal benefit would be the preservation of the science of ethics on the
level of practice. It clarifies and adjudicates familiar moral notions, rather
than abstract moral concepts whose definitions and status remain vague.

Well and good. But all the controversies are over the exceptions. Does this position not imply that if exceptional circumstances that justify theft become prevalent, then theft will become less frequently reprehensible and more respectable? Alternatively, could altruism, one day, with a change of circumstances (that would turn exceptions into rules), become less admirable? This is like saying that there is no logical reason why a rare disease such as sickle cell anemia should not become an epidemic in the future. Unless, of course, we argue that social and natural human conditions will never change so drastically as to make theft honorable as a rule and reprehensible in exceptional instances; nor will truthfulness become reprehensible as a rule and honorable in rare cases. These, however, are no longer ethical propositions but unproven and unprovable statements.

Rules and exceptions are always dependent upon a particular context and universe. Any change in that context and universe may turn exceptions into rules and vice versa. In the context of the normal genetic structure, sickle cell anemia (a result of an inherited shortfall of certain amino acids in the hemoglobin of human blood) is quiet rare, but if the genetic structure is somehow altered that form of anemia may become a robust and dominant trait. Gold is a rare metal; but it is not as if the nature of gold requires scarcity. That is a result of the specific geological conditions of the earth. It is entirely possible that in another planet gold is more plentiful than copper without any disastrous consequences! In any event, ethicists inevitably harbor sociological and psychological assumptions such as the following: "The world produces human beings who are actually inclined to form social systems in which traits such as truthfulness, fulfilling promises, generosity to friends, and tolerance of enemies are better matched with the rest of the social system. They make life easier and more enjoyable by contributing to the order, stability, and balance of the society and by facilitating the attainment of positive ends," or "Virtues are more conducive to human perfection than are vices."[5] In other words, if traits such as lying and breaking promises would better serve the desired order, stability, and evolution of the society, they would be more agreeable and morally advisable. However, in the worldview of moral philosophers, the latter possibility is a mere conjecture and fantasy. The day will never come when deception and theft would make the society more stable and human beings more perfect. This, however, is far from certain.[6] What better evidence would one need than the presence of exceptions in all moral rules? If flaws are possible in one place, they are possible everywhere. A leak in a dam that is not blocked by a spadeful of dirt can in time defy a horde of elephants.[7] True, if truthfulness and dependability were universally, necessarily, and naturally good, then they would be free of the tangle of ephemeral individual and collective human conditions. However, as we have seen, this perception of morality is untenable. It leaves the door open to extrinsic factors that could transpose our definitions of good and evil. A moral society does not necessarily copy the conventional morality of a particular society, but it has its own appropriate and idiosyncratic form of morality. Therefore, the current science of ethics is a discipline for humanity as it is, not as it could be. Analogously, the current science of physics belongs to the existing world not to every possible world, which is why its theories are not logically necessary and timeless.[8]

Human beings have correctly concluded that in this world honesty, moderation, generosity, and courage make life more pleasant and harmonious than dishonesty, excess, greed, and cowardice. If we were to closely examine all moral virtues, we would discover that they have one common denominator: They mitigate conflicts and clashes and promote a psychological and social peace.[9] The malefic souls will quarrel far more frequently than the beneficent ones. This, indeed, is the secret of the wickedness of the former and virtuousness of the latter: had it not been for the stability and balance of the collective life of human beings, the two groups of traits would be indistinguishable. Accordingly, people have found out that mildness, humility, compassion, and truthfulness are not fitting or useful for all circumstances and for everyone. Sometimes, indeed, morality itself recommends against such behavior. The criteria for choosing one over the other are borrowed from elsewhere. In other words, morality is subordinate to the world and society. It serves human life. If life changes, morality, too, will have to change.

The disturbing and misleading notion here is a conception of morality that places it, along with metaphysical rules, above the events of this world, endows it with an impervious quality, yet deems it fit for the circumstances of every society. Such a morality, if it indeed existed, would not admit of exceptions. The fact that moral rules are shot through with exceptions is itself the best refutation of the belief in an impermeable morality. Therefore, ethics follows and fits life, not the other way around. Every form of life has its own morality and every position has its own etiquette. It should not surprise us if lying is sometimes advisable; if mildness, confidentiality, profanity, and kindness to kin are found to be appropriate with some people and inappropriate with others; if the ethics of war and the ethics of peace are different;[10] if industrial and traditional societies have different values; if altering people's mores and values would require altering their way of life. It takes an immense struggle to embrace the existing science of ethics and its variations, to avoid sacrificing actual morality at the altar of an imagined inviolate morality.

That imagined morality, even if it is actualized, will work no miracles, for it sits above mundane life, soars above the reality of ordinary human beings, bypassing the minute exchanges in which human beings are constantly entangled. It will not solve any problems.

Different situations require different mores and manners.[11] Everyone is aware of this, yet few are aware that these mores are not only prescribed

for those situations but that they are also generated from them and in-
here in them. The mannerisms fit the situations because they are born
from them.

Exception-admitting morality is part of life. It is a follower and a servant. Any pain or pleasure that affects life will affect morality. Since I
surmise that some readers are still inclined to invoke moral commandments as omnipresent, impermeable tyrants demanding obedience from
life, I should like to reiterate: Do not be distracted by such thoughts. That
kind of morality is but an impossible dream, a chimera.

The preceding arguments should please those who believe in deriving *ought* from *is*. They too believe in extracting morality from reality.
This is the meaning of appointing society as master of morality. Unless, of course, they claim that not every reality deserves to serve as
the foundation of a morality, that the only realities appropriate for this
task are those whose moral worth has been established! (And, of course,
this constitutes neither a paradox, a vicious circle, nor an abandonment
of the original idea. They may even demand that reality be so precisely
and exhaustively defined that it would admit of no exceptions. I wish
them luck!) In any event, the second proposition on the nature of morality has no impact on this or that philosophical theory of morality,
for it concerns the cause, not the reason. The argument on the plausi-
bility or implausibility of deducing *ought* from *is*, however, concerns
the statement of reason, not the cause. Human morality fits human life
and emanates from it. At this point saying anything further about right
or wrong is unwarranted.

This argument leads to a further issue: The subordination of ethics to
life is not contrary to acknowledging responsibility, the reality of good
and evil, and the prominence of values in human life. It is true that
morality is an effect whose entire existence is contingent upon and subordinate to its cause. It functions without the express permission, knowledge, or intention of human beings. However, people are free to imple-
ment it. It is the free and deliberate action of human beings that admits
of praise or censure. It is the knowledge of the good and evil and the
direction of ensuing action that leads to virtue or vice. None of these are
inconsistent with the above assertion that the ethics (and the science of
ethics) of each group of people emanates from their way of life and is
suitable to them. This violates neither the assumption of free will nor
the possibility of praise and condemnation of acts. Morality is governed
by the collective way of life, but it also governs individual action.

I can empathize with those readers who may now be asking: has any
part of morality been spared? Has the devastating flash flood of relativity left a single sublime and suitable ideal worthy of sacrifice? What are
we to do? just as we contemplate an invincible morality, invincible arguments are presented to the contrary. Then, as we turn to existing
morality, they are shown to be riddled by irremediable flaws. As we try

to darn the torn texture, they tie our hands by the idea of the "innate indeterminacy" of morality. As we console ourselves that our moral conscience guarantees constancy, we are reminded that this very conscience approves of the local nature of moral rules and that it adjusts itself to numerous forms of morality and society. As we start to get attached to this prevailing "rule of rarity of multiple coincidences," we feel mired in its infirmity and frailty. As we try to usher the caravan of life on a path free from deceit, duplicity, conceit, and rancor, we are taunted for our gullibility.[12] As we demand to stay in our present station, we are lectured on the inevitable historical and industrial progress and development. As we decry the amorality or immorality of modern society, we are reminded of the farcical nature of our beliefs, that there is more than one kind of morality. We are made to feel so bound by and drowned in life that we can seek and desire nothing that is extraneous to it. Life appears to be self-sufficient, self-sustaining, and self-perpetuating. Morality too is within and from it. Outside this world there are no ideals and no morality, only death and desolation. The greatest ideal is life and nothing else. It is the only goal. No one has been offered anything beyond that.

Inevitably, a number of sages and radical teachers of ethics vociferously reject such arguments. They profess to save people from the quagmire of a corrupt and oppressive life and guide them to a utopia free from pollution, poverty, and profligacy. They now hear that a life without pollution and corruption is not possible, that pollution and corruption cannot be deemed universally evil, and that society is full of forces opposing morality and virtue. Finally, they are told that virtue and vice themselves are neither definable nor appreciable outside the structure of a given society.

Is there an outlet anywhere? Is there the slightest hope of freedom from these inauspicious logical manacles? We tried the sterile scrutiny of moral notions and found it a path to oblivion. Not only is it incapable of laying a new moral foundation, it is likely to subvert and scuttle the existing morality. Let us now examine a third path.

The third response divides deeds into two categories: those that have a moral identity [virtues and vices] and those that do not. Neither group is exempt from moral judgment. Their only difference is linguistic and nominal. Still the distinction is immensely significant and consequential, just like naming days and months. So long as we have not attached a particular label to a day, it is indeterminate. But as soon as we have designated a day as Friday, it is immediately clear that it is a holiday, and so on.

There are two categories of names. On the one hand, there are nonmoral names: shopping, sewing, cutting, laughing, watching, studying, yawning, walking, working out, talking, and so on. These names do not carry a moral value in themselves. They do not impart inherent goodness or evil. It is not clear in advance whether studying, for example, is good or bad. Thus we may have two kinds of studying: good studying (advisable) and bad studying (inadvisable). The same goes for the other terms. On the other hand, there are moral names that do imply goodness or evil: tyranny, justice, and moderation belong to this group. There is no such thing as a good justice and a bad justice. Justice is that which is good. Goodness does not depart from justice. Immoderation is that which is bad. Badness inheres in it. At this juncture, we face some ambiguous words. Are truthfulness and deceit moral names or nonmoral names? Are they any different from eating and sleeping? How about envy, violence, insult, compassion, love, and homicide?

We have vilified deception, violence, insult, and envy for so long that it has become a matter of habit to consider them as evil. Compassion, on the other hand, hinders us from demoting its namesake from its habitual status of goodness. The stunning beauty of the truth, however, lies beyond the veil of habits. The veil has to be torn asunder. Analysis and deliberation recommend this bold step. Ethical philosophers who divide lies into admissible and inadmissible categories concede that lying is a natural name of the act, not a moral name, that it reveals the objective, not the moral properties, of the act. Lying means speaking an untruth. No moral categories are used in this definition; no moral rules are thus imported. The same is true of violence, which is harming another person; or insult, which is humiliating another human being; or jealousy, which is desiring the misery of another individual; and so forth.

To consider eating and sleeping desirable or undesirable, depending on the circumstance, does not trouble anyone's moral conscience, but to consider jealousy and violence desirable or undesirable depending on the circumstances violates our habits of thought even though it is commonly believed that violence is not universally reprehensible (as in the case of legitimate defense) nor wishing less bounty on the ingrate is always improper. Here again is the temptation to try and define actions and attributes such as jealousy and deceit so comprehensively and inclusively as to specify all their conditions and exceptions and to restrict their use to so restricted an area that they would have virtually uniform application and carry their moral values on their shoulders and admit of no exceptions whatsoever. Then such and such a form of violence would be reprehensible everywhere, and such and such a form of truthfulness would be admissible in every case. But we have seen the sterility and unreasonability of such a project before. Let us add here that even if we were to attach a hundred stipulations to the natural name of an action, we would still have a natural name not a moral one. We would still reach an action that has two possible outcomes: admissible or inadmissible. In order to reach an unambiguous moral value or action, we need a moral name. Only this will end our quandary. Moral names, in reality, refer to no specific action or natural disposition. They are attributes of natural actions, and they determine the moral worth of a specific natural action. Justice is not a name for any natural action. It is not like truthfulness, mildness, verbosity, impatience, and selfishness, which describe natural actions and dispositions. The same goes for courage, moderation, and wisdom (names for the three cardinal [Platonic] virtues). Just and unjust persons do nothing but give, take, eat, haul, and so on. But one party's exchanges are considered just and another's unjust. This is why there are no moral values attached to eating and hauling, but there are crystal-clear rules concerning unjust eating and hauling as such, rules that are in no need of further inspection and inquiry.[13]

Justice, according to ethicists, is the repository of all other virtues. The three cardinal virtues—courage, moderation, and wisdom—are moral names for judicious and temperate use of human energies. That is why they are rightly subsumed under the title of justice and are its auxiliaries. The same is true of the categories subsumed under vice (cowardice, recklessness, lust, and sloth) that are the names of injudicious uses of human faculties. None of these are names of natural actions. There are moderate, courageous, and prudent actions, but there is no particular deed named moderation, courage, and prudence.[14] The moral name of just desire is moderation. The moral name of just spiritedness is courage. The moral name of just reasoning is wisdom. That is why there is no such thing as good and bad moderation, good and bad courage, and good and bad injustice; but there are such things as good and bad violence, good and bad breaking of promises, good and bad deception, good and bad jealousy, and so on.

It looks like we have reached the desired solution. The insurmountable walls are breached. We were looking for them on the earth of natural names, but we found them in the heaven of moral names. The defect has been in our methods, not in the names.

We intended to clarify the moral virtues and vices in such a way as to make them universally applicable, thus we tried to specify and record their every vicissitude to make them invulnerable to change. Tightening the ropes, however, did not fasten and awaken the science of ethics but suffocated it. Now we understand why all that scrutiny has been in vain. We have been trying to paint moral faces on natural names that by nature could not depart from their natural identity. We had lost our way. Our goal was a different one all along. Justice, moderation, and courage— universal goods—have been our objectives, and no deed will partake of them unless it is good. Nor will there ever be any exception or decline in their goodness. This is guaranteed in advance and no sophistry and force can revoke it.

Now, our moral pedagogues and revolutionaries also seem to have found some solace in this. The heavenly ideals seem secure from earthly elements and safe in their eternal sovereignty. It looks like moral sermons and crusades have a new lease on life, have escaped their confines, and look reinvigorated. It still seems possible to call humanity to justice and courage and to await, design, and erect a utopia of justice and moderation. For after all, if the moral worth of deeds such as truthfulness and deceit is variable, the moral worth of justice and courage is constant. Who cares if our heavenly city warrants lies and insults under certain circumstances; it never condones injustice and immoderation. If we may not recommend unconditional truthfulness, sincerity, and compassion, we can, nevertheless, recommend unconditional courage, moderation, and wisdom. If there are no absolute rules about violence per se, there are absolute rules about unjust violence. If there are no absolute rules about love, there are absolute rules about moderate (just) love. If there is any relativity, then, it is because of natural names, not moral names.

Again, it looks like we have approached ideal precision and stability. Not only are justice and injustice eternally and morally distinct, every natural name that comes under their aegis will find eternal moral determination as well. How distant is this life-inspiring and solid morality from the weak and moribund morality we once held![15]

Alas, the impermanence of Christlike sovereigns. If they do not rise on the cross, they rise to the heavens and disappoint the hopeful. Those who restrict justice to truth, sincerity, and so on crucify it on the cross of exceptions; and those who place it above human affairs and temperaments send it to the heavens, where it cannot heal or restore. We have learned that justice and moderation are not, in truth, the names of any actions. An invitation to justice is not an invitation to any natural and specific action. Thus it becomes possible to proudly engage in any deed in the name and under the facade of justice. This is what makes justice so sublime in definition and so powerless in action, so invisible and inaccessible. Foul tempers, lies, and insults are not missed by anyone, but who is to tell us what just and unjust traits are? It is easier to accuse people of homicide than to accuse them of unjust homicide. There is not as much controversy over the definition of deceit, insult, profanity, and defamation as there is over the definition of justice, right, and injustice. Those attributes that have a clear application have a hazy definition, and those that have a clear definition lack clarity of application. Nor does it help to combine the two categories to dissipate one's darkness with the other's light; the result of such a combination would, regrettably, compound the murkiness and darkness of both categories. This is analogous to the anecdote of a fair lady who proposed to marry an unattractive sage so their children would inherit her beauty and his wisdom. The sage, however, was concerned their children would inherit his looks and her wisdom!

We stated that every society has its own kind of morality and that if other societies do not have our kind of morality, they cannot be accused of lacking in morality and virtue altogether. A society full of deceit and disloyalty can be moral and virtuous (provided that exceptions become rules, which is not, in principle, impossible). It was this kind of talk that offended the ethicists' conscience. They could not stand by and witness so much inferiority, subservience, and variability in morality; this is what set them on the quest for a firm, durable, and glorious morality that would not slip or buckle under, whimper, or retreat in the face of tyranny in the first place. Let's put the matter in a different way. What is wrong with a society in which justice sanctions murder, false accusation, deceit, and depriving the accused of the right of self-defense? Can such a society be deemed unjust? Apparently not. It looks like justice is not contrary to any of the above. If murder is not contrary to justice, neither is torture and deceit. The above traits are names of natural actions. Besides, justice itself is a moral name; it cannot contradict a natural action. To be sure, good temper and bad temper, truth and falsehood, violence and civility are natural names; thus an invitation to one will preclude its opposite, but justice precludes none. They can all be placed under the canopy of justice and portrayed as just. It does not help to resort to the Aristotelian notion of the golden mean in the definition of justice and moderation either. It will lead to another dilemma that requires a solution of its own.

Do you see the impasse we have reached? Both types of morality we have presented seem to have ended up in the same predicament: the utter humiliation of morality rendering it devoid of content and subservient to alien elements: in one case to cultural contingencies and in the other to abstract moral attributes. The distinction between moral and natural names was not entirely futile, but rather than yielding a solution to the dilemma of morality, it demonstrated the poverty, deception, and bluster of the claim to eternal, abstract, and universal morality. Although it looked quite exalted on the surface, it was worse than the temporary, transient, moribund, and circumscribed laws:

> Pithy as pistachio, it was presented,
> skin upon skin, as onion it was, when tested.[16]

The failure of this latter kind of morality is much more disappointing than the impotence of the former kind. The latter failure resembles falling from a much taller ladder. It is bone crushing. If one doubts the possibility and actuality of such a version of morality, one can observe a multitude of political systems in the past and present that have justified just about any form of corruption and indignity in the name of establishing order and justice. One may also observe the clever evildoers who, while violating a moral rule present an array of philosophical apologies and moral justifications for their evil deed. One is inclined to salute the innocent and the ignorant, who have no access to such immoral and profane wit, living in a fool's paradise, distant from the inferno of the hellish cleverness.[17]

What is to be done? The heart is satisfied with neither natural nor transcendental ethics. It can neither endure a deceitful society nor can it escape such an inferno with the help of justice and temperance. If the former preaches accommodation to concrete social requirements, the latter demands conformity to abstract moral requirements. This latter is, of course, more bitter and disappointing.

How about changing the formulation of the question altogether? Let us ask what will happen if we reject an entire society, along with its requisite morality? What moral principle would this refusal violate? It is evident that neither a natural and subordinate morality nor an exalted and eternal one would be able to restrain a society bent on evil. What if we establish a supermoral principle that states that any society that turns moral exceptions into rules advocates deception, oppression, duplicity, war, and carnage; and that any society that depends on such depravities in order to operate would be morally repugnant and condemned along with its hellish complex of relationships. Evidently, two distinct levels of judgment are involved here: one concerning individual deeds and the other concerning the totality of deeds. It is possible for individual acts of violence, torture, and carnage to be "just" under certain circumstances, yet a system, as a whole, that depends on those acts should not be judged moral and acceptable. This is what that supermoral principle states: we do not want a system that depends more on vices than on virtues, even if those vices have their own place and function in the system, fitting it, supporting it, and guaranteeing its survival. In other words, to be moral means nothing but following these exception-bound moral rules. No society in which moral virtues are abandoned can be a good society. There is no higher cause that would justify smothering these rules. Therefore, the clearest sign of a wicked society is one in which these rules are abandoned under one pretext or another.

Therefore, there is no higher morality than the existing morality. By "existing morality," I mean our familiar exception-bound moral rules. Following these moral values is the best guarantee of justice and desired moderation in society. The history of human vice is replete with moral violations and deceptions perpetrated in the name of a higher morality and justice.

To escape a society full of deception, duplicity, and intrigue, we are obliged to refuse any system that needs and regularly rationalizes them. Inevitably, then, we need to reject any subterfuge and pretext that would justify such a system. We should refuse to acknowledge any moral, political, and social system that invents and breeds such devices. The best and the only manifestations of justice are in these moral rules. Where these rules enjoy no respect and exposure, justice, too, has no sovereignty and identity. The Stalinist regime was not evil because its goals were repugnant or because of the injustice of its individual acts of terror, accusation, and extraction of false confessions. Even if all these were judged to be just and necessary measures to ease the "birth pangs" of socialism, it would still be a contemptible and improper regime, for it needed such methods for its survival. A system that needs to abort exception-bound moral rules in order to secure its existence, balance, potency, and stability is a fundamentally immoral and corrupt system. The important thing is to acknowledge that both natural (subordinate) morality and the eternal (detached) morality are incapable of judging such a regime. The former permissively blends morality and society and the latter, with its metaphysical moral universalism, adjusts to all social and moral realities, for it endorses any possible social morality and rejects none. It presents such an angelic, abstract, and featureless image of justice, moderation, and wisdom that it seems capable of being incarnated in the body of any beast. Thus it makes morality subject to, rather than sovereign over, tyrants. One needs to believe that there is no such thing as a higher court of morality. Morality is not a parliament that dissolves itself. Such a parliamentary image of morality would be an oxymoron. The subordinate morality, then, must be taken as a sovereign. Let's not squander our actual assets in anticipation of an imaginary windfall. One of the misfortunes of the contemporary world has been that reformers, philosophers, and misanthropes[18] have, in the name and under the pretext of reform, attacked existing morality, accusing it of being a handiwork of the powerful, the affluent, the "bourgeoisie," the clergy, or the weak. (A host of thinkers and leaders from Marx and Nietzsche to Hitler and his ilk have participated in this attack.) The outcome of their efforts, however, was that the unscrupulous despots, transgressors, and scoundrels became more brazen, sophisticated, reckless, and fallacious; as a result, the same feeble morality that would occasionally keep the flame of righteousness alive in the path of a traveler fluttered and dimmed. Neither Nazi Germany (that utilized the teachings of Nietzsche and later, of Heidegger) nor Soviet Russia (that followed the teachings of Marx and Lenin) were capable of evolving a morality worthy of acknowledgment, let alone dedication of the pure of heart. This, in spite of the efforts of scores of "venerable thinkers" who were recruited to provide a moral defense for such regimes. The confrontation of the empathetic intellectuals with these regimes constitutes one of the most instructive lessons of human history.

Never before had thinkers been caught in such a agonizing moral snare as in Soviet Russia. They could plainly observe the fate of those who were immolated in the pit of Stalin's rage; those who made humiliating confessions; those who were prevented from publishing their "bourgeois" ideas; those who were presented to the nation as "enemies of the people"; and those who were imprisoned, tortured, purged, and exiled. The quantity and the quality of these "traitors" and "enemies" was such that the veracity of tales of their treacheries and travails seemed exceedingly suspicious, dubious, and questionable. But, at the same time, the anticipation of the imminent eruption of the promised spring of social justice and the desire to "take a refreshing drink after the afflictions of the past" had so gripped their minds, the idea of the "inevitable" collapse of capitalism had so captured their imagination, finally, the propaganda (presenting the state as the sole criterion of truth and falsehood) had so impaired their judgments that they actually pretended not to notice the obvious realities and suffered in silence. No one (save the brave few) had the integrity and insight to cry out: This emperor, whom people are trying to cover in order to prove their own sanity, wears no clothes! This is not a blooming orchard but a wasteland in which thorns are called flowers and flies, eagles. A large number of these intellectuals were truly desperate and perplexed. They were waiting for a just, humane, egalitarian, and cultivated "socialist" regime to break the polar night of history and to launch the new history of humanity. Were they to take their gaze away from the unprecedented historical vista of the imminent realization of the highest human ideals in order to point a finger of accusation and disclosure at the irregularities, iniquities, depravities, and corruptions surrounding them? Were they to condemn the flower bed because of a few thorns? Had Lenin not quipped, "To make an omelet, you need to crack a few eggs"? What further bewildered the sincere intellectuals (the insincere ones aside) was a belief in a higher morality. A morality that became, in the end, the very essence of immorality. Thus, in the name of this imaginary morality, they condoned all the real vices around them. In anticipation of the birth of a new brave humanity, they forgave all the character assassinations, political cannibalisms, and crimes against freedom and virtue. They did not realize that justice is nothing if not realization of moral rules, and, as such, it has no other manifestation but these moral rules. A system that suppresses this morality has no virtues and deserves no support. Even today, there are those who, in their critique of other societies, follow complex and improbable lines of argument and, striking a philosophical pose, try to minimize or deny their moral failures, attributing them to historical contingencies and the reversal of human morality, and the eclipse of the eternal truth.

Whether or not these allegations are true, they all have one common denominator: their uselessness (if not outright danger). Marxists, too, derided the bourgeoisie as humanity stood on its head, an anachronistic anomaly. Such bombastic abstractions have always been used by various (sometimes mutually exclusive) causes. They have bred hordes of effusive, ineffective, zealot advocates and defenders. Since all such claims are abstract, their social embodiments remain obscure as well. In contrast, a truly authentic and virtuous individual and society needs no other hallmark than the practice of the (familiar) exception-bound moral rules. In order to gauge the corruption of Western capitalist and socialist societies, there is no criterion other than reference to these moral regulations. Even if we believe that these abstract principles will live up to their promise and not prove "cover for a hundred buried vices" of their incompetent advocates, why should we abandon manifest moral signs and resort to principles that remain hidden, obscure, and cryptic? A society, whether it is in the West or on Mars, is base and reprehensible if it admits of deception, duplicity, defamation, usurpation, violence, harm, empty sermonizing, greed, treason, disloyalty, prevarication, distrust, bribery, niggling, burglary, conceit, contention, derision, oppression, self-righteousness, wastefulness, ignorance, poverty, cowardice, hunger, hubris, cruelty, etc. In other words, a society is morally condemned if these traits are rules rather than exceptions. Even if we judge such attributes as functionally necessary for the degree of social development of such a society, still it will not escape our judgment because the abovementioned supermoral principle will condemn such a society, along with its morality. This is true of societies that breed vices that fit their way of life, let alone societies that import vices incongruous with their way of life! This is the proper method of judging the morality of a society, not burying one's head in the sand and turning a blind eye to the sun and moon. Quaint intellectual meditations that have no effect but obscuring the truth have turned into an advantage for the inept and ambivalent and into a real hazard for the seekers of the truth. They travel unbelievably sinuous paths and resort to strange indigestible analyses to expose a supposed moral contortion in the West, ignoring at the same time, and quite deliberately, the clearest criterion available to them. Thus, they deceive others and offer them wooden swords to fight real battles.

> Since life's "goal"[19] has been concealed,
> Each is beating a different path afield.
> Each is burning in a different pyre,
> Each, a butterfly, round his own fire.[20]

The same is true of a Marxist society. Neither the highest aspirations for the ideal humanity nor the most sophisticated philosophical justifications would be sufficient for the constitution of a desirable society. The highest aspiration for humanity is a society that does not scuttle the highest moral aspirations, but subordinates all of its affairs to moral dictates. The deepest analysis is one that does not paralyze morality, but explicates and exalts it. The most judicious judgment is that which installs moral rules as the criteria of judgment and turns away from clandestine, complex, suspicious, and chameleonlike criteria that are easily manipulated by the masters of might and idle fallacy. The highest human beings are those who are the most humble in the temple of moral principles and who never place themselves above the truth and morality.

All of the systems that consider themselves authentic are confronted, in rare moments of clarity, with the soul-searching and the heart-wrenching question: To what extent are we allowed to sacrifice the truth at the altar of survival? Morally, what are the limits of staying above morality?

Legally, how far can we disregard the law? In short, survival to what point, to what end, and at what price? The responsible servants, advocates, and supporters of such systems, too, have a right, and a responsibility, to contemplate these questions and to worry about the answer. The candid answer is that survival is warranted so far as no moral rules are turned into exceptions; so far as the system does not consider itself the embodiment of and a monument to the Truth. No other criterion has the potency and forthrightness of the one just stated. The temptation of perseverance until the end of a certain historical epoch, or until the realization of the ideal justice, allows a system to adjust to every abomination and depravity. In reality, the most oppressive and wicked regimes have perpetrated the worst inhuman inequities under these same slogans.

We are approaching the culmination of this speech. What we meant to state was that a morality that is adjustable to all circumstances is no morality. What saves morality from such a death trap is a supermoral principle that installs the exception-bound rules of morality as the very foundation of morality, so they will never decline or relax. In other words, there is no morality higher and more accurate than the existing morality. There is no higher altar of ideal morality in which to sacrifice the actual morality. A society in which moral exceptions have become rules is, by definition, an immoral and wicked society. In other words, justice, wisdom, moderation, and courage have no embodiments other than the prevalence of these moral rules; wherever the lantern of these rules is extinguished, the light of those virtues will be dimmed. For those virtues are not to be found in a higher world. All these arguments and locutions have but one referent: appeal to a certain kind of morality that is indispensable for this world and without which everything will be lost.

The most egregious treachery of degenerate tyrants against a subjugated people is not depriving them of their wealth or robbing them of their rights but introducing them to wicked ways so that when they take power they adopt these vicious ways of government and use them to stay in power at any price and by any pretext. This is the very nature of defeat of a people by their former tyrants, even if it resembles victory.

In any case, here is the synopsis of the argument. First, even if there is such a thing as an ideal morality, it is the same thing as the actual morality. Second, the actual morality is amendable but not eradicable. Third, if there is to be an invitation to morality, it will have to be toward concrete and accessible rules not toward some abstract ideas that bend to any conceivable form yet solve no specific moral dilemma. Fourth, if there is to be a struggle, it should be against the bases and antecedents that cause moral exceptions to become rules and vice versa and the ideas that promote an alien and abstract "higher" morality. Fifth, if there is to be a judgment, it should be based on moral commands that yield the most sincere, generous, and straightforward responses to the most dexterous forms of subterfuge and sophistry.

This is the essence of moral practice in society. It is, indeed, analogous to the scientific practice in nature. As such, it is a useful guide. This is a humble vision of morality apropos of fallible human beings who are far from being Gods. It is not the human morality but the divine morality and justice that adjusts itself to all societies. It behooves us, fallible creatures, to act as fallible creatures not as infallible gods. One should leave God's work, God's morality, and God's affairs to God. This is the meaning of reliance on God (*tavakkol*).[21] And peace be upon you.

8

The Idea of Democratic
Religious Government

Modern science explains the world as if it were not created by a god, not denying his existence, but rather finding no need to postulate it. In other words, it is assumed that even if there were a god, science would nonetheless be able to explain the world without relying on his existence. Nowadays science seems to have left its imprint on the behavior of the individual and the conduct of government as well. In the political culture of liberal secular societies, governments and individuals act as if there is no god, proceeding in utter indifference to His existence or nonexistence, never weighing His approval or disapproval of their policies and behavior. Political struggles and deliberations are designed to satisfy human beings alone.

In this respect modern liberal democratic governments stand in sharp contrast to the religious governments of the past. The religious governments of yore (in the age of the Catholic popes and Moslem caliphs) supposedly attended exclusively to divine, not human, mandates. At most, they saw people's satisfaction as contingent upon and as a natural by-product of God's satisfaction. Conversely, today's liberal democratic governments pursue people's happiness to the exclusion of God's approval. Yet perhaps we can enjoy the freedoms of modern democratic government without ignoring the existence of God.

The problem of religious democratic governments is threefold: to reconcile people's satisfaction with God's approval; to strike a balance between the religious and the nonreligious; and to do right by both the people and by God, acknowledging at once the integrity of human beings and of religion. The task of democratic religious governments is, obviously, much harder than that of democratic or religious regimes.

It is immediately evident that we are faced with the problem of God. The central and fundamental questions are: (1) Does God exist? (2) If God exists, does He have any rights? (3) If God exists and has rights, must those rights be upheld? Surely, those who are mindful of human rights cannot be indifferent to God's rights, if such exist, nor can they neglect His existence and rights in the conduct of human life. It is by no means less significant to be concerned with the rights of God than with those of human beings.

For Whom is this a question?

Although secular thinkers may not be oblivious to these concerns, they seldom if ever raise the question of God's rights in discussing human rights, preferring to concentrate instead on securing people's contentment to the exclusion of God. One may summarize modern secular arguments about God's rights as follows:

A. God—assuming He exists and assuming He has specific rights—can defend or petition for His own rights with utmost might. Unlike weak and helpless humanity, He needs no recourse to others' patronage.

B. It is impossible to do injustice by God. Even if human beings do not observe His rights, still they cannot be said to have harmed Him. Defending human rights has a moral dimension—the defense of the oppressed and the deprived whose rights are violated—that does not enter into the defense of God's rights.

C. Believers and nonbelievers still argue over the existence or nonexistence, attributes, and deeds of God. These controversies have undermined traditional certainties about Gods' existence. But this is a contest of faiths, not of intellects. Neither side judges the other's arguments according to purely rational criteria, and this alone renders the problem unresolvable. It therefore seems unjust and unfair to impose one side of the argument on all parties, as if it were a certainty, and to force everyone to observe all its consequences. One cannot ask everyone to believe, to the same degree and in the same sense, in the same omnipotent God. Consequently, one may not ask everyone to observe the rights of such a God. Tolerance [*tasamoh*] is the best solution in this situation. The public sphere should be expansive enough to allow a coexistence of religious and secular people, free from antagonisms that result from unequal rights and the imposition of one side's belief on the other.

D. Assuming God exists, ascertaining His rights is impossible. Each religion invokes a different god and each claims a monopoly on the truth. How is the knowledge concerning their truth or falsehood to be obtained? How can we establish what God exactly expects from us? Once again, governments should be neutral toward various religions. Governments as regulators of public affairs ought to concentrate on preserving people's common rights and leave theological issues to the citizens' private and inner lives. Thus even if governments are still concerned with the questions of truth or falsehood of different religions and the supposed rights of God, they should remain impartial, guaranteeing the freedom and security of the contest of opinions, while scrupulously maintaining the separation of politics and religion.

E. Religion should, above all, be humane. Just as the people serve their religion, religion should serve its followers. Justice can not be religious, but religion should claim justice, truthfulness, and humanity among its attributes. Hence, in order to become acceptable to modern humanity, the intrinsic imperatives of every religion must be harmonious with these extrinsic characteristics.

No one should be compelled to tolerate inhumanity, mendacity, and injustice in the name of God, history, patriotism, or any other shibboleth. Mining the humanitarian resources of a religion is more important than ascertaining its privileged divinity. In fact, it is humanity's right to reject inhumane religions and even to contest their claim to true religiosity.

F. Since there is no way to derive *ought* from *is*, people's rights should not be decided on the basis of their actual aptitudes and talents. Such a policy could easily foster racism and other assorted biases. Human rights should be based either on humanity's ultimate ends as revealed by the Creator (an impractical alternative for the above-mentioned reasons) or on people's autonomous determination of their achievable objectives, combined with governmental respect for certain rights and obligations that facilitate the attainment of those objectives. Natural rights simply mean principles whose observance promotes a more humane, rational, secure, prosperous, and fulfilling life. Rational ends such as justice, order, and welfare and deliverance from discrimination, strife, prejudice, fratricide, ignorance, hunger, and oppression are the results of the long historical experience of humanity and a matter of consensus among all reasonable people. It is not as though any of these principles could be set aside for the sake of some religious dogma. Human beings have suffered long enough at the hands of sectarian obstinacy, bloody religious wars, bitter clashes over beliefs, and futile battles over turf. They are now increasingly inclined to recognize one another as brothers and sisters, as equals; to acknowledge common rights for all; and to refrain from relegating anyone to a subhuman status with lesser rights solely on the basis of his or her color, language, nationality, or beliefs. Being human is the only prerequisite for participation in such universal rights, irrespective of race, color, ethnicity, beliefs, language, nationality, or social class.

G. In the eyes of justice, inequality is an acquired state that precludes no religion, family, nationality, or ethnicity from eligibility for certain universal rights. In contrast, arrogating certain a priori rights to themselves, some racists, religious bigots, or ethnocentrists fancy themselves superior and justify social inequalities and dogmatic restrictions in matters of religious freedom, marriage, citizenship, and free expression.

H. History testifies that religious beliefs and rules have undergone substantial changes at the hands of religious leaders and the clergy. For example, church authorities used to burn heretics and skeptics at the stake, and Moslems used to resist the presence of women in legislative assemblies. These practices have undergone fundamental transformation. Such constantly shifting ideas can not serve as the foundation of the rights of God and man, nor is it wise to coerce or invite all people to observe them.

These are the arguments of today's secular thinkers, who are, indeed, blameless in their skepticism. Western science, philosophy, and technology have so shaken the foundations of human reason and mind, historicism has raised such a storm, and scientific and philosophical theories advanced so swiftly that no latitude has been left for stability and certitude. Tolerance in the domain of beliefs is the correlative of a fallibility in the domain of cognition that has encroached upon traditional dogmas.

The difference between the old and the new worlds is the difference between certainty and uncertainty, a distinction that accounts for the modern tendency to value human lives more than beliefs; in the old world beliefs always superseded respect for human life. People used to kill and be killed for their beliefs. Nowadays, killing people for their beliefs is deemed unacceptable and a breach of human rights.[1]

None of the foregoing arguments deprive anyone of his or her right to believe. Nevertheless, many people are troubled by an implicitly lackadaisical attitude toward the question of God, His approval, and His rights among three groups of people: those who consider religion from without; those who are still inquiring but are not yet committed to a specific religious outlook; and those who lead a secular life in a religious society. However, members of religious communities who seem immune to the relentless inquiries of those outside their faiths and who fastidiously pursue their own religious way of life find such arguments unpersuasive. Thus, the truly committed religious people take issue with two aspects of secular human rights:

- Freedom of opinion is considered one of the primary human rights. Now, conviction can breed the kind of certitude that fosters decisive action. It is such decisiveness that manifests itself, at times, in holy wars and other such crusades born of unshakable belief. Such attitudes, of course, offend the sensibilities of the advocates of human rights. Secular antipathy toward religious zeal is, in turn, bewildering to religious people. One may, of course, propose that the universal declaration of human rights advocates a particular form of freedom of opinion: the freedom of flexible opinion, not of absolute conviction. This may be an intriguing interpretation of the principle. It is doubtful, however, that it would find favor among ardent believers.

- If democratization of religious government means washing one's hands of convictions and surrendering to skeptical or secular ideas and to people's demands, to the exclusion of God, this would be tantamount to abandoning the very idea of religious government in favor of an unreligious and secular government. An unthinkable alternative for the ardently religious. How can one expect the people of strong conviction to retain their belief only inwardly, without honoring them in practice? Hence the dilemma of a religious government: it must confront a universal declaration of human rights that is oblivious to religion and the rights of the Creator, and it must contend with the demands of an increasingly secular society. Thus, religious governments cannot easily adopt all the principles and precepts of the declaration of human rights. Discord between the secular advocates of human rights and religious leaders stems from the suspicion of the latter that the invitation to democratization of the religious government will ineluctably eviscerate any religious content, rendering society utterly secular and reconstructing a faithless foundation. That is why religious regimes are willing to sacrifice democracy in order to retain their identity.

Considering the above secular arguments, the suspicions of the faithful do not seem altogether baseless. For its followers, religion yields a definition of humanity and a description of human rights that are compatible. Changing human rights requires changing the definition of humanity, not a trivial and easy affair. One definition of humanity makes religion necessary and another dispensable. Therefore, religiosity is compatible only with a particular definition of humanity and its rights. The slightest breach in this definition will destroy the edifice of traditional religion—hence the understandable resistance of religious scholars and leaders to the new definitions of humanity and its rights.

But the debate does not end here. It is valid to argue that in a secular society a democratic religious government is impossible because religious governments are not answerable to the people. In such a society, the best form of government would be a secular democratic regime. However, it is not valid to argue that nowhere and under no conditions may one perceive the desirability of a religious democracy, even in a religious society. The truth of the matter is that a religious government can be an appropriate reflection of a religious society. Indeed, in such a society any purely secular government would be undemocratic. Whether religious regimes are democratic or undemocratic, though, depends on two conditions: (1) the extent to which governments partake of collective wisdom, and (2) the extent to which governments respect human rights. A combination of democracy and religion would entail the convergence of reason ['aql] and revelation [shar']. Every theoretical achievement will have to become practically viable.

Of Concordance of Reason ['Aql]
and Revelation [Shar']

Religious scholars cannot afford to be oblivious to extrareligious knowledge. Nor can they shirk the responsibility of balancing the knowledge inside and outside religion, since many basic religious values such as truth, justice, humanity, public interest, and so on are integral to nonreligious value systems as well. If religious justifications are invoked in this context, then a circularity or a tautology will result. On the other hand, arguments that are adduced for the truth and justice of religion are generally rational, human, and nonreligious in nature, yet they are influential in understanding religion. Therefore, disregard of rational criteria and of the necessity for the harmony of religious understanding and rational findings is a breach of religious responsibility. It is reason that defines truth, justice, public interest, and humanity, that attributes these properties to a particular religion (or else it would not become a rationally acceptable religion), and that undertakes the task of understanding the teachings of religion. In these tasks, reason would be undermining itself if, eschewing its general principles concerning truth, justice, and humanity, it assigns a different set of interpretations of those principles for religion. This would be analogous to pulling the carpet from underneath one's own feet.[2] Thus, one may state the following: preconditions for democratizing religious government is historicizing and energizing the religious understanding by underscoring the role of reason in it. By reason I do not mean a form of isolated individual reason, but a collective reason arising from the kind of public participation and human experience that are available only through democratic methods.

For democratic governments, "common sense" is the arbiter of society's antagonisms and difficulties; religious governments assign this arbitration to religion, while dictatorships leave it in the hand of one powerful individual. Religion, however, never judges a situation independently; the judgment is refracted through the interpretation of religious texts, a task that falls within the domain of reason, which always harmonizes its comprehension of religion with its other precepts.

The debates concerning slavery epitomize this process. Contemporary Islamic scholars attempt, through various means, to bleach the blemish of the approval of slavery from the face of Islam. They explain that slavery was specific to a particular epoch, that its radical abolition was impossible at that time, or that its approval must have been a reactive measure imposed on Islam by the practice of other nations. All these explanations have but one purpose: these thinkers have correctly understood that slavery is incompatible with human rights and dignity. These thinkers then, through rational deliberations, have helped bestow a more comprehensive and accurate understanding of matters divine upon the religious society, an understanding that will affect its overall way of life and government. Conversely, an autocratic God legitimizes an autocratic government and vice versa. We may conclude that the appeal to religious conviction cannot and should not arrest the renewal of religious understanding or innovative adjudication [*ijtihad*] in religion. Such renewal requires extrareligious data. Therefore, democratic religious regimes need not wash their hands of religiosity nor turn their backs on God's approval. In order to remain religious, they, of course, need to establish religion as the guide and arbiter of their problems and conflicts. But, in order to remain democratic, they need dynamically to absorb an adjudicative understanding of religion, in accordance with the dictates of collective "reason." Securing the Creator's approval entails religious awareness that is leavened by a more authentic and humane understanding of religiosity and that endeavors to guide the people in accordance with these ideals. In thus averting a radically relativistic version of liberalism, rational and informed religiosity can thrive in conjunction with a democracy sheltered by common sense, thereby fulfilling one of the prerequisites of a democratic religious government.

Of Respect for Human Rights

The first issue concerning human rights is that it is not a solely legal [*fiqhi*] intrareligious argument. Discussion of human rights belongs to the domain of philosophical theology [*kalam*] and philosophy in general. Furthermore, it is an extrareligious area of discourse. Like other debates on matters that are prior to—yet influential in—religious understanding and acceptance, such as the objectivity of ethical values, the problem of free choice, the existence of God, and the election of prophets,[3] human rights lies outside of the domain of religion. Whether one agrees or disagrees with this argument, the discussion of it takes place in the extrareligious area of discourse. It is noteworthy that Islamic theologians [*motakallemin*] never hesitated to apply their philosophical theories concerning the nature of evil or predestination to their understanding of religion, even where such an exercise resulted in bizarre theologies.

As we have stated before, a religion that is oblivious to human rights (including the need of humanity for freedom and justice) is not tenable in the modern world. In other words, religion needs to be right not only logically but also ethically. The discussion of human rights is hardly cosmetic, superfluous, blasphemous, or easily dismissed. Nor is it merely grist for scholastic and casuistic discussions within seminary walls. Simply put, we cannot evade rational, moral, and extrareligious principles and reasoning about human rights, myopically focusing nothing but the primary texts and maxims of religion in formulating our jurisprudential edicts. Because religious jurisprudence [*fiq'h*] is nourished by theology [*kalam*], the extrareligious foundations of these rules must be clearly critiqued and scrutinized; mere derivation from within cannot yield sufficient stability and lucidity. Such an inward gaze will hinder the outside discussion.

The second issue concerning human rights is that every democratic religious government must be mindful of both the inside and the outside of the religion in order to remain faithful to both of its foundations. Of course, mindfulness is not necessarily tantamount to utter acquiescence. To be sure, contemporary advocates of human rights can claim no monopoly on truth and justice; nevertheless, religious societies, precisely because of their religious nature, need to seriously engage in discussion of the issues they pose. Not only did our predecessors passionately debate such extrareligious issues as the question of free choice and the question of the limits of God's rights to overburden the faithful with religious obligations, but Islamic society felt a religious obligation to allow such debates to spread and prosper. By the same token, the extrareligious debates of our day, which happen to concern human rights, must be viewed as worthy and useful exchanges of opinions in Islamic society. The partisans in these debates deserve a blessed respect, and the outcome of such discussions should be heeded and implemented by the governments.

Just as being humane is the condition of the truth of religion, so it will have to be the condition of the legitimacy of the government as well. Observing human rights (such as justice, freedom, and so on) guarantees not only the democratic character of a government, but also its religious character.

The third issue concerning human rights is the false assumption that sensitivity to human rights is a surrender to relativistic liberalism. Such an assumption is at once ignorant of the nature of liberalism and an insult to religion; it gives liberalism more credit than it deserves and religion less: liberalism is not the fount of all human rights, nor is religion their antithesis. To be sure, human rights in its modern form was first formulated by Enlightenment thinkers with no explicit allegiance to religion, no concern with God's approval, no feeling for religion as a source of discovery and justification, and thus entirely secular in outlook. It is equally true that only belatedly, as a response to the secular challenge, did the religious thinkers address this issue.

There were two reasons for this delayed reaction: first, religious thinkers, already possessing a rich body of knowledge concerning ethics, rights, and obligations, felt no internal impetus to address such problems and thus felt no motivation to join the modern debate begun by secular thinkers. Second, because the language of religion and religious law is the language of duties, not rights, religious people habitually think more about their obligations than about their rights. They concentrate more on what God expects from them than on what they themselves desire; they look among their duties to find their rights, not vice versa. However, a greater sensitivity to duties than to rights is not necessarily an antagonism to rights; it is, rather, a valuable addition to the debate on human rights and a challenge to liberalism's putative monopoly of this issue.

In any event, religious governments that are based on religious societies will be democratic only when they seek to combine the satisfaction of the Creator and that of the created; when they are true both to the religious and extrareligious concerns; and when they equally respect prereligious and postreligious reason and morality. In the elusive and delicate balance between the two realms lies the rare elixir that the contemporary world, because of its neglect, finds unattainable or undesirable.

9

Tolerance and Governance

A Discourse on Religion
and Democracy

1. The Principles of a Religious
Democratic Government:
A Synopsis

The article on "The Idea of Religious Democratic Government" [see chapter 8] alluded to a number of pivotal principles that are of cardinal significance to the architecture of religious democracy:

A. The combination of religion and democracy is an example of the concordance of religion and reason. Thus, the efforts and experiments of religiously sympathetic thinkers in the latter domain will be of use in the former. It is evident that such attempts are at once religious, useful, and well-precedented. They are by no means tainted by antireligious intentions or treacherous tendencies to supplant religiosity with worldliness.

B. The combination of religion and democracy is a metareligious artifice that has at least some extrareligious epistemological dimensions. Therefore, the exclusive reliance on the religious laws and myopic focus on intrareligious adjudications [*ijtihad-e fiqhi*] in order to confirm or reject democratic religiosity is ill-considered and unsound.

C. Whether we consider democracy as a successful method to delimit power, attain justice, and achieve human rights or as a value that tacitly embraces all those objectives, it is the religious understanding that will have to adjust itself to democracy not the other way around; justice, as a value, can not be religious. It is religion that has to be just. Similarly, methods of limiting power are not derived from religion, although religion benefits from them. In any case the question of whether or not democracy has the above advantages can only be decided outside religion, prior to its acceptance, and as a prelude to its understanding. The same reasoning holds for the relationship of religion and human rights, which is—not unlike the debate on free will—a theological and metareligious argument that influences the understanding and acceptance of religion.

D. In autocratic governments, the right of arbitration is left to the power and will of the few; in democratic governments, it is left to the dynamic common wisdom; in religious society, it is left to religion.

E. In a religious society, it is not religion per se that arbitrates, but some understanding of religion which is, in turn, changing, rational, and in harmony with the consensual and accepted extrareligious criteria.

F. Religious society is the supporter, sponsor, source, and succor of the religious politics. Without a religious society, the religious democratic government would be inconceivable.

The above synopsis provides a valid starting point and a correct formulation of—if not an actual solution to—the problem of the combination of religion and democracy. The present argument, unlike the writings of some Islamic thinkers, makes no attempt to place the entire weight of the conceptual edifice of democracy upon the frail shoulders of such (intrareligious) precepts as consultation [*shura*], consensus of the faithful [*ijma'*], and oath of loyalty to a ruler [*bei'at*]. Rather, the discourse on religious government should commence with a discussion of human rights, justice, and restriction of power (all extrareligious issues). Only then should one try to harmonize one's religious understanding with them.

2. Shared Notions of Justice, Human Rights, and Limited Power in Democracy and in Religion

In the opinion of believers, justice is at once a prerequisite for and a requirement of religious rules. A rule that is not just is not religious. Justice, in turn, aims to fulfill needs, attain rights, and eliminate discrimination and inequity. Thus, justice and human rights are intimately connected. The rights concerning government, power, and the just relationship between the ruler and the ruled are among the most significant elements of these rights. Therefore, the effort to restrain and restrict power is closely related to the establishment of justice and human rights. Indeed, the two efforts are in such constant exchange and harmony that any trouble or tension in one reverberates in the other. Justice, then, is a metareligious category, and the right and acceptable religion should, inevitably, be just. The same is true of other categories such as discovery and derivation of methods of just government, distribution and restriction of power, and the specific instances of human rights.

All of the above issues have, primarily and logically, a rational—not a religious—origin. Religion (in itself) and religious understanding (religion for us) rely on these rational precepts. Once the status of reason, particularly the dynamic collective reason, is established; once the theoretical, practical, and historical advances of humanity are applied to the understanding and acceptance of religion; once extrareligious factors find an echo within the religious domain; and finally, once religion is rationalized, then the way to epistemological pluralism—the centerpiece of democratic action—will be paved.

Sober and willing—not fearful and compulsory—practice of religion is the hallmark of a religious society. It is only from such a society that the religious government is born. Such religiosity guarantees both the religious and the democratic character of the government. Democracy needs not only sobriety and rationality but liberty and willing participation. The above rationality (which is not to be adopted halfheartedly) is realized when the innerreligious and outerreligious domains are harmonized. This rational sensibility permits the transformation and variation of religious understanding. The acknowledgment of such varieties of understanding and interpretation will, in turn, introduce flexibility and tolerance to the relationship of the ruling and the ruled, confirm rights for the subjects, and introduce restraints on the behavior of the rulers. As a result, the society will become more democratic, humane, reasonable, and fair. Expansion and contraction of knowledge, its constant renewal, the perception of truth as an elusive labyrinthine path, the recognition of man as a tarnished, slothful, and fallible creature who, nevertheless, possesses an array of natural rights have all been among the necessary prerequisites for and epistemological and anthropological foundations of democracy. If these same principles are included in religious knowledge and respected by religious people, the result will be religious democracy.[1] Practical and governmental regulations and social relationships are born out of theoretical presuppositions, just as branches feed on roots. The root of democracy is a novel insight that humanity has gained about itself and the limitations of its knowledge. Wherever this seed is allowed to germinate, the external manifestations of democracy will, inevitably, bloom.

3. The Paradox of "Democratic Religious Government": A Critical Exchange

Some critics, however, have deemed the idea of democratic religious government preposterous. They point to such phenomena and rules as gender and belief inequality in the Moslem societies, theocracy, the absolute authority of the jurisconsults, designation of death penalty on apostates, the regarding of infidels as impure, dogmatism of beliefs, and the general inflexibility of the rules of religious decrees as evidence of the inherent animosity of religion and religious government toward democracy. They further accuse the adherents of the compatibility of democracy and religion, of ignorance about the true nature of religion. (See Mr. Hamid Paydar's "The Paradox of Islam and Democracy," *Kiyan*, no. 19.)

Three dark and dangerous errors dim the horizon of judgment of the above thesis. First, Democracy is equated with extreme liberalism.[2] Second, religious jurisprudence [*shari'ah*] is severed from its foundations, quoted out of context, and then presented as evidence. Third, and most important, religious democratic government is equated with religious jurisprudential [*fiqhi*][3] government and attacked as a monolithic whole. It should be unequivocally stated that all three assumptions are erroneous.

If the debate is over the compatibility of the religious jurisprudential government, with democracy, then the sponsors of the above-mentioned regime[4] themselves avoid the title of democracy; they even take great pride and delight in opposing it, because they consider democracy as a fruit of the secular Western culture. The excerpts the critics quote from the declarations of some religious scholars and orators in order to portray religious democracy as a "paradox" reveal the critics' misperception of religious democracy, which they identify with the religious jurisprudential government.

The truth, however, is that religious law [*shari'ah*] is not synonymous with the entirety of religion; nor is the debate over the democratic religious government a purely jurisprudential argument. Moreover, jurisprudential statements are different from epistemological ones, and no methodic mind should conflate the two realms. Evidently, a jurisprudential conception of Islam has so occupied certain minds that epistemological arguments are allowed to pose as jurisprudential propositions. Democracy itself, in some circles, is treated as a religious practice, subject to ritual prescription or proscription.

Democracy is comprised of a method of restricting the power of the rulers and rationalizing their deliberations and policies, so that they will be less vulnerable to error and corruption, more open to exhortation, moderation, consultation; and so that violence and revolution will not become necessary. Separation of powers, universal compulsory education, freedom and autonomy of the press, freedom of expression, consultative assemblies on various levels of decision making, political parties, elections, and parliaments are all methods of attaining and securing democracy. Conversely, a nation that is illiterate, unfamiliar with its rights, and unable to attain them, in other words, a nation deprived of the right to criticize and choose, will be unable to achieve democracy.

Agnosticism and indecision, however, are by no means necessary foundations of or prerequisites for democracy. On the contrary, constant review, critique, and renewal of ideas and beliefs, followed by emendation, calibration, and transformation of the policies and decisions of rulers and their powers are among the routine responsibilities of democratic societies. There is no doubt that a democracy is engaged in an interminable process of choosing and examining, while a religious society believes that it has made a crucial choice and that it has the answer within its reach: it has chosen the path of religiosity and has determined to live in the shade of a religious belief. However, this preliminary decision of religious societies paves the way to innumerable subsequent decisions and arduous trials. From there on, it is religious understanding that needs to undergo constant examination. It will have to pass through difficult cycles of contraction, expansion, modification, and equilibrium:

> On the path of love, a hundred hazards lie, beyond oblivion, yet;
> So you won't say: once I reach my life's end, I'll have escaped.[5]

The venerable author of the essay on "Paradox of Islam and Democracy" observes: "Islam and democracy can not be combined, unless Islam is thoroughly secularized." This belief stems from the assumption that relativistic liberalism and democracy are identical. Democracy, however, does not require believers to abandon their convictions, secularize their creed, and lose faith in divine protection. Why should a religion that is freely and enthusiastically adopted be cast away? Why shouldn't the believers be allowed to strengthen and spread their belief? The practice that truly violates democracy is not embracing a faith but the imposition of a particular belief or punishment of disbelief. Needless to say, these practices are impermissible and undesirable in a democratic religious government. (Although some may condone them under a jurisprudential religious government.)

Mr. Paydar regards the principle of free choice as prior to human fallibility and considers the realm of ideas as "the most important manifestation of human free choice." He proposes that human beings are free to choose religion or irreligion at any time and under any conditions, thus equating freedom with indecision. The logical flaws of such an argument notwithstanding, one may point out that it still does not mean that a self-determining religious society is unfree or that religion and democracy are incompatible. It seems Mr. Paydar has not noticed that freedom does not necessitate permanent ambivalence and inability to reach, or act upon, a decision. Embracing a faith, relying upon it, committing to it, and believing in it—independent and autonomous decisions—are not contrary to the freedom of choice. This is the meaning of the theological dictum "Self-imposed restraint is no restraint."

It is not the assumption of free will or the belief in the fallibility of human beings in liberal societies that causes religion to abdicate the office of final judgment. Nor are these assumptions responsible for the neutrality of the liberal government and prevalence of the scientific and practical evaluation of religion. There is another epistemological fact that is partly responsible for this separation: Liberal philosophers consider metaphysical arguments unverifiable and unfalsifiable. Consequently, they deem controversy over the truth or falsehood of religious beliefs futile and interminable. They point to the permanence, doctrinal rigidity, and plurality of divergent religious practices as historical evidence. Therefore, they advocate peaceful coexistence of a multiplicity of belief systems. Their neutral stance enables them to dismiss the interreligious strife[6] as a futile pursuit of truth in the quagmire of delusions.[7] Or else, they view the variety and plurality of beliefs as consistent with a divine plan to distribute heavenly guidance in many disguises.

However, let's remind ourselves that these same liberal societies, their unshakable belief in the freedom of the will and fallibility of man notwithstanding, will never relinquish the reins of decision making concerning lucid and well-examined affairs to the popular whim. Nor do they warrant indiscriminate reexamination of all things. No liberal government would base its modern technology upon the Aristotelian physics or reexamine such obsolete theories as the Flogeston theory of combustion, which prevailed before the oxygen theory of combustion. Nor would it experimentally expose people to such deadly diseases as plague and small pox. No one is allowed, under the penalty of law, to free those accursed demons from their enchanted dungeons. In the meantime, a colorful assortment of religious creeds is allowed to multiply and spread. In other words, although the state in liberal governments stays neutral toward religious claims, it does not remain impartial concerning scientific achievements. It is true, then, that the liberal society is no longer a religious society but a scientific one. The same status accorded to religion and religious certitude in religious societies is ascribed to science in liberal societies.[8] The experimental, verifiable, and falsifiable scientific rules have deservedly reached such a grandeur and glory that no freedom-loving thinker would contemplate their arbitrary castigation, just as no wise and vigilant person would relegate the judgment of those scientific rules to laymen and dilettantes. Science, however fallible as a human achievement, has been so well elaborated, thanks to courageous and free human critique and refinement, that it has attained an unassailable status. This exalted position of science has not diminished human free will and dignity, nor has it curtailed, in the least, the liberal identity of the society. If in these societies religion is not an equal partner with science, it is not because liberalism considers human beings as autonomous decision makers and allows them to constantly change their religion but because it does not recognize science and religion as analogous bodies of knowledge. And this is established epistemologically, not through popular vote. Therefore, the religious attitude (relegating the judgment to the shared religious knowledge) maintains the same epistemological relationship to democracy as does the scientific attitude (relegating judgement to the shared wisdom of practitioners). Another error of Mr. Paydar is equating freedom of choice with indecision, ambivalence, irresolution, and an absence of a basis for judgment, thus declaring religion and democracy incompatible. However, religious knowledge is, potentially, as open to criticism as scientific knowledge; the authority of religion in religious knowledge is as invalid as the authority of science in the scientific knowledge. Contraction and expansion of scientific knowledge and religious knowledge share the same vicissitudes and trajectories.

Mr. Paydar has (incorrectly) surmised that liberalism is neutral on the subjects of science or religion. He has equated liberalism's skeptical credo of fallibility of human knowledge with utter neutrality. It is true that the liberal society has taken the above principles as the groundwork of its life and belief, however, in practice, as a result of those very criticisms, the society has adopted specific positions with respect to science and religion and no longer countenances their infringement.

The prophets of the liberal philosophy are not only Mill, Locke, Rousseau, Smith, Bayle, Voltaire, and (among contemporaries) Rawls and Friedman; but Kant, Hume, and—among contemporaries—Russell, Quine, and Carnap as well. The latter group should be included among the founders and supporters of the liberal society because they share the belief that unraveling the intricate knots of metaphysical questions is improbable. They go even farther by declaring any involvement with metaphysical subjects as exceeding the boundaries of rationality altogether. However, had religion enjoyed as popular an epistemological niche as science and had it not been weakened by the philosophical and scientific forays of the Western scholars; the society could have, conceivably, remained both "religious" and democratic, just as it has remained "scientific" and democratic.

Parting with metaphysics meant, for the West, parting with all of its requisites: the church and the clergy, divine laws, ethics, religious strictures, clerical government, and pious submission. In short, every religious institution that oversaw the temporal affairs in any way, was abandoned. It was such a rupture that, in Kant's words, liberated humanity from its "infancy" and placed the destiny and determination of all affairs in its hands. Thereafter, man reached an unprecedented centrality (even Godliness) in world history. Liberal freedom was freedom from the fetters of religion and metaphysics. It was freedom from divine guardianship. This freedom had an epistemological and rational basis. Liberal philosophers did not discover man's fallibility and free will. They discovered the irrelevance of metaphysics. This, their most important achievement, combined with the advent of scientific knowledge and free economy, shaped the liberal society. But, atheism, by itself, does not entail emancipation from tyranny and totalitarianism. Communism, too, professed atheism but it fostered an utterly ruthless form of dictatorship. Thus, democracy is neither a result of atheism nor an ally of it. Equating liberalism and democracy signifies, at once, great ignorance of the former and grave injustice toward the latter. The liberal democratic society has plural foundations. Its many bases, while not mutually conflicting, are far from being mutually indispensable. It is, therefore, logically possible to separate them. The idea of democratic religious society is a result of logical decoupling of democracy and liberalism. As such, it is analogous to the attempts of the social democrats to separate democracy from capitalism.[9]

The opponents of religious democracy usually conclude that since liberalism is identical with or a requirement of democracy and since religiosity has no affinity with liberalism; therefore, religiosity can not coexist with democracy. However, as we have argued above, the premise is not correct.

4. Is Faith Contrary to Tolerance?

Paydar states ["The Paradox of Islam and Democracy," *Kiyan*, no. 19]: "If a school of thought or a religion regards itself as the cradle of the truth and approaches other ideas and religions as manifestations of apostasy, idolatry, and delusion, it leaves no room for a democratic government." He then resorts to verses from the Qur'an in which Islam is introduced as the religion of the truth and righteousness, and Moslems are commanded to combat infidels, idolaters, and mischief makers and to establish the reign of the true religion on earth.

Although a discussion of intrareligious knowledge, that is, Qur'anic verses or jurisprudential rules, prior to a critique of their epistemological and anthropological foundations, is improper for this level of discussion, let me briefly reply that the democratic nature of religion is not contingent upon the relativity of the truth and that regarding the firm beliefs of the faithful as a threat to democracy is another grave error. The only thing that is required of a democracy is tolerance of different points of view and their advocates. Who says the precondition for tolerance of ideas and their bearers is the renouncing of one's own beliefs? One may consider an idea absolutely false while judging its bearer blameless, respectable, and even commendable. Consider the current debates among scientists and philosophers. They, too, do not always proceed from skepticism. It is not as though only undecided scholars allow and appreciate criticism and deem their opponents worthy of dialogue and debate. The purveyors of certitude do the same. Tolerance, as astute observers have maintained,[10] concerns believers not beliefs.

This insight emanates from a second-order knowledge, a vantage point above and beyond the battlefield of ideas, from which one can survey complex *causes and means* that make minds receptive, hearts committed, and believers devoted to ideas. From this viewpoint, we can appreciate how one dedicated and truth-loving individual, Mohammad al-Ghazzali (1058–1111) turns his back on pleasure and power, endures years of agony, asceticism, and relentless search for the truth, and finally arrives at the validity of Sunni Islam, while another, Saint Francis of Assisi (1182–1226), spends his youth in pursuit of worldly pleasures[11] and is ultimately set ablaze by the love of Jesus and is led to a new life of mysticism and monasticism. Neither were, in the least, derelict in their respective quests, even though they reached different results. So it is that the "battle of seventy-two denominations" is excused, and combatants (but not their ideas) are absolved. Each is deemed praiseworthy and honorable in his or her own place. Furthermore, divine guidance is believed to spread so widely that all the seekers can bask in its blessed rays. "Excusing the battle of the seventy-two nations" is the wise counsel of our righteous sages and is not a result of their "liberal-mindedness," faithlessness, or skepticism. It is the result of their profound philosophical anthropology and their intimate knowledge of the intricacies of the human soul.

Democracy requires one to divert one's gaze from the earth of "reasons" toward the heaven of "causes." Separating the truth and falsehood, embracing one and rejecting the other belongs to the dominion of "reasons;" just as tolerance and endurance are results of appreciation of "causes."[12] There are causes for one person's faith and another's faithlessness; one's admittance to the "path of good reputation" and another's rejection."[13] It is for this reason that the faithful whisper in their prayers: "O God, our nurturing teacher, do not lead our hearts astray, after you have guided us." Imam Hussein, the grandson of the prophet, in his "prayer of 'Arafah," praises God for granting him the blessing of Islam and for not relegating him to life under evil rulers who blasphemed, broke covenants, and opposed prophets. Verily:

In the affair of the rose water and the rose, it was predestined,
That one would become the bazaar's harlot, and the other, nobly curtained.[14]

In any event, recourse to causes neither sacrifices reasons nor propagates retreatism and fatalism. It is among the precious teachings of our sages that combining free will and causality is as feasible as combining fatalism and causality, and thus, attention to causes does not usher in fatalism. What a thorough blessing it would be to preserve the hierarchy of concepts, to keep cause, reason, and fate in their respective places, and to refrain from sacrificing one at the alter of another. Religious tolerance is based upon such a wise and subtle understanding. It has nothing to do with relativising truth, abandoning faith, certitude, and free will, or equating truth with falsehood.

This error has plagued numerous well-meaning thinkers who, having missed the distinction between reasons and causes, have assumed that the condition for tolerance is abandoning all commitment to principles. Confronted by the objection: How do you justify "commitment" to the principle of tolerance itself, they have stumbled, ineptly, into the unavoidable trap: "Well, that is an exception," thus reaffirming the validity of commitment to principles and weakening their own argument all in one strike. The truth, however, is that the only condition for tolerance is abandoning infantile and immature attachments.[15] Failure to leave the first-order world of reasons for the second-order world of causes leaves one in the narrow womb of one's own mind and times, oblivious to the splendor of the greater world of causes and means, ignorant of the handiwork of the "work master of destiny," and unable to excuse "the ascetic who has floundered on his path."[16]

Concerning the issue of fighting the idolaters, the least one may say is that it happens to be a rule concerning the epoch of the advent of religion [ta'sis], not that of the era of establishment [esteqrar.][17] A large number of Shi'ite jurisprudents have, indeed, proscribed the initiation of jihad during the epoch of "greater occultation."[18] There is much more to be said on the philosophy of this verdict. However, so long as the place and the status of jurisprudence is not sufficiently critiqued and determined, resorting to juridical arguments in the realm of epistemology will obscure more than illuminate matters.[19]

In any event, Paydar is right to conclude that "the government has no right to impose a religion on its citizens. Nor should it have the prerogative to dictate a particular interpretation of a religion to the adherents of that religion." He errs, however, in regarding "the essential ambiguity of the truth, and man's inalienable free will" as proof of his conclusion.

5. The Inalienable Freedom of Faith Entails Freedom of Religion

Faith is a matter of exclusively personal and private experience. We embrace a faith individually just as we confront our death individually. We have communal actions and rituals, but not communal faiths. Expressions of faith are public but the essence of faith is mysterious and private. The domain of faith is akin to the arena of the hereafter, where people are brought in individually: "And everyone of them is brought to the day of judgment individually"[20]

Faith and love are of the same grain. In the fabric of faith, enthusiasm, love, and testimony are intertwined. One adores in seclusion, loves in seclusion, and testifies in seclusion. Faith, too, is hostile to partnership for as Rumi avers: "Hail love, the splendid destroyer of partnerships."[21] There is no such thing as collective adoration, love, and testimony, just as there is no such thing as forced adoration, love, and testimony. True faith is contingent upon individuality and liberty. Their decline is tantamount to the decline of faith, just as their rise amounts to the rise of faith. This melodious song that emanates from the minaret of wisdom is the same marvelous image that is inscribed on the canvas of guidance: "There is to be no imposition in faith."[22] This means that the hand of tyranny is unable to sow the seed of religiosity in the soil of hearts. Neither king's decree nor reason's verdict can beget or augment faith or love. "The threshold of love is far above the realm of reason."[23] Coercion has no place here; this is the domain of magical enticement.[24]

One may order human beings to act uniformly and plainly, but what can one say of faiths that are more elusive and animated than angels and which do not venture out of their solitude and seclusion? How naive is the ambition to dominate such nimble brave angels as these who do not tear asunder their veils and do not become one another's slaves. They bow neither to uniformity nor to disclosure. They accept neither force nor partnership. They abandon neither individuality nor liberty. Only a witless stalker would attempt to trap such impalpable prey as these.

Prophets have came in love to enchant the hearts of the pure and the virtuous. Their miracles were meant to "subdue the enemies"[25] not to terrify hearts or inculcate faith. If they ever demanded any outward obedience and submission, it was on the strength of the enticement of hearts. Their reign was over souls not over bodies. It was the breeze of the followers' spirits that fluttered the flesh, animating and invigorating the faithful.

The prophets founded a faithful-spiritual community, not a legal-corporeal society. They started from faiths and hearts, then proceeded to rites and obligations. They were aware that one may base a legal-ritual society upon force and imposition. However, it is not as easy to steer such a society toward faith. One may use coercion in enforcing religious regulations, but how can one inculcate faith? Is action without conviction, body without soul, appearance without essence worth all the torments and sacrifices of the prophets? Their quarry was to attract and acquaint the brisk, free, and impalpable faith with the hearts of the faithful, thus suffusing them with humility and devotion, both spiritually and physically. They radiated, like sunshine, upon hearts and let the inner heat glow through frosted limbs. Their interlocutors were ardent hearts, their method was enchantment, the outcome of their mission was consensual faith, not fearful obedience. They knew themselves and explicitly told their interlocutors: "How can we compel you, while you are reluctant?"[26]

The heart of a religious society is freely chosen faith not coercion and conformity. Faiths vary and fluctuate along with people's personalities.

This is true not only of religious faiths but also of religious understandings. Everyone has a specific relationship to God and in the solitude of his or her own soul whispers secret prayers and hears subtle replies. There is no end or similitude to these whisperings. Religious society is based upon free and invisible faith and dynamic and varied understanding. A seemingly religious society that lacks faith is an oyster without the pearl, a face without the soul, an appearance without the essence. It is neither desired by the prophets nor envisioned by the wise. That harlot of the bazaar [shari'ah] will be worthless if she does not seek the shelter of this veiled beauty (faith). Any hand that rubs liberty from faithfulness and dynamism from religious understanding, whether by usurpation or by plunder, harms the very foundation and meaning of religious society. To compel individuals to confess a faith falsely; to paralyze minds by indoctrination, propaganda, and intimidation; and to shut down the gates of criticism, revision, and modification so that everyone would succumb to a single ideology creates not a religious society but a monolithic and terrified mass of crippled, submissive, and hypocritical subjects.

How could one segment of religion, its legal code, contradict the other, its holy book, thus keeping the adherents from free and deliberate choice of religion, refusing to conform to the spirit of the religion, and neglecting the dynamism of religious understanding and the freedom of faith? How can religious law force the followers into a fearful faith and a static perception of religion? How can it be content with erecting a purely worldly and external order and, in the name of battling blasphemy, stifle the freedom of faith? Such a religious law is as unsteady, unhealthy, and wayward as a body that does not obey its heart and mind.

Paydar's argument notwithstanding, the above decree to kill idolaters and apostates, whatever its rationale or philosophy, could not have been issued to make people hypocritically adopt a faith; to force them to abandon research into religious matters under the threat of the sword; to induce them to hide truths they may have attained; to use any pretext to bludgeon scholars and free thinkers; to favor unmeditated and duplicitous faiths over examined and truth-loving doubts; to throw truth-seekers into the pit of oblivion upon the slightest hint of curiosity and doubt; to snuff the last remnants of courage out of thinkers within the walls of dogmas and ossified axioms; to tie down the feet and wings of the instinctively inquisitive understanding and thought; to replace willing faith with its nemesis, hypocritical and fearful piety; and to prefer the closing of mouths to the opening of hearts. Neither God nor his prophet desire such a religiosity that begets neither worldly prosperity nor otherworldly salvation. One may base a totalitarian and a terrifying ideological government on such premises not a secure religious government. Religion is meant for understanding and willing embrace not for dread and reluctant submission.[27] The virtue of religion lies in its capacity to induce enchantment not horror.

People may be compelled to act in unison, but they may not be made to understand religion uniformly. They may be compelled to confess a faith, but they may not be forced to accept faith in their hearts. Like wild flowers in nature, faith will grow and flourish wherever it wishes and in whatever fragrance and color it pleases. The faithful community is more like a wild grove than a manicured garden. It owes the fragrance of its faith to this wild independent spirit. To harness this spirit is to strangle it. It is in this sense that a religious society, based upon free faith, dynamic understanding, and individual presence before God, cannot be but democratic. Thus, fearful and forced compliance with religious law should not be taken as the touchstone of a religious society. Once religious law, a fundamentally earthly science, is in Al-Ghazzali's words severed from free and courageous faith, it will turn into an utterly worldly science, unfit for an ideal-faithful community. It would be an instrument of a secular reign over bodies, not of a spiritual command over hearts. Still, in Al-Ghazzali's wise and judicious words, "the heart is beyond the jurisdiction of the jurisconsult."[28] The affair of religion is of the heart, not of the limbs.

6. Democracy: The Spirit and the Letter of Religion

Political philosophers have, at times, declared democracy antithetical to liberty and liberalism, seeing in it the dictatorship of the majority (Hayek) or the rule of a minority in the name of the majority (Mill, Dahl). Although democracy, regardless of the way it is defined, is a form of lawful government that seeks to curtail the arbitrary excesses of lawbreakers, it induces people to curb some of their appetites in order to attain security and prosperity. The law is inimical to unconditional freedom but not to democracy. Some other thinkers who have contemplated the relationship between religion and democracy have considered the existence of religious law and the divine status of the ruler as a barrier to democracy. They have interpreted the rigidity of the religious rules as evidence of religious tyranny.[29] The defenders of religious democracy, on the other hand, have resorted to the plurality of religions and schools of thought in religious jurisprudence as a proof of religious tolerance and compatibility of religious society with democratic pluralism.[30] In a similar vein, many Islamic revivalists (such as Abdoh, Mowdudi, Ghazzali,[31] and so on) have resorted to the religious approval of consultative assemblies [shura], the principle of consensus [ijma'], the primacy of the common good of the faithful and the public interest [maslahat], and the innovative jurisprudence [ijtihad] as evidence of the presence of democratic ideals within religion and religious society.[32]

There are other contemporary thinkers, however, who still distinguish democratic and religious governments by the tendency of the law to follow people's whims in the former and the fixed divine dictates in the latter.[33] In all these debates *shari'ah* remains the center of the controversy. It is as though the religious nature of society and government and all their other attributes were entirely contingent upon *shari'ah*. It is true that democracy is basically a method for government and restriction of power and that power is harnessed by—human or divine—law, but it should be remembered that religious society and government owe everything, including their legal systems, to a more fundamental fact: the faith of the faithful. If this faith collapses or is distorted, the governmental and religious regulations would be no different from a secular system. Islamic jurisprudence, for example, is equally applicable to religious and secular societies. The true realization and appeal of the religious law, though, abides in the belief of the faithful, a faith mingled with individuality and liberty and awash in dynamism and change. It is amazing that some consider the democratization of the religious government contingent upon the secularization of religion and religious law. Such advocates remain confined in a jurisprudential concept of Islam. Instead of regarding law as religious, they view religion as legal. Instead of considering body as spiritual, they deem spirit as corporeal. This immense intellectual barrier has darkened and inverted their vision of the religious society. Speak to them about "religious democratic government" and they will hear "jurisprudential democratic government." What is more, they deem jurisprudence impervious both to people's will and change. Consequently, they dismiss democratic religiosity. These persons neglect faith, the most autonomous element in religion, and religious understanding, the most human and essential basis of religiosity. They quarrel over the body and neglect the soul that sustains it. What authenticity and ground would religious law have if it disregarded the freedom of faith and the humanity of understanding, refused to base its precepts upon these, and neglected to harmonize its regulations with them? Liberal democracy draws inspiration and strength from the authentic axiom that states: human beings are naturally free and unique, their appetites and opinions are irreducibly disparate and interminably dynamic, and restraining this multifarious heterogeneity is neither possible nor desirable. Is the continuous renewal of understanding of the religion and the plurality of faiths less than that of appetites? Is the religious society not, by nature, plural and pluralistic? Those who have endured ebbs and flows of the heart, avalanches of doubt, clashes of belief, surges of faith, the violence of spiritual storms, and the plundering swell of visions that restlessly and ruthlessly assail the delicate sanctuary of the heart understand that the heterogeneity of souls and the wanderings of hearts is a hundred times greater than that of thoughts, tasks, limbs, and tendencies. Belief is a hundred times more diverse and colorful than disbelief. If the pluralism of secularism makes it suitable for democracy, the faithful community is a thousand times more suitable for it.

You contemplate the law of religion, I bid you to comprehend the law of the law:[34] You have seen the water, now look through the water to see the *water*.[35] You speak of bodies forcefully subdued, I bid you to think of hearts that submit freely. You respect uniformity, emulation, and obedience to religious jurisprudence and jurists, I implore you to appreciate the complexity and colorfulness of belief, liberty, subtlety, and the agility of faiths and volitions. How inferior is body to soul, dirt to heart! Truly, the religious community is plural and pluralistic by nature. The plurality of religious sects and factions is but a coarse, crude, and shallow indicator of the subtle, elusive, and invisible pluralities of souls. Only after one enters that realm will one experience the wisdom of these sagacious words: "There are as many paths toward God as there are people (or even as many as people's inhalations and exhalations)."[36]

Surely, the faiths of the emulators, not unlike their minds and their actions, are uniform, tame, and suggestible. But how about the faith of the sages and lovers? And which is nobler? A religious society becomes more religious as it grows more free and freedom loving, as it trades diehard dogma with examined faith, as it favors inner plurality over outer mechanical and nominal unity, and as it favors voluntary submission to involuntary subservience. This is the spirit that breaks the tyrannical arm of religious despotism and breathes the soul of free faith in the body of power. Verily, the religious jurisprudential government over a society of imitators is as remote from the spirit of democracy as love is from patience and the devil from the Qur'an. And this is exactly what forces critics to compose biting and bitter diatribes against the possibility of reconciliation of religion and democracy. Let me, then, declare once and for all: A religious government over a faithful and alert society that respects liberty and dynamism of religious understanding cannot help but be a democratic society.

It is evident that the discussion has progressed from the possibility to the necessity of the coexistence of religion and democracy. We no longer merely claim that a genuinely religious government can be democratic but that it can not be otherwise. However, this claim can only be made about a religious reign over hearts not a jurisprudential rule over bodies. We advocate a community of the brave and the faithful not a society of submissive emulators. We speak of hearts that are lovingly, sincerely, securely, and freely immersed in faith; hearts that seek a beloved and merciful God who "looks into inner states not outer expressions."[37] One may force the bodies of the faithful, but not their souls. One may unify their behaviors, but not their minds and faiths. The religious society is not one which people can approve by deed and deny by heart. That is why we state: A religious government is inconceivable except over religious people, but a jurisprudential government is feasible over both the religious and the nonreligious.

Does this mean that a religious society disdains outward representations of religion [shari'ah]? Far from it. The above arguments merely proclaim that the application of religious law is not the sole touchstone of a religious society. Evaluation of such a society should proceed from its spirit, that is, its morality and faith not its appearance. Therefore, the debate over coexistence of religion and democracy should be conducted at the level of the roots and essence not the branches and appearance of religiosity. If it is established that the religious society, due to the nature of religiosity, the inherent freedom and irreducible plurality of faiths, and the dynamism of religious understanding is consistent with, even in need of, democracy, then religious jurisprudence should follow rather than compete with the above conclusions. Power, too, should be in service of this exalted truth. Power in a religious society is the guarantor of the faith; what good is it if faith is obliterated? Conversely, faiths needs the shade of safety and liberty to last and to prosper. A (religious) government that does not believe in protecting the security and freedom of faith or the dynamism of religious understanding forfeits its claim to religious legitimacy.

7. Law, Religious Law, and Democracy

Jurisprudential and religious decrees that are inspired by theology and expand and contract along with changing material needs, worldly considerations, and human knowledge are the laws of the religious society and, as such, play a pivotal role in consolidating and calibrating the scales of religious democracy. Without them, the design of a democratic government would be incomplete and unrealized. In a democracy, as Thomas Paine once stated, government belongs to the law not to the sovereign, and the legitimacy of government lies in its adherence to the recognized and imperative laws. Defying and weakening the law amounts to undermining democracy. Therefore, protecting religious ordinances and edicts will, without doubt, strengthen religious democracy. If religious democracy is (despite its detractors) feasible and reasonable at all, it would be unattainable without respect for religious regulations. The protection of religious ordinances [shari'ah] strengthens religious democracy in the following [three] respects:

- *Through protecting the identity of the religious society.* It is true that a majority of the religious people seem to care more about ritual obligations (such as ablutions, prayers, and pilgrimages) than about ethical duties (such as truthfulness, patience, and abstinence from derision, intrusion, and avarice) or about the principles of the faith (such as the attributes of the almighty, the nature of evil, and the wisdom of the prophets). They perceive the glory of religion in meticulous observance of its ritual minutiae and seldom inquire about the origins and principles of religiosity. They fancy the husk of religiosity as the master rather than the servant of the core. Thus, they gauge religiosity according to the degree of compliance with the religious rituals. Still, it is also true of all religious societies that, if the husk of religiosity deteriorates, the core will sooner or later perish and religion will wither away, except in rare circles of the wise. Through protection of the outward appearances, the fragrance of religion will reach even the weakest of nostrils and the faithful will gain a better insight into their religious existence and identity.[38] Pilgrimage to Mecca, public prayers, and religious duties such as calling others to good deeds and calling them away from evil are among the graceful actions that have such blessed effects.

- *Through expanding legal discipline; debilitating tyrants; equalizing the rights of the noble and the commoner; favoring public good over individual interests; guaranteeing a minimum of moral strictures concerning rights, duties, justice, and equality for the citizens.* The least advantage of the law is its chastisement of ingrates and miscreants, its transformation of coercion and punishment into management, and its debunking of tyrannical rulers who would dare to manipulate the law. These are, however, as was mentioned above, among the least benefits of the rule of the law. One may achieve equality as easily by subjecting everyone to an oppressive law, by dispensing, as it were, "the wine of inequity in equal portions." Justice before the law is not the same as justice of the law. In other words, instituting a just legal system is different from applying the law with equal justice. The rule of the law over the social system does not guarantee its justice. Still, lawful juridical and political systems are much closer to democracy than they are to tyrannical, autocratic, absolutist, and irresponsible governments.

Even Karl Marx, an ardent critic of modern legal systems of government, attacked democracy as a deception of the bourgeoisie, not because he distrusted the formal legal system of democracy per se, but because he regarded its substantive laws as servile to the interests of the capitalists (and hence unjust.) He did not dispute the (apparently) equitable application of those laws but their historically reactionary nature. He viewed the apparently just and formal implementation of the law as a disguise for their substantive injustice. It was as if the ritual trappings of the courts, the elaborate mannerism of judges who administered justice through an intricate web of legal jargon and norms, and dazzling legislative assemblies that hashed and rehashed minute details of legal bills, all worked as a giant smoke screen to obscure the real reasons for the institution and implementation of laws and the justice and injustice interwoven in it all. Marx, the relentless critic of the "superstructures," derided bourgeois democracy not the true proletarian "progressive" democracy as such.

- *Through augmenting three auspicious and provocative sensitivities in society.* The jurisprudential and legal doctrine of religion promotes respect for the inclusive and lofty notions of right and justice and for the equitable implementation of laws. Once these precepts—that is, right, justice, and due process—are subjected to brave, rational, and critical scrutiny, rationalization of jurisprudence and democratization of the law will follow.

Democracy, as was mentioned before, is a method of harnessing the power of the rulers, rationalizing their policies, protecting the rights of the subjects, and attaining the public good. This method consists of peaceful transfer of power, legal impeachment of rulers, separation of powers, establishment of a parliament, public education, freedom of expression, freedom and plurality of political parties, powerful and autonomous press and media, public elections, consultative assemblies on every level of decision making, and the like.

The debate over the most effective method of government—including restricting power, attaining public good, and embracing the notions of right and justice—is an inseparable part of political and legal philosophy. It is exactly at this juncture that rationality, the main foundation of democracy and successful management, invites religious law to a dialogue. Debates concerning justice, human rights, and the methods of government can not be resolved through intrareligious debate. Like the arguments concerning the objectivity of ethical values and nature of free will, they are extrareligious arguments that deeply influence the understanding and practice of religion. Just as the above issues are enthusiastically debated by theologians, the controversies concerning human rights, meaning of justice, effective methods of government, and restriction of power are the daily staple of debate for the modern community of believers. Let religious understanding constantly renew and correct itself in light of these meditations. Let the legal and jurisprudential schools of thought harmonize their achievements with these novel insights.

Surely, in the minds of the faithful, no religious edict could be unjust, contrary to public good, or vain. Religious decrees that are so found will be corrected and revised in accordance with the lofty principles of justice and right or through careful and prudent deliberation. Therefore, the entrance of the element of public good in legislation and jurisprudence [in Iran], and the appointment of a committee to discern it, is a harbinger of democratic thought and action. It is a clear indication of an important discovery: adopting a worldly approach to an issue (religious jurisprudence) that has always been worldly.[39]

What makes the critics suspicious of the jurisprudential rule and its potential compatibility with democracy is the image they have constructed of it in the mirror of their own illusions. To begin with, they take one section of religious jurisprudence [*ibadat*] that concerns religious rituals (in their specific sense) as an adequate exemplar and index of religious law in its entirety. In fact, this section of religious jurisprudence possesses neither a powerful sociogovernmental role nor an easily identifiable worldly application. Second, the critics detach religious law from its ethical, theological, and epistemological foundations. As a result, religious law appears as a stagnant and dense edifice, an impenetrable and mysterious fortress whose lords dourly dominate the mind and demand absolute submission from society and history without any flexibility and tolerance. Both assumptions, one may assert with certainty, are false. A penetrating and critical glance at the status and the epistemological position of religion, fecund fountainheads of religious jurisprudence, and the eventful history of its evolution reveals its true nature and essence. The religious laws concerning social transactions [*mo'amelat*][40] are all susceptible to worldly rationalization and calculation; they would be useless if they were otherwise. That which is worldly, natural, and human should be treated as such. Thus natural and secular norms and principles of rationality and humanity are all applicable to religious jurisprudence. Any jurisprudential school of thought that does not provide the necessary tools and mechanisms to cope with historical ebbs and flows will collapse during times of ruthless turbulence. Religious jurisprudence is circumscribed, coated, and protected by faith, prudence, justice, right, reason, and morality. Thus it has the capacity to withstand violent contractions and expansions without failing as its history testifies. One should not be unduly concerned with the fate of the religious jurisprudence anyway; it is quite secondary to the essence of religiosity. If one does justice to theology and other branches of human knowledge that are prior or parallel to religious jurisprudence, the required open-mindedness and objectivity for such an endeavor develops. That is, if innovative critique of the principles and freedom of investigation are obtained, religious law, too, will find its proper niche and will be able to fulfill generously and effectively its desired duties by harnessing power and devising effective and corrective methods of government.

8. Religiosity, Rationality, and Democracy

Following Max Weber's conceptualization, the "rationalization of the world" is understood in terms of "disenchantment of the world."[41] This has meant banishing the metaphysical elements and solely relying on scientific methods. Given this understanding of the term, it is obvious that reconciling religiosity with rationality seems paradoxical. Thus any reliance on religious jurisprudence which relies on religion, revelation, and ultimately on heaven seems antithetical to democracy. It is as though power and law would be automatically synonymous with absolutism and despotism and would contravene the rule of the people (that is, democracy) unless they originate in and follow human interests and interpretations and are totally transparent to human reason.

The above assumption originates in the ignorance of the true nature of religion and religious law. Religious jurisprudence, however divine and ahistorical its origins, inevitably becomes historical and assumes a worldly application. Human beings elaborate it through their free faiths and evolving understanding of the principles of right and justice and derive whatever practical lessons they need from it. True enough, if we place religious law above the principles of right and justice (and not only practically but epistemologically as well); if we fail to establish independent moral standards (such as public interest and justice) in interpreting religious law; and if we cut it loose from its theological roots and refuse to consider jurisprudence of principles as a precondition for jurisprudence of details, we will then arrive at a religious jurisprudence that is at once antidemocratic and ineffective. Religious jurisprudence, however, is inseparable from religion. Free faith and dynamic religious understanding are inseparable from free, just, and reasonable jurisprudence. Such a jurisprudence, then, all its heavenly connections notwithstanding, will not be in the least hindered in administering justice on the earth. Indeed, in a religious and faithful society, religious jurisprudence will be more effective than a secular jurisprudence.

The faithful delegate their right of legislation to God. It is in this sense that the law of the religious society is understood as heavenly. However, the right to comprehend divine laws and to harmonize them with prudence and justice are not thereby abdicated or renounced. It is in this sense that the confrontation of the faithful with religious regulations is analogous to the confrontation of humankind with nature. The fact that the former, in each case, is surrounded by the latter does not preclude the attempt to mediate and ameliorate the environment through technological and conceptual devices. Religion and nature alike, despite their initial sternness, are generous enough to compensate for their initial severity. Despite their formidable determinacy, they are pliant enough to embrace numerous modifications and new and diverse forms.

The arguments concerning the primacy of religious law, however, presuppose the dependency of human rationality on prophetic instruction and thus the paralysis of the collective reason in dealing with worldly facts and values. Hence, there exists the expectation that the mission of the prophets include minute religious laws and regulations. However, we may view humanity's need for divine guidance and the mystery of prophethood in an entirely different light.

The mission of the prophets would, thus, involve accelerating human spiritual evolution, perfecting moral virtues, facilitating and interpreting spiritual experiences, edifying human beings, teaching the wisdom of the Qur'an and esoteric philosophy, reminding people of their true origins, their divine covenant, and their final destiny, bringing the path of humanity closer to God, augmenting justice, eradicating tyranny, crushing pharaonic arrogance, teaching the lesson of servitude to God, and preparing the conditions of a blissful end. This is how some theologians have understood the role of religion. Religion, in this interpretation, will assume an entirely different character and mission that excludes methods (but not values) of government and endows religious law with an entirely new identity and trajectory.

The idea that religion and democracy are mutually exclusive has its roots in another illusion as well: the belief that in a democracy everything is subject to referendum and debate and that nothing has a solid and a priori "foundation." This is false. Is it not true that democracy is desired to attain justice, human rights, and restricted power? Is it not true that democracy is built upon a particular vision of humanity and history, elaborated by social and political philosophy and science? Take the principle of voting. Is it arrived at through voting? Can one start with no presuppositions and still achieve all the wondrous and precious blessings of justice, right, and wisdom? Of course not. To begin with, the society should freely and deliberately attain a novel understanding of humanity and come to respect and desire certain exalted and noble goals (values). Then it should find a proper and effective system in order to realize those goals (methods).

The proposition that "democracy means the use of specific means to attain unspecific ends" is a fundamentally correct assertion that lends itself to misunderstanding. Far from denying the a priori principles of democracy, it is meant as a response to those who believe means justify ends and thus misguidedly characterize a totalitarian system that purportedly dispenses justice, and human rights, as a democracy. They are reminded: "Method" is of essence in a democracy. It is not evident, from the outset, who is right and who deserves certain privileges and powers. The "convict" is the person who is recognized as such through the legal process and the "ruler" is the person who is elected as such by the vote of the people. In other words, the convict is not defined as the person who is "really" guilty, nor is the ruler the person who is, in truth, the most qualified. Reality, here, follows the method of discovering the reality. This method is fundamental and universal in the sense that no one can follow a private method. It is in this sense that democracy may be said to have a determined method toward undetermined ends. The indeterminacy, however, refers to instances and specific cases not the basic principles and criteria of democracy, which, like the fundamental precepts of jurisprudence, are determined, honored, and inviolable.

This is true of the religious society as well. Not everything is left to the contest of human opinions. People with independent will and discernment, and with complete freedom and awareness, extrapolate certain principles of ethics and pragmatics from their religion (such as renouncing alcohol and gambling in Islamic societies). Although the origin of these principles is believed to be heavenly, they happen to be willed and desired by human beings. Thus heaven and earth are reconciled and the severity of the paradox of religiosity and rationality is reduced. It must be emphasized, though, that any assumption of inalienable a priori rights for rulers to preempt laws or any presumption of the rulers' legitimizing role over the system is contrary to democracy. No degree of sophistry can establish otherwise. It bears reiterating, then, postulating "specific results" is contrary to democracy. It is not predetermined who among Moslems will be the ruler. Rulers need to be "designated" through rational methods. That is why appointing religious judges to this office, without regard for people's will and vote and without utilizing democratic methods, is incompatible with democracy. It is not only the right but the duty of religious people to elect their own rulers through an equitable method and to restrict the power of their leaders so that their lapses of policy and deliberation are minimized and their transgressions democratically restituted or retributed. The ultimate right of the people to govern, that is, to manage rationally the society in such a way as to reduce errors of deliberation and policy making, shall not be abrogated under any circumstances. No error may be repeated or justified on the basis of an a priori or divine right. The government of the people is a government fit for the people, not for Gods. It is established and demolished through the will of the people. This will is, in a religious society, nurtured and inspired by religion and religious reason, but the religious edification and inspiration does not diminish the democratic nature of the religious government in the least.

9. Morality, Religious Morality, and Democracy

Since the a priori principles of democracy are endemically moral, democracy can not prosper without commitment to moral precepts. Respect for the will of the majority and the rights of others, justice, sympathy, and trust are among the pivotal principles of democracy. Slackening these bonds will endanger the life of democracy in any society. The revolt prone prosperity of some contemporary capitalist societies has been threatening their morality and therefore their democracy. That is why sympathetic voices are beginning to call for a return to virtues in such societies, for no civilization has survived without them. It is here that the great debt of democracy to religion is revealed. Religions, as bulwarks of morality, can serve as the best guarantors of democracy. A religious society that is sensitive to moral corruption and rectitude is better equipped to be the witness and judge of its leaders and a more vigilant critic of their abuse of power. Democracy is based on checks and balances and, as such, is designed to be responsive to the perils of power. However, this equilibrium depends on the leaders' moral (and not merely legal) obligation to combat corruption. No legal system can appoint another legal system to police it, that would lead to infinite regress. Only morality can solve this dilemma. Those in positions of power need an internal guardian.[42] It is in such a moral system that the law would be respected, effective, and consistent in form and substance. Here democracy reveals its immense potential to eradicate corruption. Whereas dictatorship and totalitarianism are corrupt in form and substance, democracy, without an intrinsic alliance with life-sustaining moral principles, will be no more than a mere facade. Some two hundred years ago, Alexis de Tocqueville understood this. "Although religion has no direct role in the government of the American society, he observes, it should be considered among the basic foundations of the political system of the country."[43] Of course, he did not mean that religion is identical with politics but that "religion in the United States guides morality" and morality is the best bulwark of democracy. Tocqueville considered egotism, extreme individualism, excessive preoccupation with one's own family and friends at the expense of the public good deleterious to American democracy, which, he believed, owed its political success to the essentially religious and moral belief that all are responsible to the society and thus forbidden from drilling holes of self-interest in the collective vessel of felicity. In a similar vein, the late Richard Niebuhr, the well-known contemporary theologian (d. 1962) regarded the biblical concept of "covenant" more pivotal to the edifice of American democracy than the secular notion of "social contract." The latter connotes self-interest, while the former embodies trust, moral commitment, and a pure sense of responsibility. It is, thus, a better asset for the survival of democratic institutions.[44]

The same religious moral precepts (that have, in our cultural past, occasionally justified a decadent retreatist mysticism) can develop into the best champion of democracy. The religious denunciation of wealth and power can provide a suitable setting for a peaceful life, ameliorate the clash over material interests, and encourage rational measures that would curtail the alluring accumulation of temptations of riches and power that may test the rectitude of hearts and faiths, enticing them to throw dust in virtue's eyes and renounce right for the sake of might. Democracy grows and prospers better on such a soil. So long as the moral values do not find a practical and disciplined form and an effective method of application, so long as they remain mere words they will be sterile, even corrupting. The philosophical anthropology of religion, too, reveals the harmony of religious values with democratic values. What can a religion that characterizes human soul as compulsive, negligent, frail, despairing, and impetuous teach other than the lesson of tolerance and humility? What way would it recommend other than the path of compassion and prudence?

10. A Look Back and a Look Forward

We are approaching the end of our discussion, and a brief summary is in order. This essay originated in the question of the possibility of combining democracy and religion; but it went on to articulate their affinity and need for each other. Notions of liberty, faith, dynamism of religious understanding, and rationality of worldly affairs were evoked to attest to the possibility, even the necessity, of such an auspicious reconciliation. Religious morality would be the guarantor of a democracy, where the rights of the faithful to adopt a divine religion would not vitiate the democratic, earthly, and rational nature of the religious government. A distinction between democracy and the liberal philosophy helped demonstrate that the convictions of the faithful do not impede religious tolerance. Recognizing the primacy of general epistemological and theological axioms over the specifics of religious law determined the status of each; the emphasis on the necessity of maintaining the equilibrium between the religious and extrareligious domain illustrated the role of rationality in the domain of religion and took the critique of democratic religiosity out of the jurisdiction of religious law. At the same time, legal discipline was recognized as a contributing factor in religious democracy. A religious reign over hearts was distinguished from a legal rule over bodies. Free and willing faith and untamed and independent understanding were found to be the essential characteristics of a religious society and the outward ritual aspects were recognized as secondary effects of the above. In none of these discussions were the boundaries of the domain of extrareligious discourse violated. Religious jurists and exegetes were never invited to enter the arena of theological and religious debate. The question of religion was deemed too important to be trusted to uncritical legal exegeses cut off from autonomous rational principles.

The role of rationality in the arena of religion has, thus far, been that of a timid and discreet servant of understanding and defense of religion. However, defense and affirmation cannot be complete without critique and analysis. The enterprise of rationality is an all-or-nothing project. One may not employ reason to attest to the truth of one's opinions, without leaving the door open to its fault-finding critique. The attempt to enjoy the sweet affirmation of reason without tasting its bitter reproach is pure self delusion. Writing books in defense of women's rights, human rights, and the system of government in Islam, summoning reason to affirm and defend the truth of one's arguments, while turning a deaf ear to rational critique of the rest of one's beliefs exemplifies a half-finished enterprise that falls far short of the requirements of reasoned discourse and the standards of rationality.[45]

Invitation to religious democracy is an invitation to the thoroughgoing project of religious rationality, a rationality that contains gains along with losses. It is an invitation to a determined methodology with undetermined results, an invitation to examined versus emulated religiosity. It is true that in religious societies imitation prevails, appearance takes primacy over essence, and the apologetic reason rises above the critical reason. However, these mind-numbing emulations and thought-killing rigidities have always been decried and condemned by the anguished and the vigilant. The invitation to religious democracy is an invitation to the realization of the freedom of faith, respect for dynamic understanding, and the establishment of a system that fosters and invigorates such ideals.

In democratic societies, the path of examined religiosity is more open and inviting. Those who appreciate the value and sanctity of religion and the glory of investigation will never doubt that a single examined faith is nobler than a thousand imitated, shaky, and weak beliefs. "The religious despotism," a term perceptively coined by the knowledgeable jurisconsult, logician, and theologian of the last century, Ayatollah Na'ini, is indeed insurmountable except by the help of such a rational democracy. Religious despotism is most intransigent because a religious despot views his rule not only his right but his duty.[46] Only a religious democracy that secures and shelters faith can be secure and sheltered from such self-righteous and antireligious rule.

10

The Three Cultures

We Iranian Moslems are the inheritors and the carriers of three cultures at once. As long as we ignore our links with the elements of our triple cultural heritage and our cultural geography, constructive social and cultural action will elude us. I will later argue that our social thinkers and reformers have all seen themselves somehow entangled in these over-lapping cultural webs and have sought to weave their way out of them. I will also argue that the immense cultural aberrations that have caused us to miss important historical opportunities originated in the confluence of these three cultures, with one aspect of our cultural heritage eclips-ing others and thereby causing various obesities and ailments in the cultural physiognomy of our nation.

The three cultures that form our common heritage are of national, religious, and Western origins. While steeped in an ancient national culture, we are also immersed in our religious culture, and we are at the same time awash in successive waves coming from the Western shores. Whatever solutions that we divine for our problems must come from this mixed heritage to which our contemporary social thinkers, reformers, and modernizers have been heirs, often seeking the salvation of our people in the hegemony of one of these cultures over the other two.

The Significance of the National Culture and the Hazards of Nationalist Extremism

There is no denying the importance of our national culture. Our people were Iranians before they accepted Islam. Theirs was an idiosyncratic Persian culture with distinctive literature, religion, folkways, and customs. They remained Iranians even after becoming Moslems and accepting the intellectual and religious bent of the Shi'a creed. Our Iranian essence was not absorbed in the digestive systems of religious or Western cultures; many of our native customs and folkways have persisted, especially the Persian language, which is one of the most important foundations of our nationhood. There are few nations whose language has remained constant for ten centuries. Our literati and poets have accomplished the remarkable feat of preserving, enriching, and perfecting this melodious language which is the reason for the continuity of the Iranian nation. Today we recite the poetry of Ferdowsi and Rudaky, composed more than a thousand years ago, and find that it speaks to us still; so we commit them to memory, use them in our daily conversations, and find delight and wisdom in them without the slightest hint of estrangement.

Consider this verse of Ferdowsi: "In the name of the Lord of soul and reason"; or Rudaky's poem starting with "[Alas] my teeth all crumbled and fell out." Are these not in our own vernacular? In contrast, challenge a German or English native to recite, let alone understand, the German or English written one thousand years ago. For the readers of contemporary English even the writings of Shakespeare require extensive annotation—and Shakespeare wrote only four centuries ago; those who wrote before him appear even more arcane and obscure.

Yet the twine of our nationality is firm and enduring. The writings of Abulfazl Beihaqi, who wrote a thousand years ago, do more than teach us history; they teach us our language as well, and an agreeable and charming language at that! Unlike such pre-Islamic Iranian sects as the Manichaean or Mazdaki faiths which have now perished, the main creed of pre-Islamic Iranians, Zoroastrianism, was recognized by Islam and to this day flows as a minor brook alongside the mainstream of Islam in Iran. Barring the area of religion (which was deeply dominated by Islam), many of our customs and folkways have preserved their ancient vigor, and we remain their witnesses and inheritors. Our calendar[1] is uniquely Persian, Nowrouz[2] prevails as our most important holiday, and our literature is permeated with expressions born of ancient Iranian rites and customs. Citing the usage of Persian idioms, some have maintained that such sages as Hafez[3] and Sohrevardi[4] had national/Zoroastrian tendencies. There is no doubt that Hafez used such nouns and expressions as *jam-e jam* [jam's crystal bowl], *soroush* [divine muse], *pir-e moghan* [the elder of the magi], *mogh bacheh* [the young magi], Jamshid, Pashang, Siavosh, Dara, Keiqobad [all mythological characters in Ferdowsi's *Shahnameh*], *khosravani-soroud* [the kingly song], *golbang-e Pahlavi* [the melodic voice of *Pahlavi*—the pre-Arabic Persian]. But it would be an overstatement to argue that Hafez yearned to revive the pre-Islamic ideas, especially at the expense of sacrificing Islamic thought.

In any case, there were those who tried to revive this pre-Islamic culture in all its purity and entirety, as if they saw their mission for salvation of the people of this nation in this endeavor. At the dawn of the constitutional revolution (1905), when we were gradually learning about Western ideas, there appeared some intellectuals and writers whose main project was opposition to Islam and "Arab contamination." They believed that all of the problems of Iranian society—which lagged far behind the caravan of civilization—originated in the Arabs' influences and the remedy would be to return to our pure national pre-Islamic culture. This group insisted that a foreign thought is foreign, regardless of its origins. Thus Islam, being the product of foreigners and belonging to Arabs, is an unbecoming patch sewn on our culture. This attitude arose spontaneously from certain writers and thinkers like Akhound Zadeh[5] at the birth of the constitutional revolution, led to condemning Islamic thought for its Arabic origin, and found formal state sponsorship during the reign of Reza Khan.[6] It also found such uncompromising and powerful advocates as Kasravi[7] and Hedayat.[8] Monarchy as a form of sovereignty is part of Iranian culture, and we all witnessed how much Iranian culture was emphasized to bolster the rule of Mohammad Reza Shah Pahlavi.[9] We observed how a group of literati and historians entered the service of the monarchy, and how, in the name of establishing the authenticity and superiority of the Iranian race over the aliens, they perpetrated inequities, deceptions, and the worship of false idols. Their mission was to promote the pure Persian, to expel every Arabic word from books and peoples' daily language and to propagate a form of "extremist nationalism." Academy of Persian language, a worthy institution in itself, also followed extremist paths and attempted to wipe out the religious culture under the guise of cleansing the vestiges of alien cultural domination. Until the last days of Mohammad Reza Shah's rule, the chairs of Persian literature were occupied by scholars who would not tolerate a single Arabic or non-Persian word (the names of Dr. Mohammad Moqaddam or Sadeq Kia, two of the professors of Persian language, come to mind). I specifically named Dr. Moqaddam because he pronounced his last name as "Moq Dom" meaning "the tail—or follower of the magi." Due to his bizarre hatred of Arabic language, he developed an improper and unscientific obsession with following every non-Iranian word to Iranian roots. He would argue that Plato[10] is the same as our own Fereidoun[11] and Aristotle[12] none other than our own Rostam![13] Although some of these arguments were made in jest, they also had firm roots in decadent nationalism, a turning away from rich foreign cultures and an inflated sense of cultural self-sufficiency that they dubbed "returning to one's own authentic identity" or "sitting at home and turning out the foreigners." Such poets and writers as Mir Zadeh Eshqi, Sadeq Hedayat, Zabih Behrouz, and even Said Nafisi fed the flame of this spectacle and started resuscitating the Iranian heros of pre- and post-Islamic times, wailing and sighing for the days of the shahs of yore. Exhuming Babak, Maziyar, Abu Moslem, Al-Mughanna'[14] and the rest, writing novels about them and lavishing on them all kinds of accolades, they strove to endow Iranian culture with so much pomp and majesty as to leave little room for other cultures. Ferdowsi's *Shahnameh* is most grievously abused in the midst of all this. *Shahnameh*—or as Ferdowsi himself dubbed it, "Nameh-ye Bastan" (the ancient epistle)—is our most precious linguistic document. But this gem fell into corrupt hands and turned into the bible of racist pride. That is why even today some do not dare acknowledge the worth of the book and its author. Indeed, the service that Ferdowsi has rendered to Iran and the Persian language is such that no amount of praise would suffice.

So far we have related the story of those who focused on the ethnic culture and sought the resolution of our problems in putting distance between the national and religious cultures. There was a certain policy at the time of Mohammad Reza Pahlavi to bring Zoroastrians of India to Iran. Of course, Iran is a haven for Zoroastrians and as Iranians they are welcome to come here and live in peace whenever they wish to return. But those policies had a different political aim: fattening one part of our cultures while starving the rest.

Coming to Terms with Western Culture: Beyond "West Toxication"

The second culture which we faced at the outset of the constitutional revolution was Western culture. Of course, Moslems had touched base with the culture of the West once before, at the onset of the Islamic culture's glory, when Moslems expanded their empire and were gradually acquainted with the thought of the foreigners, especially the Greeks. That was the era of dynamism in Islamic culture; it possessed ample power to absorb and entice; its attitude about foreign ideas was that of a victor dealing with the vanquished. Dauntless and fearless, with able and discriminating hands, Moslems took the foreign thoughts, ground them up in the sharp teeth of their minds, and consigned them to the digestive system of their reason; they discarded the tainted while keeping and utilizing the pure and the good.

Alas, after that first era of dynamism, this roaring river became stagnant and even putrid as it ceased to flow. The second time, about a hundred years ago, when we Moslems faced Western culture (this time an invading culture armed with the weapons of science and technology), we were quite weak. This time, too, Western culture found its advocates among us, and many both within and without our borders loudly asserted that the salvation of Iranians and those left behind the caravan of civilization and progress lies in following the culture of the Westerners, in loving them, prostrating before them, and begging them to ease our pains and solve our problems.

It is undoubtedly true that no one was at fault for the arrival of Western culture in our country. This was the encounter of a strong culture with a stagnant and feeble one. In this encounter, we had nothing left in the storehouse of our religious and native cultures save a few dried up formalities, habits, and conventions. Inattentiveness, poverty, hunger, ignorance, and tyranny reigned. If we had a few thinkers among us, they were too few and insignificant to swell a countertide. Thus, when the current of well-groomed ideas of the French Revolution, outfitted with the weapons of science and technology, entered this country, they found no hindrance or resistance and proceeded to enchant and mesmerize us all. The Western-engineered and Westernized regimes such as (our) Reza Khan and (the Turks') Ata Turk fueled this fire. The coming of Western culture to our land was neither caused by historical determinism nor did it indicate the end of a historical era in our culture: it was the result of our weakness and the West's strength. The encounter with the West caused various reactions in our people, one of which is captured in the concept of *gharb zadegi* [West toxication].[15]

Two groups among us have used this concept, and each means something different by it. The main champion of the this concept was the late Jalal al-e Ahmad[16] who developed it in his book, *Gharb Zadegi*. This book (that became very popular among intellectuals and those concerned with the national destiny due to its content as well as its having been banned by the government) alerted us to the onset of a case of terminal cultural cancer. What Al-e Ahmad meant by West toxication was the coming of Western customs, manners, and technology, causing our eviction from our native home, the sacrifice of our noble and gracious traditions at the feet of the Western practices and industry. It meant the nauseating imitation of everything Western even at the expense of immolating the most eminent cultural assets and legacies of our own: speaking with their tongue, thinking with their brain, looking through their eyes, and wailing their pain. For these reasons, the message and slogan of Al-e Ahmad was "back to traditions." He argues that the only way to stand up to this fierce Western tempest is to hold on to our traditions. The victim of West toxication turns out "effeminate, trendy, rudderless, lacking in competence and personality." A feral child snatched from the native cradle "apes the Western ways."[17] In Al-e Ahmad's view, we have a chain of national traditions that constitutes our identity, and if we do not preserve them, we will be assimilated in the Western culture. Not a traditionally pious man, Al-e Ahmad opposed neither Western science nor technology. He had first turned his back to religion, but his aversion toward religion gradually diminished. Religion was significant for him only as one of the components of the tradition: it was Al-e Ahmad's respect for tradition that attracted him to religion, not vice versa.

Such was Al-e Ahmad's intent in discussing the concept of *gharb zadegi*. But there is a different school of thought that was a different interpretation of the concept of *gharb zadegi*. It maintains that our Islamic and native cultures are long past their prime, that they are exhausted and depleted. In this view the Islamic and native cultures are incapable of revival and renewal, having been superseded by the West. For this group *gharb zadegi* means sharing in the historical destiny of the West. This meant the swallowing of world history by the West and a deterministic, Hegelian swallowing at that. The subject here is not the superficial changes in customs and folkways, the encroaching corruption of the West, or even the Europeanization of Iranians. Rather, it is the necessity of the arrival of one epoch and the passing of another; no one can hope to change a historically determined fate by kicking and screaming. In this sense, *gharb zadegi* is not an illness nor the blight of aping the West (à la Al-e Ahmad); it is a historical destiny. It is the turning of our history into "matter" for the "form" of Western history.

The above meaning of *gharb zadegi* has a series of practical consequences quite different from those that would follow from Al-e Ahmad's version. The former is flexible and implies a critical approach to the Western culture. It says that a calamity, or to put it more accurately, an accident has occurred but one must keep ones head: the West must be carefully examined but vigorously resisted. The useful elements must be absorbed and the harmful rejected. Traditions must be evoked as a bulwark of resistance, and the slumbering culture must be awakened. But the second interpretation inspires passivity and feebleness of merely observing ones own predestined fate. It never attempts to separate the West's wheat from its chaff. It regards the coming of Western culture as an earthquake, above human will, beyond human knowledge, and impervious to prediction and control. This interpretation is based on a certain Hegelian and Spenglerian philosophy of historical determination that instead of questioning the domination of the West, passively acknowledges it and invites people to do the same. By considering *gharb zadegi* a necessary and ineluctable fate, it envisions human beings standing in front of history with both hands tied.

When the philosophy, science, technology and literature of the West flowed into the world of Islamic Iran, nothing retained its previous shape: the walls crumbled as exchanges intensified. Western customs, rites, worldviews and philosophies wafted through us and was enthusiastically received. At the outset of the Constitutional Revolution, Western liberalism attracted the attention of the thinkers and social reformers. The slogan of the French Revolution, "Liberty, Equality and Fraternity," were in the minds of the framers of the Iranian constitution. In the words of Mokhbereddoleh Hedayat in his *Khaterat va Khatarat*, each revolutionary kept a treatise about the French Revolution in his bosom and wanted to play the parts of a Robespierre or a Danton. The founding of the parliament, the writing of the constitution, the formation of the constitutional government, the separation of powers, and the propagation of Western-style liberties, including religious tolerance and the rights of religious minorities, were all the manifestations of the liberalism of Western culture.

Since the 1940s another progeny of the Western culture, Marxism has also flourished in our land. With the gradual increase in the oppression by the government, different armed and unarmed groups equipped with this ideology grew here and there. It is important to remember that these groups, liberal and Marxist alike, believed the salvation of Iranians to lie in embracing Western ideologies alone.

The Status of Islamic Culture in Iran

Having briefly discussed the above two cultures, we will now turn to our Islamic culture which is qualitatively and quantitatively the dominant culture of Iran. Our religious culture goes back thirteen hundred years. Iranians have lovingly embraced, nurtured, and developed Islamic thought and culture, never abandoning it and endowing its literature with new riches. Our folkways and customs, art and architecture, wedding and divorce, education and edification, entertainment and amusement, sorrow and joy, schooling and literature, all accepted the cast and content of Islam. If our judiciary and government did not conform to the Islamic form, under the Islamic Republic they do.

The Question of Identity

Now, the important questions that arise are the following: where among these three cultures does our identity lie? What did those saviors and reformers mean by "salvation" and "identity"? What does "cultural identity" mean, anyway? Is it possible or desirable to aspire to a true and pure cultural identity, and in that case which of our three cultures would be closer and more loyal to us, which more faithful to our "true identity"? Which one subverts it and takes us away from ourselves? Is it a duty to remain loyal to and preserve the old culture? Is there such a thing as cultural repentance? Is any nation permitted rebellion against parts of its own culture? Is there an opportunity and an avenue for intercultural exchange, or must cultures keep their windows closed to one another? Is it right to advocate the hegemony of one culture over others? What does "returning to one's authentic self" mean, and in whom and what does that "self" consist?

As we know both Al-e Ahmad and Shari'ati spoke of returning to our own culture, as did many other third-world intellectuals and reformers such as Julius Nyerere, Secotre, Aime Cesaire, Frantz Fanon, and others.

I do not know of any of these thinkers and social reformers who did not include this appeal in their writings and messages, calling their people to a sort of "return" to their authentic culture. Now the time has arrived for us to determine our responsibility toward these calls and these cultures. I am certain that the message of our reformers or social thinkers shall not find resonance in our society as long as they do not determine what this elusive "identity" means, on what it depends, and how we must deal with our mixed cultural heritage. The idea of "returning to ourselves" has engendered a great deal of confusion. Some understand it to mean a return to the villages and the system of serfdom. Others read a decadent and extremist nationalism into it and wander off to revive dead and absurd myths and creeds. Yet others find in it a charge to turn their backs on other cultures and denounce them. And a few have opposed or ignored the concept altogether because of its vagueness.

If we agree that assimilation in an alien culture, seeking to become like them, dressing like them, and adopting their tone is an illness, to which the slogan of "return to thyself" proposes a cure, we need to answer a few questions: Is learning from others necessarily bad? Is it possible to return to the past? Does every turning to the other wipe out one's identity? Does every return to the past restore our true character? Do "self" and "other" in cultures substitute for right and wrong? Did Arabs who persisted in their ancestral and ethnic pagan heritage and ignored the call of the Prophet to monotheism choose the right path? Would it have been wise if we Iranians had rejected Islam of the Arab Prophet just because it belonged to the foreigners? Did the call of the prophet of Islam aim to save the people or Arabic culture?[18] Ought the social reformers seek to revive a particular culture? Finally, where did this doctrine of the revival of tradition and culture originate and for what wound is it a balm? The truth is that as long as we do not view identity (including cultural identity) as a dynamic and evolving matter, we shall not find answers to any of these questions.

The Question of Cultural Allegiances

The source of these problems is the baneful equation of identity with rigidity. One who has squandered half of a life languishing in isolation and iniquity must not use the pretext of persisting on one's identity to continue a slovenly and secluded life. One must seek purification in exchange with others. After all, rebellion against oneself is also a part of one's self. Rectifying one's identity is part of one's identity. Becoming, is also a part of Being. And this implies causing oneself and ones culture to "move." And in this movement lies all manner of blessings. If movement means anything, it means avoiding imitation. It does not matter whether one imitates one's past or the foreigners. Exhuming extinct and wicked customs and beliefs cannot be called revival. Returning to one's authentic self can not be accomplished by reposing in ones ancestral tomb. Throwing away offensive, impoverished, and false conventions and convictions must not be equated with selling off one's identity, alienation, and self-degradation.

What causes fear of other cultures is the lack of a strong cultural digestive system and also the misconception that each culture is an indivisible monolith, accepting one part of which equals accepting the whole. Dispelling this illusion is not very difficult, and as soon as the mind is released from its spell, gates of insight and blessing will be opened, and the mind shall embark on the path of critical selection. It is said that one must stand on one's own feet (meaning one's own culture and tradition) before attempting to engage other cultures. However, we must ask who is this "self"? For the imitators this is whatever is bequeathed to them: religion, country, local conventions and customs, and so on. But truth seekers consider all of these as open to review, revision, repentance, and rebellion. For them, questions of right and wrong and public interest are more important than blind imitation. In this manner, a new self will be born who will clean and ventilate the house in broad daylight, instead of shutting its door and boarding its windows to protect it from robbers.

These questions and answers will be posed only for those outside the culture looking in. They will not impinge on someone who has not yet become aware of the encounter and distinction of cultures; who has not yet peered through the shelter of the one's own nationality, religion, conventions, customs, history, language, literature and art; and who has not yet formed a picture of a different people and a different culture. Everything such a person says, understands, and experiences originates entirely in his or her own culture. Such a "self" is created entirely by local history. The above questions will arise only with recognition of the possibility of multiple selves and the attendant anxiety of cultural choice. We do not have a "fixed" ethnic or religious "self," these identities are fluid and expansive. With vigilant eyes, brave hearts, and able hands the multiple selves can be merged.

Our task is to discover—if not reconstruct—who we are instead of assuming the answer at the outset. Yes, we are actual people with set identities. We have common interests, predilections, conventions, opinions, and values, and these combine to make up our collective "identity." Our particular ways of seeing and tasting, sensitize us to experiencing things as sweet, bitter, fair, and foul. The pleasure we take in the poetry and language of Saʿdi,[19] the loyalty we feel for our own home and country, the relationship we have established with our history, and our pursuit of common goals has raised a roof of ideas, values, and views upon us as they have bound us together: this is our culture. Whether we know it or not, we are the offspring of this cultural geography, but there is a gulf between what is and what ought to be. It does not follow that since we have been such, we must therefore remain such forever. The one who does not question remains the same, but the one who questions shows with this very questioning to have achieved self-awareness, to have peeked out of the cozy blanket of one's culture, and to have looked at oneself and others from the angle of admonitory learning ['ebrat']. This person can no longer embrace and maintain a received identity but must examine, revise and adjust it.

The difficulty arises when some people unreflectively assume a fixed and eternal cultural identity and distinguish friend and foe accordingly. Such people never realize that the self must be created, that it does not come prefabricated and maintenance-free. Of course one of the materials for the construction of the self is our (modified) past identity. But loving one's native culture (a blameless sentiment and a sign of cultivation itself) does not mean spurning all that is not native to it. This is how some declared Islam to be a foreign element. Instead of illuminating who this "us" is; they assume that our pure Iranian identity is the sole referent of this pronoun. Had there been the necessary and adequate debate about our identity, it would probably have become clear that Islam (like many other things) is a part of "us." This argument does not amount to washing our hands of our authentic self but exploring its boundaries. This is no mean task. The bid to "return to oneself" will remain an empty slogan at best (and a slayer of culture and a source of stagnation at worst) if the boundaries of the self remain unspecified, if flexibility is denied. We cannot countenance a "return to the self" that is counterposed to the reconstruction of the self.

The Question of Cultural Property

Is all that has flourished outside our culture alien to us?[20] Is every word not coined by Persians alien to the Persian language? Is every science not accessible by Iranians unworthy of learning? Here is the encounter of the self and other. Must we count as alien whatever we have not nurtured? Islam is part of us, belongs to our national culture, and has strong ties to our cultural identity only in the sense that it has fused and united with us, but it did not originate in Iran. The Iranian embrace of Islam was willful and voluntary; it was not forced on us. Islam fused and united with us, entered into our very essence, and to this day fortifies our contemporary culture and identity. A comparison of the advent of Islam in Iran with the rise of communist and socialist systems in Eastern Europe can be quite instructive. Communism was born in Europe and then found a motherland in Russia. From there it was exported to other countries, accompanied by carnage, coercion and an assortment of circumstances contrary to ideology that trumpeted its concern for justice. But communism remained an alien implant wherever it prevailed. It does not matter whether this was due to its innate incompatibility with human nature or its incompetence in resolving economic problems, historical conditions, and the conspiracies of enemies. Even in its motherland—Russia—those who lived under its yoke for seventy years were never content with it, did not willingly absorb it, and discarded it at the first opportunity. Communism was alien to these people, regardless of its geographic origins. It originated in Europe: in Brussels, Paris, and London. Then it found a strong practical agent and an enforcer in the person of Lenin, who found the situation ripe in Russia and established it there. Later, Stalin stabilized the system with cruelty and bloodshed. Milovan Djilas discusses the same period with a hint of dark humor.[21] According to some accounts, Stalin slaughtered close to five million people, including the former commander of the Red Army, Leon Trotsky. Yet his efforts were futile, for communism never became part of the Russian self. The collective acceptance of an idea (especially when it is just and right) is the same as its incorporation into the collective self. A peoples' consent is not arbitrary, nor is it based on a whim; it presupposes affinity in substance and resonance in spirit. Our hearts and minds are our wealth. Whatever satisfies the reason and wins the heart is by definition ours, even if it has traversed thousands of leagues or thousands of years to reach us.

We were born in Asia, in Iran among the followers of Islam. Thus we are at once Asian, Iranian, and Moslem, each a different aspect of our culture. Yet just because a culture happens to nurture us, we can not deem it as the absolute truth, worthy of unconditional support and the guarantor of our entire identity. Nor can we deem what has not grown in our soil as the incarnation of absolute falsehood. The mature human being is born only after emerging from the cocoon of local loyalties to look at one's culture from a critical distance, keeping the ledgers of reason and love separate.

Those who propagated the decadent, deterministic, and historicist version of the idea of West toxication among us were themselves feeding from the same trough that fed the followers of extreme antireligious nationalism. Both maintained that the West has reached the end of its road and that Islam has been depleted. It is noteworthy that they have borrowed both of these ideas from the Western sources! If we intend to fight the West with this weapon, we have to fight Islam as well because it too has come from the outside. Some even argue: do not complain of West toxication; first think about Arab toxication; we were stung by the Arabs more severely than by the West.

Let us not use the categories of ours or theirs in the realm of culture. Instead, our primary criteria should be categories of right or wrong, good or bad. Instead of "construction of the self," we have talked about "return to the self," spawning confusion and quandary. We have quarreled over cultural ownership rather than distinguishing truth and falsehood, correction and corruption. The final criterion for counting a cultural value or practice as our own should be this: It has to be right and good, and it must have been willingly adopted by our people.

The Question of Cultural Repentance

No ancient cultural trait can claim our automatic devotion on the sole ground of having grown in our soil; each culture must disavow certain elements of itself. No part of our culture (religious, national, or Western) can be defended in absolute terms. There are elements in all three from which we have to repent, and all three are in need of renewal and borrowing. On this score they are all the same; none is so complete as to eclipse the others.

Thus those who sought to weaken, put to sleep, or kill a part of our mixed cultural heritage in order to make other parts more salient have not served our people well. They were reactionary nationalists, radical Westernizers, or unschooled defenders of Islam. Some Iranians could not countenance the [pre-Islamic] Nowrouz holiday or the giving of pre-Islamic Iranian names to children. In the name of cultural purity, some Egyptians went in search of pharaohs. In Saudi Arabia, they revived people like Abu Lahab and even named a street after him. This is the same Abu Lahab that God curses in the Qur'an saying "may his hands be cut off." Should the call to "return to yourself" be understood as a return to infancy or infamy? Should the brutal autocratic pharaohs in one's past be the source of pride or shame? Absolute monarchy was an undeniable part of our Iranian heritage, but our people opposed it in the name of religion and of combating injustice and of defending liberty of human beings. This example of successful and cherished cultural repentance proves that cultural identity is not stagnant. Clutching traditions in order to hold still in the contemporary storms is advisable only if those traditions are not rotted. To judge whether this is the case is a task for the caring, insightful, and sober thinkers of today, not the uninformed and dogmatic prisoners of the traditions of yesteryears. How can building on the foundation of soggy traditions bring stability? And what sort of identity can it award us?

What passes for religious culture among us is in need of a great deal of revision and repentance as well. All manner of intellectual superstitions prevail among us under the guise of religion not the least of which is disrespect for national customs. Similarly, many ethical concepts of religious origin are adulterated or truncated to assume an ugly and frowning countenance. Examples abound: *sabr* [forbearance], *shokr* [giving thanks for God's mercy], *qena'at* [frugality], *tavakkol* [relying on God's mercy], *zohd* [asceticism], and *amer-e be ma'rouf* [calling the people to noble deeds]. For many years resignation in the name of awaiting the coming of the Imam-e Zaman (Lord of the Time) was propagated as a religious duty. If these are not part of our religious culture, what is? Those who do not recognize the plague of superstition afflicting religious culture have not yet crossed the threshold of reform. For many years the ostensibly religious rites of *rouzeh khani* [stylized recitation of the sufferings of the martyrs during the month of Moharram], *qameh zani* [blade beating], and *sineh zani* [breast beating] prevailed among us.[22] Did anyone dare to oppose these as contrary to religion? For many years, the preachers elicited tears from people by reciting the passion of Imam Hossein.[23] In the late Shari'ati's words, they have transformed blood into opiate allowing the supposed stimulative to degenerate into a sedative.

Those who claim that our religious culture should dominate our other cultures must determine what is meant by religious culture; they must define which parts are to be accepted and which rejected? Popularity does not equal cultural identity; it may equal a false identity. The late Motahhari had an apt analogy. He would say God has called *taqva* [piety] our garb. There are two considerations here: the garb protects us, but we, too, must keep it in good repair. The same is true of religious and national culture. We must rely on it as it relies on us. Just like water, which cleans but itself needs to be cleansed. Whose task is it to cleanse the cleanser?[24] The constant process of purification of water in nature consists in its constant rotation and movement. What we said about national culture also applies to religious culture: it is wrong to discard something just because it did not originate within our religious domain. Just last year one of our religious journals satirized the Nowrouz holiday in the name of the religious culture. To delight in the Nowrouz is neither against the religious law nor contrary to reason; on what basis is it then opposed?

Sometimes we see that respecting the Persian language is justified on the grounds that it is a carrier of Islamic culture. This alone would be reason enough for respecting the language. But even if Persian did not have this honor, it would still have been worthy of love and respect. Nothing nurtures the soul and body of Iranians like this language. It is a window to our hearts and music to our ears; it is our fathers' voice, our poets' verse. And these are reasons enough to offer it the highest seat of honor. The same is true of other aspects of our national culture, including the Nowrouz holiday, the solar calendar, Ferdowsi's *Shahnameh*, Shi'a jurisprudence, Islamic erudition, Rumi's *Mathnavi*, Greek philosophy, Newtonian physics, traditional music, fine crafts, and mechanized production. These are all parts of our culture, and they are so intertwined that even Esfandiyar is unable to undo them.[25]

Now let us consider Western culture. In order to justify embracing Western science and technology, some have attempted to trace the roots of these sciences to Moslems. They have claimed that Europeans borrowed such disciplines as mechanics, medicine, pharmacology, philosophy and astronomy from us and embroidered them into their present form. I do not propose to challenge this claim—indeed I would endorse its gist, ignoring the trivial and incomplete form in which it is often presented. But, I would like to invite you to consider its origin. Those who make this claim wish to demonstrate that Western science and technology originated among us, that they are "ours," ergo, worthy of acceptance. You see that the same twisted logic operates here as well: if something has not sprouted in our midst, it is necessarily alien to us. This logic does not allow cultural exchange of any kind.

A Final Note on the Difference between Servile Imitation and Critical Exchange

We do not mean to neglect the significance of preserving authenticity and rejecting cultural imitation, intimidation, and alienation. We distinguish between servile and dignified varieties of exchange. Our aim is to warn against two pitfalls: blind emulation and blind rejection. Pursuit of fads spurns or injures ones own cultural taste. Those who constantly search for novelties; who spurn their own customs blindly; and who imitate others in manners of dressing, entertaining, talking, celebrating, home decorating, mate selecting, eating, judging, evaluating, and creating art are bereft of authenticity. Yet living in the presence of a multiplicity of cultures and tastes is healthy. Different cultures have created a diverse and colorful range of beauties, talents, arts, literatures, rites, and glories. Every cultural phenomenon is beauteous and sweet in the eyes of its culturally trained beholders. Preservation of authenticities does not imply the perpetuation and revival of the offensive and superstitious customs of one's predecessors. It means active participation in cultural creations and taking delight in the best of one's native culture while constantly attempting to improve. There is no shame in choosing to maintain or abandon certain element of ones culture on the basis of investigation, insight, and critical inquiry.

Of course, in the world of affections, affinities, customs, and tastes there is little place for rational debate. But we can insist on rational choice in the world of ideas, rational speculation, ideologies, and worldviews; it is here that we should abandon our ethnic parentage and seek the authority of reason alone. In this world, blind imitation is forever condemned, whereas the rational search for truth is eternally noble. In matters of convention one may follow ones native tastes, affinities, and ways, while in the realm of thoughts and truths, one must follow the rules of rational discourse. Unification of all cultures is neither possible nor desirable. To preserve the diversity of cultures will expand opportunities for evermore colorful creations.

Let me summarize. First, the reformers who intend to serve this country must not take as their point of departure the assumption that what has not originated among us is necessarily alien to us. Second, they must not seek to establish the hegemony of one culture at the expense of others. Third, the criterion for belonging to a culture has nothing to do with its native origins. Fourth, each culture contains elements for which it must repent and aspects it should uphold. We lean on our culture as much as it leans on us.[26] Fifth, the esteem in which we hold our multiple cultures depends on opening them up to one another and on purging them from added superstitions and unwanted elements. Sixth, respectable exchange in cultural matters must not be confused with blind and servile emulation or cultural subservience. Seventh, the alleged humiliating determinism of history must be condemned. We must stand in the agora of cultural exchange, fit, able, and willing to assume the task of defending the truth. We must not deem our ethnic and Islamic culture as terminus, but as a point of departure. Here I end my oration and bid you farewell and leave you in God's care.

I I

What the University Expects from the Hawzeh

In this distinguished gathering of the university community, I would like to open my discussion of the relationships between the university and the Hawzeh, delineate the distinctive characteristics of each, and outline the expectations of the university from the Hawzeh.

This day, which is dedicated to the unity of the Hawzeh and the university, expresses the aspiration of healing the unfortunate rift between these noble institutions. This ideal of unity germinated in many a beneficent heart at the outset of the cultural revolution[1] but was present even at the dawn of the Islamic revolution. Notwithstanding the causes of their separation—history's fate or the enemies' force—it was hoped that the university and the Hawzeh would rediscover each other and join forces to serve the nation by cutting through its thicket of scientific and intellectual problems.

Much has been said about this potential union and how to advance it. Thirteen years after the revolution, this union is still sought after in both communities. What is the intent of those who desire such a union? What will be its final shape? Many symposia have been convened to explore these questions and the ideal of unity has yet to be realized. Speaking as an empathetic and compassionate observer, I intend to touch upon a few points in this area, outlining the characteristics of the university and the Hawzeh and the reasons for their separation. I will also propose a few practical steps for achieving this much discussed rapprochement.

The defining characteristic of both institutions is the same: education. The university is an educational institution based on textbooks, teachers, and students and so are the seminaries in Qum and Najaf. Both institutions have long histories. But while Hawzeh has a longer tradition that stretches for centuries, the university in its present form is less than a century old. The latter has of course had predecessors in the Qajar period,[2] but we had nothing resembling a university before that. This is an imported institution, a foreign plant whose saplings we have borrowed and planted in order to sit in its pleasant shade, as we do today.

Although the Hawzeh and university appear to share an educational mission, the essence of their curricula are very different. The disciplines taught in these institutions are fundamentally dissimilar: the education at the Hawzeh is geared to a certain attitude that is absent at the university. Since this is the source of the differences between the two institutions, any attempt to unite and unify them must start here. The disciplines taught at the Hawzeh are related to or associated with religion. This is true of those disciplines that are directly related to religious texts (i.e., interpretation of the Qur'an [tafsir] or religious jurisprudence [fiq'h] as well as the prerequisites of such studies and the related disciplines such as philosophy and theology [kalam]. These are all nonempirical disciplines; their content is different from those taught at the university, where mostly empirical (natural as well as human) disciplines are taught.

Significant though this difference is, the dissimilarity between the Hawzeh and the university do not end here. In contrast to the university, the Hawzeh teaches subjects predicated on faith, which is impervious to criticism and opposition. Herein lies such a disparity of atmosphere and attitude among the students and the curricula of the two institutions as to make their alliance, let alone unity, profoundly problematic.

Please note that I am not saying there is a dearth of critical analysis and lively debate in the religious seminaries. Nor do I contend that the university is above reproducing clichés or that it is always humming with genuine inquiry and critique. Quite often the reverse is true: the seminarians, schooled in a dialectical tradition, are likely to enter into serious and lengthy debates with their teachers, whereas our university students have been trained in the passive routine of taking notes, passing exams, making grades, and going home. The practical, real-world virtues and flaws of each institution are not at issue here. The critical point is one of principle: in the seminaries the students' and teachers' a priori commitment to the original texts and sacred sources precludes criticism and doubt. It is possible to question and even reject the opinion of one's professor in jurisprudence [fiq'h] but if the argument is based on the unambiguous purport of a "tradition" [revayat] whose imputation to the sacred sources is established, then the gates of criticism will be shut and the case will be considered closed.

It has been said that the gates of jurisprudential innovation [ijtihad] are closed for the Sunni Moslems. This only means that they refrain from transgressing or even criticizing the edicts and rulings of a handful of their jurisprudential authorities. But this limit appears to the Shi'ite jurisconsults as well, except they stop at the authoritative edicts of the

Imams. This "stopping," for which each school of thought adduces justifying reasons, occurs in both schools of jurisprudence: the former stops at the opinion of a fallible authority and the latter at that of an infallible Imam. Our earlier remarks about the lack of critical thoroughness applies not to this issue but only to the study of the original sacred texts. In these interpretive [*tafsiri*] and hermeneutic [*ta'vili*] disciplines, you are allowed to ransack any opinion with ruthless curiosity, but up to an impassable red line, beyond which no one is allowed to advance. The interpretation of sacred texts is based on an important presupposition: we do not read them to undermine, replace, nor to criticize them; we strive to understand them. We do not even entertain the possibility that they might have faults and flaws. We assume these texts as perfect, hallowed, and sacred; they are beyond the reach of controversy or scientific inquiry, which thrives on discussion and criticism. But at the threshold of the sacred understanding, we presuppose submission to the holy texts. More importantly, we think that this submission will promote a degree of insight and discernment that would be inaccessible to those who spurn, defy, or rebel against the sacred truth. This is the main presupposition of the religious sciences: a carefully circumscribed receptivity to criticism. This self-enclosure is not necessarily a defect or a sign of decline; it is, however, a hallmark of these sciences.

Now let us consider the sciences studied in the university. It is true that a typical undergraduate student in physics, economics, or philosophy has not yet attained sufficient erudition to effectively question the theories that underlie these disciplines. It is even less likely that such a student could emulate the authorities of the field by originating a new paradigm to supplant the old one. But in principle the gate is open for such a development. Empirical disciplines have no "red line" that the students and professors are forbidden to cross; no theory is considered sacred or above questioning; no authors are immune to criticism. The atmosphere of the university intimates to the student and the professor: "If you are qualified, your mind can wander freely; you have the right to take an ax to any belief or conclusion in order to build newer, better ones; there is no authority in science blocking the free, chosen paths of thought."

Ladies and gentlemen, here in the university you are steeped in such an atmosphere, whether you appreciate it or not. So it would not be unreasonable to claim that the university is a domain of defiance that recognizes no boundaries to criticism and inquiry. In contrast, the Hawzeh not only recognizes such boundaries in theory, but it also constantly applies them in practice. The submission or lack thereof, however, applies only to the principal sources and not to all ideas.

Without a proper and thorough analysis, this fundamental difference of views could amount to an unbridgeable chasm between two institutions. The university can scorn the Hawzeh as stagnant, reactionary, and antiprogress. The Hawzeh can counter by hurling the university similar adjectives of abuse: relativistic, West-toxicated, and faithless (which it has done before and immediately after the Revolution). As a result of such misgivings, justified or not, neither side harbored a very high opinion of the other. This mutual intolerance resulted not merely from ignorance but from different views molded by different disciplines. Since each is valid in its own domain, it would be fruitless to consider replacing one with the other or unifying them without the requisite preparations. Let it not be said: "What is the difference? Both sides engage in study and research!" There is a qualitative difference between the activities of these two institutions: one, predicated on faith, requires obedient understanding; the other based on the spirit of science, requires not faith but criticism.

The other difference between the two institutions is the Hawzeh's access to power, and this is no trivial detail. After the revolution the clergy took over the nation's management and formulated its governing political theory (the guardianship of the jurisconsult), which requires a Hawzeh-trained clergyman with the rank of the grand jurisconsult to be the supreme leader of the country. Because we have a religious government, the ties of the Hawzeh to the centers of power are organic and profound, giving it the last word on matters of state. It is self-evident that the religious government entails the empowerment of the clergy and the Hawzeh; the religious disciplines actually empower those who possess them. The clergy become judges and occupy seats of power; representatives of the supreme jurisconsult [*Vali-e Faqih*][3] gain supremacy over the laity and are singularly sanctified without suffering the slings and arrows of media scrutiny that afflict everyone else.

The empowerment of the clergy (and in particular the jurisconsults) in religious governments is not a novel affair in our cultural history. The quarrel of some philosophers, mystics, and poets with the jurisconsults has not been merely academic but has been based on real differences of perspective on religious issues. But other challenges have abounded as well. The jurisconsults were the ones occupying the seats of power in society. Since the government was run by religious laws, those who knew these laws were entrusted with the reins of power. Theologians, philosophers, and historians were not in favor, nor did they have the prestige and wealth accorded to jurisconsults. The poverty of the former and the riches of the latter is an enduring theme of our critical literature. A great deal of literary rebuke has been heaped on the worldliness of the jurisconsults and their love of judicial and political power. Hafez has bitterly denounced both the jurisconsults and the Sufis who had forged alliances with the powerful: "Behold, the town Sufi gorges on many a dubious morsel / May the rump of this craving beast remain ample." This is a harsh verdict indeed. To eat dubious food[4] is the result of cultivating alliances with the powerful and of caring little about what is religiously proscribed or prescribed [*halal* or *haram*]. In the following, Hafez names some of the religious and government occupations: "I am no Judge, professor, picket or jurisconsult[5] / Why should I interfere with the drunkards' cult?" Even such prominent jurisconsults as Feiz Kashani, who was also an expert in historical attribution of holy traditions (*mohaddeth*) and a mystic (*'aref*) is equally outraged by the jurisconsults and monastic leaders:

> These jurisconsults who appear as brothers on the outside
> Are all foes of one another's faith, if you look inside.
> These monastic lords who do not harbor a scintilla of sincerity
> Rob the faith of each other's disciples out of envy and venality.

The Arab poet states: "Our judge is either blind or pretends to be lost / Stealing the holiday[6] as if it is the orphans' trust." The above depiction of those closely tied to power must serve us as sobering admonitory evidence: they demonstrate how a scholarly environment—religious or otherwise—with easy access to power can invite corruption and abuse. In Iran the religious seminaries did not exemplify this problem up until the revolution, but they do now. I do not claim that the graduates of regular universities do not find influential jobs or that they are barred from positions of power. But their situation is not comparable to that of the clergy, who interfere in any affair as deeply as they wish and practically run the country. A town's leader of the Friday Prayer [*imam jum'ah*] or a member of the clergy can make or break any major government project. The clergy [*rouhaniyyat*] has always been an organized party; now it is a party in power that has eliminated all of its rivals.

The third difference between the Hawzeh and the university is that the seminarians, dealing as they do with the common people and the public, prepare more than rarefied nourishment for the elite. They do not deal merely with students' scientific questions; they face the masses and are given the noble task of their edification. The requirements of addressing the masses are different from those of scholarly discourse.

One of the most important tasks of the Hawzeh is to train preachers who can give a speech or "go on the *menbar*."[7] They must be able to guide the people using simple and accessible language, fables, examples, and poems in order to convey moral commands, religious wisdom, and catechismic principles. There is now no faculty in the seminaries dedicated to the art of preaching even though this is one of the duties of the Hawzeh; this vocation falls to the talent and initiative of individuals. It would be preferable if suitable people were chosen and trained for discharging this task—but here I do not wish to address the problems of training public orators. Rather, I would like to stress the potential pitfalls of an educational institution aspiring to promote public speaking (which consists of influencing public opinion, often at the expense of rational discourse). Universities do not suffer from this problem since they do not promote populism and persuasion; they have not been asked to guide or maintain people's faith. The task of the university is to train specialists and to cut through scientific knots; their disciplines are immune to vulgarization.

Let us turn to the blights that beset the Hawzeh from the three sources discussed above. The first characteristic (the sacredness of one part of the Hawzeh's learning) is highly contagious: it can spread to other disciplines taught at the Hawzeh down to its language of instruction—Arabic. Since the Holy Qur'an and the Tradition harking back to the infallible ones are above questioning and critique, this aura of inviolability may gradually envelop the edicts of this theologian or that jurisconsult as well. In time, many of the mundane things are sacralized by association to the point that no one dares to question them. We occasionally witness this in our seminaries. Claims to the contrary notwithstanding, the gates of critical analysis are actually closed in many occasions. They are closed not only for the outsiders but also for the insiders of the Hawzeh who do not dare to challenge current or ruling opinions. We all remember the impassioned uproar over the publication of *The Eternal Martyr*.[8] The author was mercilessly battered for daring to challenge a popular view that had gained an undeserved patina of inviolability; they made an example out of him for all would-be reformers. The sacredness of the views of Majlesy,[9] which prevented Allameh Tabataba'i[10] from writing his exegesis on *Bihar al-Anwar*, is another instance of this contagion of sacredness. The least damage of this contagion is shielding scholarly views from independent examination and analysis. The ossification and decline of a scholarly institution, begin when the authorities in the field come to think of themselves as the guardians of an unexamined and unscrutinized heritage. Here, too, lies the origin of the discrediting in the eyes of the outsiders. I openly declare that most of the current theological views taught in the religious seminaries are unexamined and merely taken for granted. If the Hawzeh decides to clean house, we shall see that many of these views are open to revision. But this airing out can proceed only in an open atmosphere cleansed of pseudosacredness. The proper domain of the sacred is the divine; when stretched into the domain of human knowledge, it serves neither the human nor the divine.

One of the most important reasons for the resistance against my theory of "the hermenutical evolution and devolution of the religious knowledge" was the fact that it recognized religious knowledge as human and treated it as a humanly gained wisdom. The implication of this thesis is that the disciplines of the Hawzeh are as prone to criticism and skepticism (by the experts, of course) as are the rest of the sciences. This view is based on solid foundations and requires little elaboration. Yet this theory has caused a tempest beyond the confines of the academic debate. Because it refuses to consider mundane disciplines as sanctified and declares the equality of all of the sciences that have human origins. The unity between the Hawzeh and the university can not become a reality unless the former, recognizing the human and mundane origins of its scholarship, refrains from treating (in theory as well as in practice) merely human opinions as infallible, divine edicts. The union of the two institutions of higher learning will remain shallow and cosmetic as long as the Hawzeh clings to this exalted self-image. The essential condition for this unity is their mutual acknowledgment as equally human institutions that are equally susceptible to criticism. Merely human and fallible jurisconsults, clergymen, and theologians reside at the Hawzeh, not God, nor the Prophet, nor the blessed Imams. Whatever they produce is nonsacred human knowledge. The sacredness of the Qur'an and the Tradition do not rub off on the knowledge and erudition of the seminary scholars.

How can there be union as long as one resides in the heavens and the other on earth? The least precondition for friendship and alliance is equality and accessibility to each other. The sages have rightly observed that there can be no friendship between master and slave: Where there is no equality, there will be no friendship. A master may cast a benevolent glance in the direction of a slave out of pity, but he can never be his friend. True fellowship presupposes the resolution of the differences. It is the function of love and fellowship to raise the differences and to equalize: "Hail love's feast where / A king sits facing a beggar." People expect the Hawzeh to frankly admit the human nature of its learning and dismiss the insinuations that the residents of the Hawzeh are directly linked to God and his Prophet, that their contemplations are directly inspired by God, or that they share in the stature of His messengers.

Assuming a sacred and nonhuman origin for religious learning (presumably for preserving religion) on the one hand, and relying on rhetorical sermons to pander to the masses on the other, makes for an odd concoction, a repugnant, disquieting and dark picture of religion. If even rational arguments do not merit sacred stature, why should we endow it on mere sermons?

Sometimes the disciplines that are taught in the Hawzeh become sacred. Take, for example, Mr. Motahhari's charge against Iqbal Lahori[11] that the latter was steeped in Western and not Islamic philosophy. I accept this: Iqbal, educated in England and in Germany, had only a sketchy knowledge of Islamic philosophy. But despite taking the label of "Islamic" and claiming undue sacredness, what is taught in the religious seminaries under the rubric of Islamic philosophy is nothing but a variation of Greek philosophy and is but one among a dozen or so philosophies in this genre. It is neither the best nor the only possible philosophy. As a kind of human knowledge, Islamic philosophy, that has been borrowed and assimilated by Moslems, is to be respected but not worshipped.

Besides, we must ask whose philosophy is "Islamic"? That of Al-Farabi or Fakhr al-Din Razi or Sohrevardi or Mulla Rajab Ali Tabrizi? These authors, after all, espoused different philosophies. To regard Islamic philosophy as a unified entity is as misguided as regarding Western philosophy as a monolithic. There, too, we find that the views of Descartes, Hegel, Bergson, and Russell are as different as night and day, and yet they are all varieties of the same Western philosophy. The first harm of regarding Islamic philosophy as sacred is the neglect of other philosophies. It has been assumed that other philosophies, having been based on blasphemy, generate only blasphemous ideas, while the Islamic philosophy produces good Moslems. At the same time, within this Islamic culture there have been renowned scholars who denounce Islamic philosophy as blasphemous. I do not wish to enter the debate over whether Islamic philosophy helps or hurts the faith. I would rather ask, Why create such an uproar over a human-made science? Philosophy is, after all, philosophy: it has nothing to do with piety or impiety. Of course, it would be a different story if we were talking about theology (*kalam*) but, alas, these days it is not terribly in vogue in the Hawzeh. It is noteworthy that the philosophical debate that has gained a veneer of sacredness combats its opponents with such zeal as to label them "Satan." Mulla Sadra has dubbed his response to Ibn Kamouneh's critique "the stoning of the Satan—*rajmi Sheitan*." Philosophy is nothing other than a number of questions, answers, debates, and arguments. If both sides are equally versed in the discipline, why call each other names? This is how another problem is created: a simple question (*so'al*) can turn into a scandal (*shobheh*).[12]

Today *scandal* is a term for which no equivalent can be found in the culture of the university. It refers to a question raised by a young seminarian [*talabeh*] that appear to challenge orthodoxy. As soon as a question is dubbed a scandal, it loses its essence. While a true question prompts one toward research, the value judgments associated with a scandal—that is, a satanic question—calls forth suppression and concealment. By contrast, a question must be kept in mind and spread in order to stimulate further research. A society without questions is dead; a science without them is stunted. Any scientific institution which debars questions from crossing a certain threshold on pain of turning into scandals and which treats the carriers of such questions as disreputable and untrustworthy shall decline. A scholarly institution must foster critical intellectuals not mere scribes who memorize and repeat lessons. Such intellectual cowardice harms everyone.

The blight of an educational institution is transforming questions into scandals while its glory consists in encouraging its members to question—not in theory but in practice. Routine learning and innovative research are twin exercises: the victory of the former over the latter is a disease that must be prevented. Like dreaming, questioning is involuntary; it cannot be considered religiously allowed or disallowed (*halal* or *haram*). Rather, a question must be held dear as a guest (of the mind as well as of the scholarly community) and not simply dismissed. The essence of the unity of the Hawzeh and the university of which we shall speak below can be gleaned here: They must share a single method of dealing with questions.

The prestige and importance that has accrued to Arabic writing is another blight of the Hawzeh. Should a member of the university community decide to become familiarized with the Hawzeh, he or she shall encounter either forbidding Arabic texts—that conceal all the labor and toil that has been spent on them—or a simplistic book (written in Persian) for mass consumption. Serious scholarship is published in Arabic, yet our Hawzeh-taught Arabic is not current and has no appeal for Arabs. There is no justification for the Hawzeh's practice of teaching only Arabic texts and excluding Persian ones. Mr. Tabataba'i's Persian *Ravesh-e Realism* is surely more profound than his Arabic *Bedayat al-Hikmah*.[13] Yet only the latter is taught at the Hawzeh. Did Mr. Motahhari's reputation suffer because he wrote in Persian? Would the university professors' publications become more scientific if they wrote in English or French? Would this facilitate the relationship between the Hawzeh and university? The usual arguments—that legal texts are studied only by jurisconsults who are already familiar with Arabic or that ancient books in religious law [*fiq'h*] are in Arabic—do not justify continuation of publishing books in the areas of *fiq'h* and principles of jurisprudential logic [usul] in that language. As the lessons are conducted in Persian, the texts must also be written in that language. Persian is now testing its strength for carrying the load of modern sciences; it must also be retooled to bear the disciplines of the Hawzeh, including religious law (*fiq'h*), philosophy, jurisprudential principles [usul], and exegesis [*tafsir*]. If a book excels and is of use, it will be translated into other languages. Tending to our own people must take precedence over seeking the recognition of the others.

Now we must turn to the complications of mixing scholarship with power. I shall touch upon three main blights here. The Hawzeh is tempted to fill up the logical holes in its arguments by invoking power and finally becomes an apologist for power: by abandoning critical analysis of theories of government, by issuing edicts in favor of the political authorities, and by closing debate on politically sensitive areas. For instance, it would be a sure sign of impoverishment in the Hawzeh if pros and cons of the doctrine of guardianship of the jurisconsult (*velayat-e faqih*) are not allowed proper consideration. Do not say, "This power does not need to be limited because it is now wielded by the righteous rulers." This is true, and I have no qualms about their good intentions or their dedicated service, but I also know that as human beings they require critique, advice, and correction. The powerful are in a greater danger of slipping when they enjoy support of an intellectual and scholarly community; that simply rubber-stamps their deeds and suppresses critical impulse. Two incidents come to mind in this connection: the first is the criticism of the members of "the council of guardians" [*shoura-ye negahban*] for succumbing to political favoritism in the wake of the elections for the "assembly of the experts" [majles-e khebregan]. Some defended the council on the grounds that they are supposed to be just and thus above playing politics. This is an odd argument indeed. The just do not deliberately transgress, but they surely can err. They are just *people* not just angels! As human beings, they are capable of all manner of error. To say otherwise is an unjustifiable apologia for the powerful.

Another example is a recent critique of the central bank's policies authored by one of the scholars of the Hawzeh, Mr. Azari-e Ghomi, and published in the journal *Nour-e 'Elm*. The author calls the director of the central bank to the correct path of Islam and regards his experts as unqualified for the task of solving the economic problems of Islamic society. I am not concerned with the substance of this argument. But the very fact that this criticism came from a scholar at the Qum seminary is admirable. I wish we had more cases like this to show that the Hawzeh, far from kowtowing to political authorities, acts as an unyielding reformer and critic.

Now we come to the problem of populism, which is harmful both scientifically and morally. Those who do not practice what they preach become the subject of endless rebuke and ridicule because preachers have a special place in people's hearts. The slightest inconsistency between their words and deeds will cause disillusionment and deep distrust of religion. The clergy, who have become as prominent as the midday sun, can not assume to have the trust of the people if their public pontifications are undermined by private practices of a different sort.[14]

The lavish clerical attention to image and deportment and the proliferation of titles and honors are yet additional moral plagues. But the resulting damage to scholarship, also known as mass toxication (*'avam zadegi*) is, in the words of Martyr Motahhari, worse than being overrun by floods or stung by scorpions. This blight turns the potentially progressive clergy into a reactionary and conservative clique that considers any new idea as a scandal [*shobheh*] or a harmful innovation [*bid'ah*] and that denies the benefits of growth and progress. There is honor in siding with the people, but is there any in following them? I know that these words will displease some people who will incite others to oppose me. But in addressing these harsh realities, I only seek God's grace and speak out of heartfelt concern: why is the Hawzeh so insensitive to many unreliable or forged traditions, superstitious tales, and offensive banalities that are printed in books and uttered on the pulpit? What purpose do these serve except sustaining the superficial and superstitious religiosity of the masses? Why has the Hawzeh saved all of its irritability for a few compassionate observers who are attempting to abolish superstitions? What have they done about the scholarly annotating and editing of the books of the tradition (*hadith*) literature? A collected volume of these traditions in their present form would indeed make a most antireligious text.

I am not implying that the Hawzeh should alter the existing books without the permission of their authors. These books have historical value and must be preserved in their present form; after all, they reflect the traditional beliefs and activities of our people. If the contemporary Hawzeh does not share those beliefs, let it critique and revise them. Our scholarly predecessors have fulfilled their duty; why don't our contemporaries perform theirs? Could it be that attention to public sermons and the desire to win the approval of the masses has paralyzed them? Consider the case of *Mafatih al-Jinan*.[15] Can we find a single scholar in the Hawzeh who believes that a toothache is caused by a tiny worm that can be dislodged with prayer?[16] There is an abundance of this kind of absurdity in our books of *hadith*. The university community expects the Hawzeh to confront these issues. Why don't they candidly declare their stance with regard to the modern world, science, and morality? Why do they keep reprinting and reciting these traditions from the pulpits, only admitting that they are undocumented, dubious, and even concocted when confronted by critiques? Is it enough to analyze critically only the legal traditions [*revayat-e fiqhi*]? Are not moral and religious traditions in need of scrutiny as well? If someone has to criticize them, why don't the scholars of the Hawzeh take the first step? It will be more difficult to either deflect or admit the criticism if others preempt them.

In my address to a group of seminarians at the outset of the revolution, I said that we all agree that there are many problems in the texts taught at the Hawzeh. If you do not correct their mistakes, someone else will, leaving you on the horns of a dilemma. If you try to defend their errors, you will be hard put because you know that they are indefensible, and if you accede to the criticism, they will ask, "Why did not *you* point it out first?" For instance, I mentioned that the late Sadr al-Mote'allehin[17] expressed an improper opinion about women in his *Asfar-e Arbaʿeh*—which is not a religious book in the narrow sense of the word. The late Mulla Hadi Sabzevari[18] writes on the margins that the author has included women among beasts because they really belong in the genus of animals but that God has given them the appearance of human beings so men are not repelled and desire to have intercourse with them.[19] I respect the sage, but I have no respect for this statement. This book is currently studied and taught in our seminaries. I said to the seminarians: "If you do not criticize this argument, someone else will. This is not an Islamic or a religious idea, nor is it based on a Qur'anic verse or a *hadith*. It is not even humane; it is utter nonsense. Should we ignore and condone this sort of foolishness until it, too, shrouds itself in a veil of sacredness and defies criticism? Neither the texts nor the disciplines of the Hawzeh are sacred; all are subject to revision. The editing and annotation of ancient texts continues at the Hawzeh, but this does not extend to revision and criticism of the same texts. The uncorrected book is raw material; it is a historical artifact. But such a book must be subjected to revision and critique if religion is not to become a historical relic or a curiosity in a museum.

There is no such thing as a sacred book in any of the university disciplines. There are, of course, historical books of little scientific consequence that are edited and published for historical value. But in the university, we do not publish, teach, or recommend inaccurate and erroneous books as a matter of course. The unity in methods of critique could be one of the main common denominators between the university and the Hawzeh, heralding further comity: if the two institutions learn to deal with questions and disciplines in the same way, they would be able to correct each other's mistakes and complement each other. The unity of the university and the Hawzeh does not consist in adopting each other's curricula, or in a group of students becoming seminarians or vice versa. Of course all of these are desirable, but they amount to superficially grafting the two institutions; the true union can be realized only though their methodological unity.

Again, let me illustrate. Yesterday was "Women's Day," and we heard many public sermons through the media and from the pulpits on the exalted status of women and Islam's recognition of their glorious position and rights. But you all know that most of these are "rhetorical niceties," not arguments based on genuine research. Our seminaries must once and for all clarify their position regarding the rights and general image of women in the traditions [revayat] passed on by our authorities [mohaddethin]. These are the kind of traditions that no one dares to recite on the pulpit. A scholarly institution needs candid answers. To sweep things under the rug[20] may be a good practice in the world of politics but not in the world of scholarship. A cure must be found. The problem should be solved; it will not do to dissimulate and improvise.

Only when a scholarly institution is tainted by populist concerns does it exercise "discretion," lest the people lose their faith. It must be stated that the Hawzeh is not the custodian of people's faith; it is only responsible for teaching the religious canon and directives. The blight of any scholarly institution with populist interests is the lure of cosmetic and apologetic thinking. You can see this phenomenon in other countries as well. I recall a recent sermon that I attended in a New York church. It was so removed from the essence of Christianity and so nicely packaged in popular wrappings that with just a few adjustments it could have been delivered anywhere, including here in Iran. This sort of dilution appeals to the masses but repels serious religionists. Religion has a natural beauty; it does not need embellishment.

Let me also relate another story about the late Mr. Taleqani. At the outset of the revolution, a Cuban delegation came to visit him. Later the press quoted the spokesperson for the Mojahedin[21] to the effect that he introduced Islam in a way that the members of the delegation declared, "If this is Islam then we are all Moslems." One may think that it is a feat to present Islam in such a way, but this is nothing but cosmetics. Such a maneuver is beneath a spiritual scholar, even if it comes directly from the heart. I must also add that I have no confidence in the truth of this story and mention it only for heuristic reasons. In Rumi's words: "And if this passage is not that of Ptolemy / Then my response is not addressed to Ptolemy." It must also be added that for obvious reasons the expectations of the scholars of religion are much higher. One does not expect their level of purity and virtue from everyone. They are not supposed to "Advise people the world to denounce / While hoarding grains and silver for the nonce."

But I do not wish to leave the wrong impression. It is not as if we wish only to list the faults of the Hawzeh or to establish the superiority of the university. What we say is meant to bring these two revered institutions closer together and to find the roots of their differences. I have proposed that our Hawzeh has better access to power, is awash in persuasion and sermonizing, and believes in sacredness of the knowledge that it transmits. For better or worse, these characteristics are not typical of our universities. The two must be aware of their differences if they wish to discover each other.

The Hawzeh may consider taking the following practical steps: abandoning the habit of stealth and concealment in matters of religious knowledge; desisting from treating questions as scandalous; and refraining from expedient speech and action that subserves political power. It must also abstain from regarding human knowledge (i.e., their understanding of the holy scriptures) as superhuman. The Hawzeh must not replace demonstrative arguments with rhetoric. Abandoning religious cosmetics, it must renounce arbitrary selectiveness in the presentation of religion, which must be presented in a scholarly manner. The Hawzeh must represent the faith in deeds as well as words. What guarantees the unity of the university and the Hawzeh is their methodological unity. Let us pray for the realization of this auspicious unity. And peace be upon you.

12

Let Us Learn from History

Is it possible to learn from history? This question reminds us of the idea of historical laws and the attempts made to falsify or verify them. It may also prompt us to think of efforts made to arrive at generalizable laws that use history's lessons to guide current and future practices to help us seek beneficial results and avoid harmful ones. There is no denying the legitimacy of such an approach: The school of history does instruct, yet it must be emphasized that the above lessons are not the only ones to be discovered there. There are two other lessons that can be learned from history, lessons that are in no way less valuable than the usual feeble deductions and predictions.

A Lesson in Epistemology:
The Ahistorical View
of Traditional Philosophy

Let us recall how Aristotle and Descartes scorned the science of history, one ranking it below poetry and the other regarding it as indelibly tarnished by the fibs and fantasies of historians. Let us also recall that logicians did not deem history—along with geography, geology, and to some extent astronomy, which imparted the knowledge of particulars—as deserving of the name of "science," a title they reserved only for adducing general statements. Until recently history had no respectable status among the scholarly circles because it was deemed incapable of being taught or learned. Some were genuinely astonished by the appointment of Allameh Mohammad Ghazvini to the chair of history at the faculty of divinity at the University of Tehran, wondering if history—which was deemed to be the domain of either memory or imagination and certainly not reason—would need a teacher![1] Also note that in our religious seminaries, the historian is never esteemed nor is the science of history ever taught or valued. The path of Ibn Khaldoun has been forsaken.

Conversely, in the occident the tempest of history has, since the eighteenth century, caused such a bluster that even the deaf hermits of the secluded dens of science have taken note of it. Since that time the sciences of man have been renamed "historical sciences" and a new epistemological vista, namely, that of historical knowledge has been opened up. Hegel saw the being in toto as historical, Vico judged knowledge to be more akin to human action than to nature,[2] and Marx offered a historical interpretation of politics and economics. Existentialism, too, fused the flowing substance of humanity with history and pondered "the historical man." The fixed substances of the yore melted; they were molded by the palm of history into the forms of historical epochs. Everything was branded by the stamp of a historical chapter, and time became one of the constituents of the substance of things. The scholars sat by the flowing brook of history and beheld the course of nature.[3] Thus did history and its philosophy gain such an exalted stature.

The science of history was also transformed by epistemological investigations. Eminent historians emerged who meticulously analyzed and scrutinized the methodology of history. The consensus of thinking in the last two centuries regarding the study of human action and historical knowledge calls for reexamining and revising the conditions set forth by traditional scholarship for the discovery and validation of knowledge—namely, impartiality, conforming to reality, and discovery of essences.

Recent historians have said that "all history is contemporary history"[4] or that "the history of each event must be written one hundred years after its occurrence."[5] This means that events become historical only after a certain period, or it could mean that "the final history of an era can never be written,"[6] confirming the view that "history is a blend of science, art, and myth."[7] In other words, we can have as many histories as historians: "History is what goes on in the mind of the historian."[8] Despite all the differences in the above citations, they all agree that history is the kind of science that varies with the scientist. Although this viewpoint was steadily gaining ground among historians and appeared more self-evident than ever, it was nonetheless a difficult idea to embrace.

For centuries, public opinion had been wedded to the conviction that the subject should be attuned to the object, not vice versa. If science were to follow the whims and vanities of the scientists instead of reflecting reality, it would be no more than a mirror of their fantasies and opinions. No, science would neither yield to caprice nor depend on a fallible mortal. Science was supposed to consist of objective truths revealed to a scientist. Otherwise, how could one separate science from myth, and truth from falsehood? How could a single truth vary with the persona of each of its seekers? How could a unitary thing abide in multiple incarnations? How could there be "middles" (i.e., stages and gradations) between two contradictory statements? The traditional view conceded that humankind can attain knowledge but that knowledge could not become "human": the truth is revealed to mankind, but it does not become their handmaiden. This way of thinking prevailed in the natural and physical sciences as well. No one thought that the earth or the sun could have multiple substances and realities, to be randomly discovered by people. No one decreed: let time pass so that the sun can reveal its true developing nature. In the same vein the ancient philosophers did not propose a historical method for understanding the allegedly unfolding nature of water, man, or fire. Hence, they did not entrust the definitions of these entities to the vicissitudes of history.

Kant, who was awakened of his dogmatic slumber by Hume, recognized the human character of our knowledge, rightly acquiring the title Father of Modern Epistemology. His main contention was that knowledge always bears the stamp of humanity. For Kant, it is an impossible dream to vanish in the embrace of the naked truth as if there were no knowing subject to capture the truth in the first place. In his view, knowledge is relative, but only in relation to the world of humanity, not in relation to this or that knowing subject.

The delicacy and complexity of Kant's arguments made them inaccessible to most people—including many scholars. Although his was a great breakthrough in philosophy, nonphilosophers did not feel its impact. The science of history had a major role in demonstrating Kant's intricate theory. Unaware of vehement philosophical and scholarly arguments, historians were one by one uncovering the unique properties of the science of history, without recognizing the far-reaching and earth-shattering implications of their own discoveries. Most significantly, the new views about the nature of historical knowledge were constantly confirmed in reality. All the assorted historical books written about the same era and the multitude of judgments rendered about the reality and realization of the same historical event affirmed the same point: historical understanding has not—and will never—reach culmination. A historical event will forever remain alive and fresh; its case is never closed. Historians never tire of investigating an era; no historical book quenches our thirst for another. Historical knowledge is born in the context of history: as the events develop in history, our understanding of them also develops. The definitive history of an era can not be written in any time; indeed, the farther we get from an event, the closer we seem to have come to its essence. Historians are forced to look at historical events from the standpoint of their own place in history. Thus historical knowledge is shaped like a stairway with infinite steps. Hence, all history is contemporary history.

On the other hand, historical books proved that historians are not indiscriminately interested in all events. This clearly underlined the role of the historian in history and the dependence of science on the scientist. The salience of this issue becomes evident when we realize that a series of events impart a meaning that can not be conveyed by the individual events. In other words, the constellation of events is as important as the individual events themselves. How could events tell us to what constellation of events they belong? Is it not the case that this task belongs to the historian? The determination of this relation is the very core of our understanding of a historical event. For instance, when we state that an event influenced the development and consummation of the Iranian Constitutional Revolution (1905), we mean that the event belongs to a series of events that influenced that revolution. It is through determining this relationship among the component events that we can rest assured that we have understood a historical development. So the art of the historian consists in lining up the events, selecting the building materials, erecting the elegant palace of history, and attending to its repair and renovation.

All of this illustrates the merging of art and science, and the acknowledgment of the legitimacy of the sciences of particulars. We thus realize that in this arena, besides discovery and description, invention and design also have a role to play. More importantly, previous understandings of an event are integrated into the history of the event itself and become one of the sources for the future understandings of it. In other words, the historical impact of an event affects not only the objective world but the subjective one as well. Future historians will investigate not only the actual consequences of an event, but also its intellectual and epistemic repercussions. This is why the disinterested and unbiased historians—with no philosophical ax to grind—bear witness to the cumulative nature of the historical knowledge. They call on the epistemologists to look into all kinds of human knowledge and to reexamine their knowledge of knowing.

The earlier, simplistic view that those closest to an event know it better has now been supplanted by a more refined theory: each group looks at an event from its own viewpoint—which immanently defines the limits of what it knows. No standpoint is inherently superior to any other. Each event creates waves—like ripples of a pebble in a pond—that widen into history and fade into eternity. Each generation receives the wave at a different distance from the point of origin and in a different pitch; each reconstructs a new picture of the original event. These pictures are infinitely numerous. The events themselves are not available for understanding as long as they are not flowing, that is as long as they are not historicized. The more they flow, the more they will grow and come to the foreground. There is no limit to the growth of this understanding.

In the realm of history, ancestors are always defined by their progeny. This retrospective glance clearly signifies the endlessness of historical understanding and the multiplicity of historical discoveries of the same event. In other words, history is rediscovered by each generation, and each time it demands a fresh "real" meaning. There is no doubt that Napoleon did not understand the true impact of his campaigns as well as we do today. This is because the waves of his feats have now expanded and whispered new mysteries in the ears of the historians. Hence the future historians will be in a better position to make new discoveries about the present.

The multitude and variety of human action in history and the gradual and self-unfolding quality of historical knowledge can scarcely be encountered in any other discipline. In its attempt to know such elements as earth, water, acid, base, blood, flesh, wood, light, and so on, the Aristotelian scientist claims to possess the totality of what can and must be studied. Thus such a scientist will dispassionately and ruthlessly ransack the object under study, pulling apart its wrap and woof to gain immediate knowledge of its nature. The science of nature conceals and obscures the position of the scientist. In this realm the activity of delineating the limits and defining the genus, species, properties, and characteristics of things gives one an immediate sense of control and victory over the object. But in the realm of history, we face the exact opposite of this. Here mastery and command come in a gradual and piecemeal manner, not quickly and instantly. Once the science of history awakens us from the trance of scientific pride and teaches us how to approach knowing and learning, we shall forever change our views about the nature of human knowledge.

Such is the noble role of a modest science like history: despite its humility and incompleteness, it generously lavishes many novel and precious insights upon the philosophers. From now on, we must think of knowledge not as a snapshot of an object that we take once and for all, but as a pond that we constantly replenish with new knowledge or a plant that we irrigate and nourish with new data. Even more importantly, we realize that in addition to human action, other things can also become the subject of historical portrayals whose gradual evolution invites our gaze and evokes our sense of familiarity. All the molds and limits must become fluid in the tumultuous flow of history; no science must be branded with the seal of culmination. We must look at everything and every happening as though it is a merchant who has not yet offered his entire stock to the marketplace of knowledge. Only in a bazaar as long as history and as wide as geography, with its endless transactions, can the wealth and wits of this merchant be judged.

It must be added that the preceding does not necessarily clash with the philosophical belief that things in themselves have substances and limits. It must also be mentioned that our argument is not akin to Hegel's view that history is an independent entity and that it is the stage upon which the Absolute Idea unfolds. For one thing, our discourse concerns the discovery of the nature of things (not their objective nature) which, as we argued earlier, occurs gradually. For another, the appeal of Hegel's view is due to its affinity with the epistemological insight explained in this treatise, not vice versa. Our view does not require imagining history as a singular person with different modes of behavior. Rather the heart of our case is to argue for the existence of a knowledge—or in Dilthey's parlance, a reason, known as "historical reason"—which could be used to enrich our pure as well as practical philosophy [*hekmat*].

A Lesson in Philosophical Anthropology

The trouble with understanding human beings is that particular individuals take the color of their surroundings, making it impossible to know their true colors. Human beings can go astray, deviate and forsake the path of humanity. It is obvious that studying an aberrant human being will not yield the knowledge of the authentic, natural, and pure subject. Philosophically speaking, the "Natural Man" can never be found: all human beings come under perverse pressures. It is obvious that studying the perverse man can not produce the knowledge of the natural and free subject.

Those who have argued that humanity is a vessel that is filled with social influences or a letter that finds meaning only in the context of a word and a sentence (i.e., society) have come face to face with the daunting nature of this problem. They have consequently preferred the examination of collectivity to that of the individual and of perversity to that of nature. Adhering to the adage: "All the game is in the belly of the wild ass," they have decreed, "know the society and you shall know the individual." It is not easy to resist this position. Where can we find the pure man, unadulterated by collective influences and untouched by perverse forces, the one who remains true to and reflects the pristine nature of humanity? The dust that has been raised in this path obscures the vision. While we cannot hope to have access to the pure essence of humanity, history allows us a brief glance. We know that the environment puts obstacles in the way of knowing humanity ever perverting it and insinuating into it all kinds of alien elements. Since people always accept the cast of their culture, it is impossible to know what they would be like had they not taken its shape.

The above problem, which makes understanding the pristine nature of an individual impossible, does not arise if the subject of study is humanity per se. Here the desired situation naturally obtains; history does not have an external Other. No external hand can be said to distort and pervert it. War can be imposed on a nation, but no war or dispute can be imposed on history as a whole. This is true even in the divine conception of history, where God's action is realized only through the essence and volition of his creatures, and where the telos of His design and beneficence leads all creatures to their respective ends. Thus the whole of humankind has moved in a direction akin to its nature. In other words, this movement has not been violent, but natural. It is impossible to say that history has gone astray. One can not regret the direction it has taken nor regard it as deviant, deplorable, or avoidable. Even if we argue that every individual has been under the strain of cultural determination and perversion, we must still admit that these forces constitute the very nature of society and history. In other words, such restrictions, limitations, distortions, and inculcations constitute the ineluctable condition of human social existence. By the same token, although each and every particle in the world of nature is under the violent influence of gravity, the gravity itself is in the very nature of the physical universe. So human beings have existed and lived in the flow of history according to the requirements of their nature; what has happened in history has been natural, not artificial. No cause, save the humanity of human beings, has propelled historical events. Nor has the interventionist hand of an external force ever encroached upon the realm of history. By contrast, when we judge a single individual, the possibility of perversion, aberrant growth, external influences, reprehensible action, and the alteration of behavior because of changes in the environment can be entertained.

Contention is a natural feature of human societies. This is not to imply that it is essential to the nature of history as this treatise does not posit a "nature" for history. Discord originates only in the structure of human beings and nowhere else. It would be absurd to think that conflict has been injected into society from some outside source, for there is no "outside" for human society as such. If this is true, then it follows that the historical arena presents a pristine natural stage for the examination of human nature.

Humanity has nowhere expressed itself as well as it has in history. There is a clear answer to the question, Why have human societies engendered war, inequity, apostasy, and sin, as well as science, worship, art, and competition? The progenitor of all these goods and evils is the nature of human life in society. Whenever human beings congregate, these phenomena emerge. A human history devoid of science or apostasy can not be manufactured anywhere, unless human beings cease to be human beings as we know them.

We must warn against the false belief that human history could have been more or less virtuous than it has turned out to be. If we believe the latter view, then we must explain why history did not traverse the alternative path. The truth is that there is no intervening agent outside history. Thus the road that is traversed is by and large the only one possible; no other drastically different way could have been taken even if history could repeat itself a thousand times. At the dawn of creation, the angels accurately divined that human society could not avoid depravity and bloodshed.[9] Nor did God fault them for this judgment advising them only that their knowledge was incomplete. Hafez restated the protestation of the angels but with humility and infinite charm:

How can we not lose our way amidst harvests of creed
When Adam was led astray by a single seed![10]
There is no escape from blasphemy in love's bower,
In absence of "Bu Lahab," whom would the hell devour?[11]
Where the Chosen Adam was struck by the thunderbolt of impudence,
How would it behoove us to profess our innocence?

In short, the countenance of humanity does not appear in the mirror of history as fair or flawless. Our definitions of humanity need to be soberly and somberly reexamined in view of the amount of greed, cruelty, wickedness, and ingratitude that humans have caused—all of which they have done willingly and in accordance to their nature, not because they have been coerced or perverted. While selfishness pervades every corner of our minds, when the time comes for self-regard, we chose as our main attribute the delusive "yearning for perfection." We do not trouble ourselves to question where and when this desire for perfection has demonstrated itself. We then try to evade the questions that this idealistic position begs by suggesting that human beings desire the good and a state of perfection but are often mistaken in identifying their instances. This would lead to the untenable position that all tyrannical, hypocritical, and wicked people have sought their own perfection in inequity, duplicity, and depravity. If this is the case, would it not be better to identify humankind as a "mistake-making" instead of a "perfection-seeking" race?[12] Indeed, we must think about why human beings make so many mistakes and about the source of this pandemic of errors, which seems to be even more firmly rooted in our nature than the instinct for seeking perfection.

We must learn from history and study rather than worship humankind. Humanity is what shows up in history, and if it were something else, it would have a different history. Let us not say that evil does not exist, when what we mean is that it ought not exist. There is an unbridgeable abyss between "does not" and "ought not." It is true that we do not relish seeing humans as tyrannical, unappreciative, unjust, and foolish and that we hope they will not be so. Yet we must recognize these defects as part of human nature. Iniquity must be recognized as a natural and permanent part of human nature and not as an erasable or incidental facet of it.

The Heuristic Value of Historical Evil

The rubbish and sewage of the cities inform us of the civilized lifestyle. These pollutions are natural and common; human life itself generates them. Refuse is a problem that must not be wished away but acknowledged and handled. This acknowledgment is necessary for understanding human life on earth. By the same token, medical and biological scientists can not avoid the study of blood, urine, etc. They do not portray the ideal man as one who is above eating or defecating. Depravities and obscenities can function as valuable methodic guides. Decadence is necessary for learning about decency; the morally reprehensible trait may turn out to be methodically desirable. Jokes, dreams, and sexual perversions—which for centuries were ignored or merely cursed and damned—have provided psychotherapists with insights into the depths of the human psyche.

Those who seek a list of man's original natural inclinations (*fetriyat*) need look no further than history, which is the best manifestation of the natural and free man. Let them not worship at the alter of humankind but observe what this bipedal beast has freely wrought with his/her two hands. Let them change themselves rather than changing the meaning of history; let them familiarize themselves with the secret of the revealed inspiration that describes man as impatient [*halo ʿ*], niggardly [*jazo ʿ*],[13] restless [*ʿajoul*],[14] unjust [*zalum*], foolish [*jahoul*],[15] and ungrateful [*kafour*].[16]

Let us remember that Satan has been granted leave to beguile.[17] Flowing like blood in the arteries of the progeny of Adam, he is eager to seduce and mislead.[18] His existence does not narrow the dominion of God; on the contrary, he is one of His custodians. God is just, but justice does not limit His domain or restrict His dominion. He is resolute [*jabbar*], but this resoluteness does not diminish His goodness. Since God has not created the world of humanity without Satan, we must not describe it as though it is devoid of evil and afflictions. Humans are companions of Satan; few are the saints who have subjugated the devil by their bare hands.[19]

Social Policy and the Insights of the Modern Philosophical Anthropology

The history of mankind is not peopled nor built up by the ideal men but by real ones who have never been innocent of apostasy [*kufr*] and immorality. Maybe the humans who determined the course of history have not been (or done) all they should have, but it can not be denied that they have expressed themselves in the way they have lived and have lived out what they were about. Through being and living, they have exercised and thus expressed the very essence of their existence. So why must we set aside humanity's ignored and ignoble qualities in our effort to understand them? We must peek through these chinks in order to discover the truth about the actual as well as the natural man. Insights garnered in this way are of particular interest to students of education and politics. The first lesson that results from this examination, and which must command the attention of political leaders and social managers, is tolerance. The lesson is that Satan is ever-present on the stage; sin has a serious standing; a little abnormality is normal; and a bit of chaos is in order. Government must be based on real human beings and practical wisdom; it must not be wasted on impossible tasks. One must not resolve to root out what cannot be uprooted nor confuse what ought not to exist with what does not exist. Only in this case would the expectations—and following them, the complaints—diminish.

The knowledge of real human beings will rectify and temper our expectations. We will no longer tear our hair out upon viewing the slightest error and aberration nor give into indignation. We will not despairingly wonder: Why people are not the way they ought to be? From now on, we will regulate our relations with human beings as they are, knowing that the existing state of affairs is more or less the best that they can manage. We shall then live in a world owned by its inhabitants and talk about them as the only possible earthly human creatures. We will no longer think that the world should have been inhabited by angels or ideal humans. The world belongs to us as we are, not to paragons of perfection, platonic ideals, and angels. We must not complain that because people are bad, collective hopes go unrealized nor fantasize that heaven on earth would be established only if an improved crop of human beings could replace the existing inferior one.

We have to limit our expectations to the contours of the actual humanity and tailor our outfits to its actual measurements. Otherwise, we will resemble the proverbial tailor who botched the dress and blamed it on the client's unfit body: "Oh, how you would marvel at my art if only you had the proper body!" If we learn the proper lesson from history, tolerance and mercy shall replace rigidity and hostility. Only then will noble realism replace ignoble superstition; only then will the rights and duties of humans be determined in accordance with their abilities. They would then be looked upon as complete human beings, not as incomplete angels or substandard humans. The definition of humans as fallible and susceptible to sin—as creatures who do not vitiate their nature by being so—is most constructive for pedagogues, leaders, and managers of society. This definition portrays reality as it is and encourages leaders to face the real profile of humanity.

It suffices to examine the horrid record of certain leftist movements that laid their foundation on idealism and ended up with hostility and cannibalism. They replaced the totality of history—where they could have learned lessons about the nature of humanity—for a pleasant dreamworld inhabited by imaginary human beings. Hence, they erected a system that aimed at erasing the indelible. Because of this, it will not take long before societies based on this delusion will join the legends of the vanished societies of the past.[20] To adore the goals and abhor the means arises from ignorance about humanity and from refusal to learn from history. In the words of Roudaky: "He who refuses to learn from the Time's flow / Shall never learn a teacher's lessons nor grow."

The Divine Prophets
and Human Nature

God's prophets mirrored His benevolence.[21] They resolved to consummate their mission while resigning themselves to the fact that they could not save everybody.[22] Convinced of the ineradicability of strife in human societies,[23] they were serene and untouched by sorrow in the face of the unbelievers' obstinacy.[24] They refused to consider themselves captains of history and culture or to impose their views in matters of faith. They were willing to see all nations as equally captivated and fascinated by Satan as well as by their own customs.[25] They spoke the truth and exposed the falsehood in order to discharge their divine duties and attain bliss in the hereafter. They did not set out to survive or win or wipe out ignorance, iniquity, and evil.[26]

These all signify the prophets' perfect realism, their insight into human nature, and their divinely inspired inner peace. Indeed, the prophets' divine certitude and their realistic knowledge of human nature resulted in their forbearance, equanimity, magnanimity,[27] steadfastness, and freedom from misgivings and remorse.[28]

The prophets came to forewarn and bring good news; none of them professed to have been appointed to obliterate evil and iniquity fully. They knew well that they had not come to denature this world and its inhabitants. The Almighty had taught them that the wicked can never disrupt or preempt the divine order.[29] Because the world is a laboratory designed to measure the forbearance of human subjects, it shall never be devoid of wickedness.[30] Let us follow the example of the prophets, who did not confuse petitioning, prudence, diplomacy, proselytizing, reform, and edification with malevolence, malice, cruelty, despair, and haste. Let us follow them by not squandering our wits on pointless pursuits.

We deal with nothing but actual humans in an actual world. Let us cut our coat according to our cloth, judiciously withdrawing into the confines of this world's means and skillfully wielding our crafts within its limits. Here modesty should be our principle, for extravagance is the same as assuming partners for God (*shirk*) and the most egregious of all depravities.[31] The preceding arguments have been stated rather bluntly and can be readily misunderstood. Hence I will attempt a recapitulation.

First, history is the most natural stage on which humankind has expressed itself. Hence, it is the best means for knowing it. On this stage, human beings have not hidden altered or exaggerated their true nature. They have not been forced to sway from their inner nature. Thus they have left in their historical wake obvious hints about their nature for the benefit of posterity.

Second, an unbridgeable gap separates the two categories of "does not exist—or the nonexistent" and "ought not to exist—or the reprehensible." What is considered evil in the world of morality may be valuable as an instrument for the methodical study of human nature. When we say things like, "sin is bad, injustice is abhorrent, fraud is harmful, lying is futile, or discrimination must be eliminated," we must not think that studying these actions are dangerous for the human sciences as well. For the students of human nature, all of these are good, useful, and helpful. While the manifestations of good and evil signify the noble and ignoble aspects of human nature for the moralists, the students of humanity interpret them as keys to the nature of humanity. Thus studying these can not be considered objectionable. It is true that vices will not benefit us in the hereafter, but their study will prove useful in uncovering the nature of humanity. The flames of emotions, fervor, applause, and censure are extinguished at the threshold of the temple of science.

It must be added that our emphasis on the importance of studying evil is due to the fact that it has been long ignored. Hatred of evil has led to neglecting its value as evidence. Therefore, in emphasizing the importance of examining evil, we insist equally on the value of investigating the good.

Third, there is an essential difference between our arguments and those of the fatalistic and deterministic school. Our views are in no way based on the assumption that history unfolds according to a predestined plan. History is made out of human choice, which emanates from human nature. Only in this sense is history "natural": it reveals the nature of humanity. There is no trace of Hegel's "cunning of reason" in our understanding of history. One hundred percent of what transpires in history is caused by human volition, not a predetermined plan. The free action of humanity is the very core and domain of history. History is human, humanity is not "historical" in the Hegelian sense of the term.

Fourth, the lesson we learn from history imparts a kind of rational certitude and insight into divine providence. This can not help bringing in its wake a certain amount of inner peace. But, of course, we can not use history for deducing guidelines for action. The history of humanity can neither instruct us about the evils of tyranny nor exhort us to fight it. Deviations and depravities are useful in describing human nature but are not thereby excused. After all, the universal abhorrence of sin, even prevalent sin, is a historical reality. We cannot turn our backs on values in the name of historical anthropology because they, too, constitute a ubiquitous reality within history. Here "moral realism" is the main doctrine. In order to act correctly in any field, we must know it well. By the same token, detailed and correct knowledge of the possibilities of humanity is necessary for adjusting our expectations. The best way to gain such knowledge is to look at human beings unadorned, the way they appear in history.

A realistic view of humanity will stop the proliferation of impossible injunctions and bridle the arrogance that inspires the wish for unrealizable and dangerous goals. It exposes the folly of idealism and thus tempers our expectations and quells our righteous indignation. How different are the experiences of two travelers in a thorny terrain: one knows it for what it is, and the other blunders in, expecting a flower garden. The phantom flowers sting more painfully than the real thorns!

The idealists are ever unsatisfied. Wailing in disappointment, impatience, despair, grief, fear, niggling, taunting, and megalomania, all result from lacking a historical perspective and from living in the company of imaginary humans. By contrast, a realistic view of humanity yields steadfastness, benevolence, humility, tolerance, resolve, and courage. The ruins of history are laden with the treasure troves of wisdom and sagacity. Educators, politicians, and economists must build their schema for real, not imaginary, humans. A realistic anthropology does not say what must be done. Rather it warns about what must be avoided.

Fifth, a historically informed philosophical anthropology studies the collectivity rather than the individual; it enters the abode of the individual by passing through the vestibule of society. The cognoscenti of this field will not regard this method as a turn toward methodological holism at the expense of methodological individualism or vise versa. Our view is consistent with both approaches. In other words, the assumption that the knowledge of the whole is prior to that of the individual or vice versa belongs to the realm of epistemology and methodology. In contrast, the discussion of factitiousness or the reality of being belongs to ontology. These are autonomous spheres. One does not determine the other, that is, one thing can existentially precede another while depending on it epistemologically. According to Avecina the science of metaphysics [*ma baʿd al-tabiʿah*] must be renamed "prephysics" [*ma qabl al-tabiʿah*]. The abstract entities, and above all the supreme God ("the Necessary Being," or *Wajib al-Wojoud*) are existentially prior to natural creatures. Yet knowledge of them becomes possible only after achieving familiarity with nature, and this is why such knowledge is called "metaphysics."

While in reality cause precedes effect, the knowledge of the effect may come before—and could be used as a preamble to—the knowledge of the cause. From this, it can be deduced that we can behold the reflection of the individual only in the mirror of collectivity. Only in history can we observe the natural growth of humanity. Thus we shall not attain knowledge of humanity as long as we avoid history. Disdaining history can only lead to the deepening darkness of delusions.

Sixth, history is littered with dissimilar shells that hold the same content. Historians attempt to break through these shells. Only in this sense can we learn about the essential requirements of human life. The molds and forms are transient, but the essences remain the same. Whatever human beings do in the future will remain in history: they are history. This history will be the necessary manifestation of humanity: nothing will happen that is beyond the pale of humanity or that is devoid of the contents of human history.

Through its actions, humanity has already defined the boundaries of its capabilities; it has thus adumbrated the future of humanity. As the world of our future is susceptible to strife, sin, blasphemy, poverty, injustice, affliction, falsehood, sickness, greed, and discrimination; it is also open to efforts aimed at alleviating or reversing these adversities through novel scientific, practical, and political means, as well as through ways yet to be discovered. Disorder and iniquity belong to history as much as order, reform, and relief. Like day and night, these polar opposites braid the same reality. The enlightened views of evil impart wisdom, certitude, and equanimity. The unenlightened ones reap nothing but depression and discord.

Seventh, a caveat is in order lest the degenerate and the depraved presume that this treatise intends to excuse their sinfulness. Here our intended audience consists of teachers, social planners, and managers. We hope that they candidly view actual humanity as it is and moderate their expectations accordingly. This treatise does in no way put the seal of approval on the wickedness of the wicked, nor does it absolve or forgive them their transgressions. Of course, humankind is susceptible to error. In other words, only humankind (in distinction to inanimate objects or animals) is in a position to err. But, first, this is a volitional act. Second, a wrong act is, after all, wrong and no explanation can make it right. Third, to avoid error is every bit as human as giving in to it. Every soul is duty-bound to avoid sin, although by experience we know that humanity as a whole shall never be without sin. This realization does not alter anyone's duty. It only improves the insight and ability of those in the business of understanding.

> If the complete acquires dirt, it turns into gold
> The incomplete acquires gold and turns into mold!
> One eats to become sheer divine light
> The other, to foment greed and envious blight.[32]

Notes

Introduction

1. We borrow these concepts from Max Weber's sociology of religion, preserving the original meanings. For Weber, emissary prophecy signified the mainly (but not exclusively) Western tradition of salvation-religions, aiming at saving the masses of people. Exemplary prophecy implied setting an example of salvation for the emancipation of religiously inclined virtuosos.

2. Mongol Bayat's work *Iran's First Revolution* explores the Transcaucasian and Azeri roots of Iran's turn-of-the-century intellectuality.

3. The twentieth-century incarnation of this agenda could be traced in the revivalism of Seyyed Qotb, Abol ʿAlaʾ Mowdudi, and others.

4. In his *The Last Intellectuals*, Russell Jacoby offers an evocative explanation of this phenomenon.

5. As Soroush recounts in our interview in this volume, he returned to Iran at the outset of the revolution and was immediately recognized as an exceptional talent. One could count many important ayatollahs among the admirers of his works. He found his immediate mission in engaging the most vociferous ideological challengers of the revolution, that is, the Marxists. These ranged from the pro-Soviet Marxist Toudeh Party to the proponents of other fashionable varieties of Maoist ideology, imported ironically by the Iranian leftist students who had returned from Europe and the United States. He succeeded in vanquishing these adversaries in a series of debates broadcast on national television and published in newspapers.

6. Universities had become arenas for physical confrontations among various political groups, many of whom were seen as counterrevolutionary. Some of these groups were known to use their offices as ammunition depots. This provided the government with the excuse to close down the universities pending a "cultural revolution." Fortunately this was of shorter duration than its Chinese namesake. ʿAbdolkarim Soroush was appointed to the Advisory Council on the

Cultural Revolution, which was charged with "cleansing the universities" of non-Islamic elements and then reopening them. During this period many professors were expelled from their jobs. Although Soroush resigned from this committee after a while, some of his critics consider this period to be a blemish on his reputation. (See the interview with Soroush in chapter 1 of this volume.)

7. Soroush is unique because he has combined traditional Islamic learning in law and philosophy with a mastery of physical science (pharmacology) and cultural science (especially philosophy of science). Other lay intellectuals have also straddled the two fields, but without exception they have been dilettantes in scholastic Islam. This had caused even the best-intentioned among them to be castigated by the scholastically trained clergy as shallow. The dismissive term used by the seminarians for such lay intellectuals has been "well read" (*ba motale'eh!*). Soroush's extraordinary memory and prodigious talents have allowed him to complete not only a two-tiered education but also to attain command of Persian literature, especially its mystical poetry. His own recent corrected edition of Rumi is considered to be one of the most authoritative in Iran.

8. This group is comprised of the above-mentioned rejectionist and reflexive revivalists. We will not concern ourselves with the nationalist and Marxist intellectuals here (except insofar as they qualify as radical laical modernists), not because they are of little intellectual interest, which is certainly not the case, but rather because they have not proven historically significant. The secular intellectuality of Iran, however, remains quite alive and vibrant.

9. In 1953 the CIA engineered a coup d'état that brought the Shah back after he had been sent into exile by the popular prime minister Mohammad Mosaddeq.

10. Soroush gave several lectures about Bazargan after his death, praising him as a forerunner of Islamic reform.

11. See his essay "What the University Expects from the Hawzeh," in this volume.

12. Qur'an, 1:30.

13. The Persian word *haq* connotes metaphysical truth or rightness, as well as civil and legal rights.

14. *Los Angeles Times* (January 1995) and *Journal of Democracy* (January 1996).

15. Nor is this manner of borrowing among civilizations a one-way street. It is impossible to study the formation of any civilization, least of all that of the West, in isolation from the direct and indirect influences of other civilizations.

16. This usage is in line with both Max Weber's lifelong project of explaining the roots of modern capitalism and with the work of his interpreters, including Talcott Parsons and Niklas Luhmann.

17. There are, of course, a few sociologists who harken back to the founders' predilections. Bryan S. Turner's unabashed defense of a materialist view of religion is a case in point.

18. Bell calls the first stage "secularization" and the second "profanation." Berger calls the first stage "objective secularization" and the second stage "subjective secularization."

19. One of the ways the contemporary sociology of religion explains the longevity of religion is through revising its founders' "holistic" view of society. Demise of religion in a particular sphere of life, say politics, does affect all the other spheres with equal force.

20. Max Weber argued that early Judaism, Christianity, and Islam all engaged in demagification of the world. To the extent that they deprived the masses of the intervention of numerous local deities, they could be said to have secularized the world, so there would be no interceding power left between man and God. Harvey Cox and others have argued that modern secularization is part of the essential mission of Christianity.

21. Martin Marty (1969) provides an example of this heterogeneity of the phenomenon by distinguishing three paths of secularization: utter secularization (France), mere secularization (Britain), and controlled secularization (the United States).

22. Andrew Greely (1996) has reported that based on a meta-analysis of surveys conducted since World War II—contrary to those who suggest that the United States is less religious than in the past and despite some decline in variables such as the literal interpretation of the Bible and attendance in mainline Protestant churches—most indicators of religious involvement have remained constant. These results lead to theories of "neosecularization" and "postsecularization" (*yamane*) positing that secularization means not the decline of religion but the declining scope of religious authority at the individual, organizational, and societal levels. There has even been suggestions of the "resacralization" (West, 1969) and "re-enchantment" (Goldstein, 1990) of the world.

23. Daniel Bell's definition of religion in *The Winding Passage* (1980).

24. The Western reader of some of Soroush's writings, including his article "The Sense and Essence of Secularism," in this volume, would be struck by the categorical tone of his argument on Western secularism. Soroush is, after all, an outsider, an "Occidentalist" philosopher, not a sociologist. The Western reader should bear in mind that Soroush's position is important, not because it is original—for the most part, it is not—but because it represents a native synthesis of the Western political philosophy with traditional Islamic precepts; and that it is articulated by an Islamic thinker with a growing and enthusiastic native audience.

25. Robert Bellah's borrowing from the Japanese antimodern movement, in his *Beyond Belief* (1970).

Chapter 1

1. Soroush was accepted in the school of pharmacology in the prestigious University of Tehran, from which he graduated after six years with a doctoral degree. [Ed.]

2. The book, *Usul-e Falsafeh va Ravesh-e Rea'lism*, is not translated into English. [Ed.]

3. A quote from a verse by Naser Khosrow Ghobadiyani, the great Iranian Isma'ili thinker and poet. The poem is about the tragic pride of a soaring eagle. [Ed.]

4. The book, *Zarreh-ye Bi Enteha*, is a work of theology inspired by the theory of thermodynamics, Mr. Bazargan's specialty as an engineer and a physicist. It has not been translated into English. [Ed.]

5. The book was first published in 1962 by the University of Chicago Press. [Ed.]

6. The brand of Marxism that was prevalent in Iran was what was known in the West as Soviet Marxism or vulgar Marxism. A southern neighbor of the

former Soviet Union, Iran was flooded with subsidized Soviet tracts that dealt with Marxism. People's Mojahedin, an Islamic organization, had adapted this facile materialistic ideology and attempted to reconcile it with Islamic and religious ideas concerning social justice. The tract in question was considered a kind of manifesto of the group. It contained materialistic epistemological statements concerning the dialectical nature of the world, society, and the struggle for social equity and justice. [Ed.]

7. Shortly after this interview, Dr. Soroush was relieved of all his positions. This situation continues at the time this book is published. [Ed.]

8. The author is reluctant to reveal the name of the plagiarist, but in the interest of clarity, it should be stated that the individual in question is a clergyman, which explains why he cautioned Dr. Soroush, a layman, against publishing the thesis but was himself unafraid to publish them in his own name. As a clergyman, he enjoys a measure of immunity from persecution as well as a certain degree of professional courtesy from the clerical authorities. [Ed.]

Chapter 2

1. 'Allameh Mohammad Iqbal Lahori, *The Reconstruction of Religious Thought*, edited and annotated by M. Sa'eed Sheikh. Lahore: Iqbal Academy and Institute of Islamic Culture Press, 1989, p. 117.

2. The two terms (*bed'at* and *badi'*) are cognates. This text is particularly rich in such arrangement and allusions. It is noteworthy that Iranian philosophical discourse is traditionally steeped in such stylistically ornate forms. The translators have taken pains to preserve and convey the poetic and syntactic flavor of the text wherever possible. [Ed.]

3. Molana Mohammad Jalal al-Din Rumi is popularly known in Iran as Molavi and in the West as Rumi. [Ed.]

4. In esoteric thought, *shari'at*, *tarighat*, and *haqiqat* are considered progressive stages of realization in religion.

5. Mohammad Iqbal Lahori, philosopher and religious reformer, is considered to be one of the most influential Moslem thinkers of the Indian subcontinent and one of the two founding fathers of the Republic of Pakistan.

6. Morteza Motahhari, the contemporary Iranian theologian, advocated reform from within the ranks of the traditional clergy. [Ed.]

7. See *The Dilemma of the Veil* (*Mas'ale-ye-Hijab*) by Morteza Motahhari.

8. Italicized terms in this paragraph refer to the expressions that are culled from the late Motahhari's own works. [Ed.]

9. An arrangement in business whereby the tenant of a store is entitled to certain extra rights accrued due to the reputation of his business.

10. The major rituals of Islam such as the daily prayers and the annual month of fasting are closely attuned to natural cycles such as the position of the sun relative to the horizon and the cycles of the moon. The problem is, given the universality of Islam, how these rituals may still be observed where the normal geographical conditions do not obtain.

11. 'Ali Shari'ati, a controversial, prolific, and highly influential Islamic modernist, and a sociologist by training, lectured in Mashhad and Tehran during the 1960s and 1970s.

12. *The Idea of Religious Revival in Islam*. The idea is that if the man refuses to divorce his wife, according to the canon, her only resort would be to renounce the faith, become an apostate, and thus be automatically divorced from her erstwhile husband. She can return to the faith afterward, of course. [Ed.]

13. The reference is to books with these titles that are published by the central Islamic seminaries in the city of Qum. [Ed.]

14. The two major sources of learning and legitimate inference in Islam are the Book (the Qur'an) and the Tradition (words and deeds of the Prophet, but also those of his family and his companions). There are two other recognized sources of legitimate inference as well: *'aql* (reason) and *ijma'* (consensus). [Ed.]

15. This is the late Mr. Motahhari's argument.

16. The reference is to a fable in Rumi's *Mathnavi* in which a difference of tongues causes a clash between three friends. They all meant to buy grapes with their common money but uttered their desires in their different languages. Not knowing that the others meant the same thing, they went on arguing in vain. [Ed.]

17. "Hermeneutic" (the English term in original). [Ed.]

18. The title of a forthcoming book by the author.

19. *Mathnavi*, bk. 3, verse 1258.

20. The author is alluding to a verse in the Qur'an that states: "Today I have completed for you your religion." [Ed.]

21. A theory that concerns the interpretation of the Qur'an, (*tafsir*), the application of logical rules of inference to religious texts and principles (*usul*), and Islamic theology (*kalam*). See pp. 18–19.

22. Qur'an 17:82. The author illustrates this point with a verse from *Mathnavi* (bk. 1, verses 691–92):

> Indications, sharp as a steel blade,
> If you don't carry a shield, run to the rear.
> Face not the diamond edge without a shield,
> For a blade won't be timid, cutting clear. [Ed.]

23. Imam 'Ali-Ibn-Hossein, the son of Imam Horssein, the great-grandson of the Prophet and the fourth Imam, according to the Twelver Shi'ite religion.

24. *Mathnavi*, bk. 3, verse 1491.

Chapter 3

This essay was presented at the seminar on cultural development at the Faculty of Social Sciences, University of Tehran (June 1994). [Ed.]

1. *Mathnavi*, bk. 5, verse 2695.

2. For a complete analysis of this point, see my "The Ethics of Gods."

3. The author is referring to the philosophical axiom that the cause does not always precede the effect. Even when two events occur at the same time, one may be considered the cause. For instance in turning a key in a keyhole, the hand and the key move at the same time. Yet the turning hand is the cause of the turning key. [Ed.]

4. *Mathnavi*, bk. 5, verse 3422.

5. *Bakht*, i.e., luck.

6. *Mathnavi*, bk. 6, verses 3839–41.

7. For a detailed discussion of the issue of the relationship between justice and causality, see my article, "Justice and Causality for Rumi," published in my *Loftier than Ideology*.

8. For a detailed elaboration of this topic, see Friedreich August von Hayek, *New Studies in Philosophy, Politics, Economics, and the History of Ideas* (Chicago: Chicago University Press, 1985), p. 258.

9. The concept of "obliviousness" has been explicated in the article, "Intellectuality and the Knowledge of the Mysteries," in my *Roshanfekri va Razdani va Dindari* (Tehran: Serat Publications, 1994).

10. Rumi likened them to the impure urine, which, while necessary in the larger scheme of things, can never be equal to pure substances like clean and cleansing water.

An astute soul addressed Jesus once:
What's the world's harshest thing? the response
Was: *God's rage, my dear*
From which Hell would tremble the way we would shiver.
But, who is secure from this rage? the astute one demanded.
The one who masters his own fury, Jesus commanded.
So the pickets who manifest their rage,
Surpass the wild beasts in cage.
What hope would they have in God's compassion,
Unless they abandon their hateful fashion?
To venture: *The world needs them, at any rate*
Is to begin a deluding debate.
The world requires urine as well.
Yet, it is no equal to the water fresh from the well. (*Mathnavi*, bk. 4, verses 113–19)

Also, he was inspired by Al-Ghazzali when he candidly argued:

Awareness trickles into this world's sight
So that the world is not concurred by envy and spite
Should awareness exceed obliviousness in this sphere
Both virtue and wickedness would disappear. (*Mathnavi*, bk. 1, verses 2069–70)

11. In my article "What Is Ideology?" I have elaborated on the concept of "ideological oblivion." See *Loftier than Ideology* (Tehran: Serat Publishers, 1995).

12. *Mathnavi*, bk. 4, verses 238–40:

The passions of this world are like dung heaps
Whose benefit the warm bathhouse of piety reaps
The task of the rich who carry it
Is to keep the fire of the bathhouse lit
Yet the pious gain purity from the sooty furnace
As they are in the bathhouse, seeking pureness.

13. Al-Ghazzali, *Ihya' al-'Ulum* (The Book of Knowledge).

14. Abu Hamid Mohammad al-Ghazzali (A.D. 1058–1111).

15. In the following, Rumi describes the situation of the worldly scholars that endowed the schools with warmth and popularity. *Mathnavi*, bk. 2, verses 2431, 2436, 2437, 2440:

> The common man seeks knowledge for the common customers's sake
> Rather than aiming to gain salvation from the world and its stake.
> The knowledge of the surfaces is devoid of life
> It seeks an audience and customers rife.
> Although, while expounding, it appears very high,
> Without customers, it shall wither away and die,
> Leave these destitute customers behind.
> In a handful of dust a good customer you will never find.

16. In his *Ihya' al-'Ulum al-Din*, Al-Ghazzali quotes some Sufis to the effect that wealth or other worldly goods are nothing but divine punishment, saying: "'Tis a sin whose time of atonement has arrived."

17. *Mathnavi*, bk. 4, verses 1189, 1191–92.

18. Al-Ghazzali, in his *Ihya' al-'Ulum al-Din* (Revival of the Sciences of Religion) in a chapter "Patience, Thankfulness, Poverty, and Asceticism," analyzes different forms of patience and gratitude and their subtle nuances and precise meanings.

19. Feiz Kashani, "The Book of Poverty and Religion," in *Mahaja' al-Baiza'* (Tehran: Sadough Publications), p. 330; Abu Hamid al-Ghazzali, "The Book of Poverty and Religion," in *Ihya' al-'Ulum al-Din*, vol. 4 (Lebanon: Dar al Ma'refah Publications), p. 203.

20. Ibid., pp. 202, 328.

21. The late Mr. Motahhari has a fine discourse on this erroneous meaning of the concept of abnegation. See his *Ten Lectures* as well as the late Dr. Shari'ati's wonderful explications of this issue. Also, please see my explication of the Sufi ideals of virtue, in my *Story of the Lords of Wisdom* (Tehran: Serat Publications).

22. The following are examples of Hafez's approach:

> I am the heavenly Adam, however, on this cruise,
> I happen to be a bondsman to the love of a beautiful youth.

Or:

> Take joyous advantage of the beautiful youths' faces,
> For on the path of life there are bandits lurking in secret places.

Or:

> We do not fault a soul for being a sensualist or a lush.
> For the beloved's hair's fine, and so is the wine's delectable rush.

23. Sa'di, "Debate of Sa'di with the Opponent," in *Golestan*, edited by Dr. Yousefi, bk. 7, "On the Influence of Education" (Tehran: Kharazmi Publications, 1987).

24. See Al-Ghazzali, "On Poverty and Asceticism," in *Kimiya'-ye Sa'adat* vol. 2, ed. Hossein Khadiv Jam (Tehran. Scientific and Cultural Publications, 1982).

25. Preferring gratitude to patience or vice versa is one of the most controversial issues in Sufism. The opinions of the Sufi thinkers on this issue are, to paraphrase Al-Ghazzali, "extremely agitated." This has reached a point that,

according to Abou Talib Makki's *Ghout al-Gholoub* and Al-Ghazzali's *Ihya' al-'Ulum al-Din*, one of the great Sufi leaders, Abol Abbas Ahmad Ibn Sahl Ibn 'Ata' (309 of the Islamic calendar), who disagreed with Joneid, another Sufi master, over preferring the grateful rich over the patient poor, was reportedly cursed by the latter and was subsequently afflicted by the deaths of his children, financial ruin, and a fourteen-year bout with madness, until he changed his opinion and agreed that the patient poor are more virtuous than the grateful rich. Similarly, Abol Qasim Qoshairi narrates that once Yahya bin Mo'az Razi lectured on the subject of the preferability of wealth over poverty in the city of Balkh and received 30,000 Derhams. One of the Sufi masters cursed him by ironically declaring: May it be auspicious for you. He was consequently accosted by bandits on his way to Nishabour, and all his belongings were stolen. Also look at Morteza Zobeidi's *Commentary on Ihya' al-'Ulum al-Din*, where seven reasons for the superiority of gratitude over patience are quoted from Abou Bakr Mohammand bin Is'hagh Sufi's *Maghasid al-Monjiat*. Hojviri's *Kashf al-Mahjoub* and Abou Talib Makki's *Qout al-Qloub*, too, have expanded on this controversy. See Morteza Zobeidi's *Commentary on Ihya' al-'Ulum al-Din*, vol. 9, chapter on the explanation of Al-Ghazzali's "Book of Patience and Gratitude."

26. Michel Foucault, *The Order of Things* (New York: Vintage Books, 1970); Jürgen Habermas, *Knowledge and Human Interest* (Boston: Beacon Press, 1971); Barnes and Bloor, *Rationality and Relativism*; Thomas Kuhn, *The Structure of Scientific Revolutions* (Chicago: University of Chicago Press, 1962); and Paul Feyerabend, *Against Method* (London: Verso, 1987).

27. I have explained this, in detail, in my introduction to a translation of Edwin A. Burtt's *Metaphysical Foundations of Modern Physical Science* (Persian translation; Tehran: Scientific and Cultural Publications, 1983).

28. The author paraphrases a verse by Rumi here to illustrate the preposterous nature of such a claim: "Not even God created such a lion." [Ed.]

29. I have critiqued the instrumental view of science in the Frankfurt School in my *Lessons in the Philosophy of Social Science* (Tehran: Ney Publications, 1985).

30. The discussion about the impartiality of science is itself a complex issue that cannot be unraveled here. Suffice it to say that the presuppositions of science may be valuational or nonvaluational. Nowadays, both of these presuppositions are identified as prescientific, presuppositional values. This has led to great confusion. In any event, both the value-free and value-laden presuppositions of science are criticizable. Furthermore, the truth of scientific theories, independent from their presuppositions, is testable.

31. I have explained the essential difference between science and other Western product in "The Distinct Thrust of Modernism," *Kiyan*, no. 20 (1994).

Chapter 4

This chapter is an edited and abridged version of three lectures in the Imam Sadiq Mosque (December 1994). [Ed.]

1. A verse of poetry by Hafez that has become somewhat of a saying in the Persian language. [Ed.]

2. A reference to Marx's famous eleventh thesis, in his "Eleven Theses on Feuerbach": "The philosophers have only interpreted the world in various ways; the point, however, is to change it." [Ed.]

3. *Golshan-e Raz*, verse 717. Also, Rumi says in *Mathnavi*, bk. 3, verse 2772: "Do not meddle with the judgment of determination, / A donkey's ear fits the rest of its constitution."

4. As Rumi stated in *Mathnavi*, bk. 2, verses 3326–27:

> Life is naught but experience of information,
> whosoever has more of it has more animation.
> Our lives are superior to those in the animal world,
> Because ours are wrapped in knowledge's fold.

5. Some scholars have expressed confusion about the Arabic rendition of the term *secularism* as *elmaniat*, literally, "this-worldliness" or "scientification." The late Motahhari, for example, in his *Islamic Movements of the Last Century* (Tehran: Sadr Publications), p. 25, has expressed this confusion. Contemporary Arab authors resort to transforming certain nouns into transitive verbs. For example, *elmania al-ijtima'* means "scientification" or "secularization" of the society; and *aqlania* means "rationalization" and so forth.

The term *scientification* is probably the most accurate translation of the term *secularism*. It denotes the scientific and practical nature of its referent. Of course, as mentioned before, secularism also connotes neglect of religion in the sense that a secular government derives its legitimacy and laws from the people, not from a divine source. The question is, however, why has this been the case? The answer lies in the essence of secularism: the scientific and rational approach to social and political deliberation.

6. I have elaborated on this theme in my translation of Edwin A. Burtt's *Metaphysical Foundations of Modern Physical Science* (Persian original; Tehran: Scientific and Cultural Publications, 1983).

7. I have detailed this concept in my essay "Livelihood and Virtue." See *Kiyan* (May–June 1995).

8. The author uses a Persian expression to indicate the absurdity of this practice: It is like beating water in a crucible. [Ed.]

9. See chapter 2, this volume. [Ed.]

10. Qur'an 17:35.

11. The fourth Imam from the progeny of prophet Mohammad according to the Shi'a.

12. In literal designation for the faculty of law in Iran is the faculty of "rights," or *hoqouq*.

13. I have described this point in detail in *Hekmat va Ma'ishat* (Tehran: Serat Publications, 1992).

14. Here a word must be added about the secular religions, that is the human ideologies that are even more dogmatic than religions. They wish mankind as servant, not of a beneficent God but of cruel secular rulers. Besides, they colonize history and nature, reconstructing everything anew. Human society in their hands is nothing more than malleable wax ready to be molded and shaped.

15. In the modern setting the task of the reformers and religious thinkers consists of familiarizing those who have exercised their right to serve God with their duties. The task of religion becomes difficult and the flight from religion

reaches its peak when the pretenders to God's throne on earth prevent the people from viewing the God of the heavens, when God gains an unsolicited bunch of bragging partners who spoil His picture with tinges of tyranny and megalomania.

16. See Leo Strauss, *Natural Rights and History* (Chicago: University of Chicago Press, 1953), and Aristotle's *Metaphysics*.

17. Strauss, *Natural Rights*.

18. Remember Avecina's dictum: "God has not made an apricot an apricot; he has (merely) necessitated its existence."

19. *Mathnavi*, bk. 3, verses 3576–77.

20. Unless, of course we speak of these not as essential things but as contingent and actually existing objects. In this case, we have basically agreed with the secular thinkers (who do not consider the religiosity of the government as essential, but only contingent). There is another way of escaping this trap. We can basically deny that there are such things as essences and thus join the ranks of Nominalists or, like Wittgenstein, supplant essences with "family resemblances" or replace the essences with "habits of mind," like the pre-Socratic philosophers and the Ash'ri philosophers.

21. The author of *Tahafat al-Falasifah*.

22. The author of *Awaref al-Ma'aref, Rashf al-Nasayeh* and *Ksahf al-Faza'h al-Younaneyeh*.

23. The philosophers' tendency toward causality went hand-in-hand with their affinity for the study of nature and vice versa. Averroes, in his *Tahafot al-Tahafot*, responds to Al-Ghazzali's argument as follows: Denial of causality is tantamount to the denial of nature [the seventeenth problem]. Also, Ibn Khaldoun simply says of the theologians who deny causality that they deny nature. See Harry Wolfson's *The Philosophy of the Kalam* (Cambridge, Mass.: Harvard University Press, 1972).

Chapter 5

This chapter is the transcribed and edited version of an address in the Faculty of Theology, University of Tehran (June 1992). [Ed.]

1. English names in the original text. [Ed.]

2. The reference is to a fable narrated by Rumi. An illiterate but sincere shepherd harbors illusory views of God as a human companion. He is rebuked by Moses for blasphemy. Moses is subsequently rebuked by God for insensitivity to the shepherd's purity of intention. [Ed.]

3. The theory of nonexistence of evil is a surefooted theory in the Islamic philosophical theology. This does not mean, of course, that evils do not exist. It means that evils are always of the nature of the absence of something positive, such as ignorance or death whose contents are evil.

4. Mr. Kianoori was the former secretary general of Iran's pro-Soviet communist party, known as Hezb-e Toudeh, literally, the party of the masses. [Ed.]

5. Rumi, *Mathnavi*, bk. 6, verses 1967–68, 1974.

6. The term *ideology* in this paragraph refers to nonliberal ideologies. The positive and negative results of liberal social systems, however, are to be attributed to the doctrine of liberalism.

7. The maxim paraphrased in the text states: "They contradict each other, therefore they are both annulled." It is derived from "'Elm al-Hadith," or the science of discerning the authenticity of narrated traditions from the Prophet. [Ed.]

8. Yazid, the son of Mo'avieh, is generally known as an inveterate hedonist, and a calif, Bayazid, the great exemplary Sufi master, is respected for his great humility and wisdom. [Ed.]

9. These four characteristics of human beings are quoted in their Arabic original form from the Qur'an.

Chapter 6

This lecture was delivered at the Shahid Beheshti University (previously the National University) at the *esfand* of 1370H (February/March 1991). [Ed.]

1. *Mathnavi*, bk. 1, verse 4157.
2. The Persian word *haq* connotes metaphysical truth and rightness, as well as civil and legal rights. [Ed.]
3. Shi'a Moslems reserve this title only for their first Imam, 'Ali, who was also the cousin and son-in-law of the Prophet Mohammad. [Ed.]
4. *Nahj al-Balaghah*, Sermon 15.
5. The Persian *morid bazi* refers to the corruption associated (primarily but not exclusively) with the abuse of the relationship between the devotees and the Sufi masters. [Ed.]
6. *Mathnavi*, bk. 2, verses 2332–28.
7. *Mathnavi*, bk. 2.
8. *Mathnavi*, bk. 4, verse 2301.
9. Rumi (*Divan-e Kabir*, elegy 633) uses the phrase "totally other" to denote an ineffable and transcendental essence:

> My sun, my moon, my sight my hearing has arrived.
> My own silver framed one, my very gold mine has arrived.
> The intoxication of my head, the light of my eyes has arrived.
> If you wish a "totally other," my "totally other" has arrived.

10. *Mathnavi*, bk. 2, verses 25–27.
11. *Mathnavi*, bk. 5, verse 167.
12. Qur'an 2:256.
13. Qur'an 11:28.
14. Qur'an 7:123.
15. Sa'di, *Kolliat-e Sa'di*, elegy 323.
16. The author relies on the familiarity of the readers with Islamic mysticism where these concepts are developed and used as a matter of course. [Ed.]
17. Rumi's magnum opus.
18. Here the author uses the philosophical term for God (*wajib al-Wujud*), which means the "one who *exists* by necessity," or "the necessary being." [Ed.]
19. Sadr al-Din Shirazi (1571–1640), known as Mulla Sadra, is a renowned and highly original Islamic philosopher. [Ed.]
20. "The Lord of Time" (*Imam-e Zaman*) is one of the titles of the living but occulted last Imam of the Twelver Shi'a Moslems. [Ed.]

21. This doctrine was first unleashed by Marxist intellectuals, who ended up as its first victims.

22. Qur'an 20:68.

23. The author is referring to the well-known Qur'anic verse: "Those who listen to the Word and follow the best (meaning) in it: those are the ones whom Allah has guided, and those are the ones endowed with understanding." Qur'an 39:18. [Ed.]

24. *Mathnavi*, bk. 3, verse 1109.

25. Qur'an 28:83.

26. The author is boldly using the politically loaded term *velayat* (guardianship) that is a keystone of the late Ayatollah Khomeini's theory of the "guardianship of the jurisconsult" (*velayat-e faqih*). This idea was later molded into the main axis of the political theory of the Islamic Republic and enshrined in the constitution of the Islamic Republic of Iran.

27. *Mathnavi*, bk. 2, verse 290.

28. *Mathnavi*, bk. 1, verse 2892.

29. Qur'an 13:29.

30. *Mathnavi*, bk. 1, verses 1373–74, 1389.

31. *Mathnavi*, bk. 3, verse 2435.

32. Only then can we sing with Rumi (*Mathnavi*, bk. 1, verses 2311–14, 1810):

> Give us a hand, buy us back from ourselves,
> Lift the veil, but cover our hidden shelves.
> Buy us back from the sordid desires of the flesh.
> Whose blade torments the bone through the flesh.

And then we may take pride:

> I heaved a sigh in the shape of a rope.
> A rope hanging in my well as hope.
> I climbed up the rope and emerged from the well.
> And became happy, ample and well.
> I was at the bottom of a well, gloomy
> Now the world is too narrow for me.
> Praises are due to you O Almighty
> Suddenly you relieved sorrows so mighty.
>
> Your blessing, keeps me in such good cheer,
> How can a cup of wine compete as its peer?

Chapter 7

1. Some contemporary thinkers have deemed this possible. See Mehdi Ha'eri Yazdi's *Kavoshha-ye 'Aql-e Nazari*.

2. Like the late Mohaqeq-e Lahiji in *Gohar-e Morad* and his contemporary disciples.

3. The author paraphrases a verse by Rumi in which the proposed cure, a vinegar syrup (*serkangebin*), increases rather than decreasing yellow bile (*safra*). [Ed.]

4. The followers of the school of logical jurisprudence (*usuliyyun*) who opposed their intellectual predecessors, the school of pure obedience to the text

(*akhbariyyun*), have used a much misunderstood expression: requirement (*eqteza*) of moral precepts in this context. Thus they say that truthfulness, for instance, requires goodness in the sense that it is good more often than not.

5. This analysis has a functionalist hue (as it seems to proceed from the effect). It is possible to offer another analysis that proceeds from the cause, such as asserting that human beings are so constituted as to prefer truthfulness to deceit. Although, in this author's view the former is more plausible than the latter, which is ultimately reducible to the former, but the present essay is not contingent upon the result of such a debate. Nor does it take a specific position in this regard. What we are concerned with here is the exception-prone nature of the ethics, and thus, their contingency upon a particular structural assumption for the humanity, the world, and the society.

6. The least problem with such a worldview is that it is unsupported by evidence. It makes statements about a future society and world that cannot be supported by rational and experimental evidence. It may be indisputable that, so far, moral virtues have been in harmony with the world and society and that they have been conducive to—or at least promised to bring about—a more pleasant and balanced life, but it would need strong scientific (and not only philosophical) arguments to establish that societies and individuals necessarily, unequivocally, and indefinitely need such a morality. Apparently, the ethicists have never felt they were bound to produce such arguments. The assumption of a constant human nature (*fetrat*) too, the weakness of its reasoning notwithstanding, is not particularly effective in this respect. An affair judged to be part of human nature is like a malleable substance that can take dozens of forms. Therefore, it can determine neither the form of societies nor the parameters of morality with any degree of accuracy and certainty. The need to communicate through language, for example, may be one of the strongest and most exclusive inclinations of human nature. Still, this basic need has given rise to more than two thousand languages and dialects in the world. Each is a specific form of the primal substance. This is another way of stating the powerful proposition that a social fact should be explained with another social fact and it is not sufficient to explain it by reducing it to its natural and psychological rudiments. Market, morality, language, etc., have distinct social identities, and it is wrong to reduce them to such motives as personal interest, desire for virtue, ability to reason through symbols, and the like. Such a reduction would beg the question why is there such multifarious manifestations of fundamental needs? Nor can we rely upon the maxim: "The independent coincidence is neither permanent nor usual." (Coincidences are rare in the sense that two or more causally independent events happen to coincided neither permanently nor in a majority of cases. Otherwise, they are causally linked.) Because such a doubtful and feeble proposition, even if true, says no more than the following: "the evil of deception, being frequent, necessarily connects deception to evil. This conclusion may be upheld (all the flaws and instances of carelessness in its arguments and allegories not withstanding) while one continues to hold morality subordinate to a contemporary world and society. For deception in this world produces its own consequences that inevitably contribute to a break down of order and loss of confidence. The point, however, is whether deception would have the same deleterious effects in another world and society, so that its evil would remain constant!

7. The expression is borrowed from a verse in Saʿdi's (the thirteenth-century Iranian poet's) best-known work, *Golestan*. [Ed.]

8. I have elaborated on this point in my introduction to the translation of Edwin A. Burtt's *The Metaphysical Foundations of Modern Physical Science* (Persian original; Tehran: Scientific and Cultural Publications, 1983).

9. For a detailed examination of this concept, see my *Manners of the Virtuous*.

10. Remember the famous and popular words: "War is trickery." While we know deceit with friends is considered a definite vice.

11. The term *manners* here means values not habits and traditions.

12. See note 5, this chapter.

13. From this, one can deduce that subsuming natural names under moral ones, pretending the latter are instance of the former (such as subsuming integrity and truthfulness under justice) is wrong and misleading. This is a practice that has severely contorted the contours of the science of ethics. How can one count forbearance, friendliness, patience, tranquility, kindness to kin, etc., (all natural names) as virtues, while counting assault, violence, cursing, backbiting, obsession with glory, and deception (all natural names as well) as vices? Unless it is asserted that the present society overwhelmingly approves of these designations. No ethicist has claimed this though. No natural deed will be described as a vice or a virtue until it has admitted of a moral title. It has to be specified: "timely and just forbearance" or "untimely and unjust lie." Only then would the moral admissibility of each be determined. It now becomes clear why some ethicists of yore were so confused in attributing a moral status to traits such as poverty and wealth and why they sometimes resorted to such quaint and curious arguments as: wealth is better than poverty because God is not poor. Wealth and poverty, as natural names, would have no moral designation until they are subsumed under a moral attribute.

14. The existence or lack thereof of a faculty called courage or justice makes no difference in this argument. The discussion is about their effects, that is courageous and just deeds, etc. The deeds indicate the faculties, not the other way around.

15. The author cites the following poem from Hafez to illustrate this point [Ed.]:

> The tall beauty whose radiance had eclipsed the sun and moon,
> Had to seek another trade, as you walked in the room.
> The bundle of sorrows that weighed on our soul,
> God sent a Christ-like figure and lifted it, whole.

16. Saʿdi's *Golestan*.

17. The author cites the following lines from Rumi's *Mathnavi* (verses 1419–22) as further illustration [Ed.]:

> Feign foolishness, for only then you would,
> Be freed of this hellish foolish brood.
> Most people in heaven are fools, hey!
> That's why our lord has thus shown the way:
> A fool's way is not to carry on and clown,
> It's to be absorbed in wonders, divine.
> Many a craft, wit, and acumen's tool

That's naught for the traveler but a bandit and a ghoul.
Most heavenly souls are from among the fool,
Thus, they have escaped the sophists' rule.

18. The original expression is "cannibals." [Ed.]

19. All Moslems pray in the direction of Mecca. This united and unifying direction of prayers is called *qiblah*, which is the word used here. [Ed.]

20. Rumi, *Mathnavi*, bk. 5, verses 328 and 337.

21. I have explained this in my book *Wisdom and Life* [*Hekmat va Maishat* (Tehran: Serat Publishers, 1997)].

Chapter 8

This is a combination of two lectures given, respectively, at the Human Rights Conference of the foreign ministry of Iran, in Tehran (1991), and at the Human Rights Conference at the Institute of Orientalism, in Hamburg, Germany (1992). [Ed.]

1. The controversy concerning the punishment of Salman Rushdie is a result of such a debate.

2. The Persian simile is that of sawing off the branch on the tip of which one is sitting. [Ed.]

3. According to Islamic theology, the principles of the existence of God and the necessity of divine guidance through prophets are matters of independent debate and inquiry and can not be accepted on faith. Therefore, they are extra-religious debates by nature. [Ed.]

Chapter 9

1. These are theoretical and epistemological foundations of democracy, not social causes of it. Discussion of the historical causes and social conditions of democracy is outside the realm of this essay. The same holds for the discussion of the impediments of democracy. Insightful critics such as C. Wright Mills, *Power Elite* (New York: Oxford University Press, 1956), and Robert Dahl, *A Preface to the Democratic Theory* (Chicago: University of Chicago Press, 1956), examine the external causes of democracy not the definition and internal nature of it. For instance, the theory of democracy, in principle, theoretically sanctions the separation of powers and free elections, but these may take place only in societies that are already poly-archical.

2. The author intends this concept in its classical and strong sense. Some contemporary authors have attempted to underline the two senses of the term by distinguishing the concepts of "Liberalism" and "liberalism." See Randall Collins, *Four Sociological Traditions* (New York, Oxford University Press, 1985). [Ed.]

3. Given the prominence of jurisprudential exegesis in traditional Islam, the author focuses on this issue. Hereinafter, the concept of "jurisprudence" implies the religious aspect of the concept in Islam, or *fiq'h*. [Ed.]

4. The Islamic Republic of Iran is the only country in which this form of government is in evidence, although the general idea is popular in other Asian and North African Moslem countries.

5. Hafez, Ghazal 314.

6. The author alludes to the "battle of the seventy-two nations;" a reference to a verse by Hafez:

> The battle of the seventy-two nations,
> admit their excuses, and excuse them:
> Not having seen the truth,
> they wandered on the path of delusions.

The phrase "seventy-two nations" refers to the common perception among Moslems that Islam has splintered into seventy-two sects. [Ed.]

7. It is interesting that the respected critic who is referring to my article "The Theoretical Foundations of Liberalism" has nevertheless failed to take this point into account.

8. The following source contains the illuminating case against the premise of impartiality of liberal governments toward science: R. P. Wolff, *The Poverty of Liberalism* (Boston: Beacon Press, 1969); also see B. Appleyard, *Understanding the Present: Science and the Soul of the Modern Man* (1993). Although the above author adopts a critical attitude toward science (that is, the philosophical approach of some scientists toward science, not science itself), still, he exposes the "science-centrism" of liberal societies. He attributes the crisis of faith in these societies to the scientific approach and predicts the advent of a "post-scientific" society where science will have a more humble status while faith will enjoy a more exalted position. Also, Allan Bloom's controversial book, *The Closing of the American Mind* (New York: Simon and Schuster, 1987), focuses on the havoc that a certain strand of liberalism has wreaked on the American society. In addition, see the works of the Frankfurt school of "critical theory," particularly, the writings of Jürgen Habermas on "ideologization of science." The upshot of these arguments is that nowadays science and scientists are no longer neutral. Therefore, "science-centric" societies have distanced themselves from the original liberal position. Finally, see Paul Feyerabend's recent publications, specifically his *Science in Free Society* (London: NLB, 1978), where the domination of science is considered as a threat to democracy. The book calls for the government to stay impartial both with respect to science and religion.

9. Edward Bernstein (the classic progenitor of democratic socialism) considered democracy a precondition for socialism, while the Fabians viewed socialism as an extension of democracy.

10. See, for example, the following splendid article on the intricate meaning of religious tolerance: Jay Newman, "The Idea of Religious Tolerance," *American Philosophical Quarterly* 15, 3 (1978).

11. The author borrows an expression from Hafez to allude to the youthful adventures of Saint Francis: "He doused the "jewel of soul in liquid ruby." [Ed.]

12. The synopsis of the argument is that reasons have to do with the proof of the truth or falsehood of beliefs, but causes deal with the process of their development. False beliefs have causes but not reasons. In theory, it is possible to fashion a faslse belief, but it is not possible to prove it. Therefore, it is possible to empathize with the purveyors of corrupt beliefs for they are caught in the maze of causes that have led them to the love of certain ideas, of whose falsehood they are unaware. However, it is not possible to join such people in their false beliefs. We can attack their "reasons" but, from the perspective of "causes,"

we may condone their inclination toward those beliefs. For more information on the crucial and precise difference between the concepts of reason and cause, and the transferability of one to the other, see my "Cause and Reason" and "Reason and Freedom," in *More Comprehensive than Ideology* (1992).

13. The reference is to a verse by Hafez [Ed.]:

They did not grant us passage, on the path of good reputation,
If you don't approve, change the verdict of predestination.

14. Hafez, Ghazal 61. This is a testimony to the tyranny of the world's whimsical ways, the luxurious turbulence of life and the frailty of the human condition; not a flash of Hafez's poetic mystification or fatalistic resignation:

My lot is no more than loving her in the secret sanctuary of my heart,
What can I say of her embraces and kisses, for it would not be my lot.   (Hafez, Ghazal 165)

15. An allusion to the verse by Rumi [Ed.]:

Inflexibility and clenching are symptoms of callowness and infancy,
So long as you remain a fetus, you're engrossed in suckling and dependency.

16. The expression is borrowed from Hafez. [Ed.]

17. These are considered, in the language of logic, not universal but pseudo-universal propositions. On the issue of the difference between the epoch of advent and epoch of establishment, see my *More Comprehensive Than Ideology* (1992).

18. Moslems, in general, and Shi'ites, in particular, believe that a savior, a guide (*mahdi*) with divine mandate, will someday emerge to restore justice and goodness to earth. The period of "greater occultation," according to Shi'ite belief, started in A.D. 921 and will continue indefinitely until "Imam Mahdi" appears. A version of the Jewish and Christian Messianism is incorporated into Shi'ite eschatology. [Ed.]

19. Later on, I will expand on the position and relevance of religious law to a theological view of prophethood and Islam's status as the last great religion (khatmiat). Suffice it to hint at this point, that jurists, in their attempt to rationalize the decree concerning the apostates have advanced noteworthy arguments that stipulate significant qualifications. For example, it is argued that when a quandary becomes universal and a doubt epidemic so that a great number of people are persuaded to doubt or leave the faith, the above decree may no longer apply. Also, that apostasy in the epoch of advent of the religion usually followed political agendas, in the sense that frequently entering and leaving the faith was a conspiracy to trivialize Islam and engage in psychological warfare with the faithful. Mohammad Ghazzali, the contemporary Egyptian author, argues in favor of religious freedom by resorting to the following Qur'anic verse: "And say, the truth (comes) from your God, so whoever wishes, may accept the faith and whoever wishes, may turn away" (Qur'an 18:29). On the subject of the apostasy that was motivated by nothing but mockery and conspiracy, he resorts to the following verse: "And a group from among the people of the book advised (others) to accept Islam in the morning and reject it in the evening, so that Moslems too would turn away from their religion" (Qur'an 3:73). Mohammad Ghazzali, *The Rights of Humanity* (Cairo: Dar al-Kotob al-Haditha Publications, 1965), pp. 106–

118. It is clear that such apostasies that had political (not rational) motives would not have subsided without punitive measures. This is quite different from a relentless search for the truth, in which case even the defiant tone of a person who is interested in the truth should be tolerated.

Motahhari, too, while commenting on the subject of "corrupt books" and establishing a chair of Marxism in the faculty of theology of the Tehran University stated: "books, however atheistic and hostile to Islam and the Prophet, may be based upon a cogent logic. . . . That is, there are people who think along these lines but are sincere in their thought. The proper way to confront such people is through proper logical argumentation." See Morteza Motahhari, *On the Islamic Revolution* (Tehran: Sadra Publications, 1986), pp. 76–77. Surely Motahhari did not intend to invite scholars who were dead or condemned to death to occupy the above chair!

I am not arguing that all jurisprudents had a uniform interpretation of the law of apostasy, or that they were all tolerant of idolaters and apostates. I know that such rationalizations are too modern to be generalizable to the mind-set of previous generations. Nor do I argue that Motahhari was able to establish the universal supremacy or reason and to transcend servile reason toward critical reason. But I am arguing that religious interpretation is capable of modernization and rationalization in such a manner as to make it compatible with democracy. Also, notice that Motahhari's rhetoric concerning freedom of thought and corrupt books is purely rational and, in the precise sense of the word, extraneous to religious legal reasoning.

20. Qur'an 19:95.

21. Rumi's poem. [Ed.]

22. The reference is to the Qur'an 2:256: "There is to be no imposition of religion, for (the path of) growth is clearly distinguished from (the path of) revolt."

23. Hafez's poem. [Ed.]

24. Thus Hafez sings:

We have conquered the land of felicity, not by arms,
We have raised the imperial throne, not by force,
We are at the mercy of the magic of the beloved's eyes,
    for again, we have laid our foundation on magical charms. (Ghazal 365)

25. Rumi's poem.

26. Qur'an 00:00.

27. The following passage from one of the late Motahhari's lectures in "Hosseinieh-ye Ershad" in 1967 sounds extremely appealing in this context:

The Prophet expects faith. . . . Has Islam come only to create an Islamic society that follows Islamic regulations? No, this is only the initial phase. Islam has come to engender faith, love, zeal, and kindness in hearts. Faith cannot be imposed on people. The verse "There is to be no imposition in religion, verily, the path of truth is clearly distinguished from the path of revolt" may . . . be addressing this issue. Who can force people into faith? (*On the Islamic Republic* [Tehran: Sadra Publications, 1985], pp. 118–19.)

28. Abu Hamid Mohammad al-Ghazzali, *Ihya' al-'Ulum al-Din* (Revival Sciences of Religion), vol. 1, chapter 2.

29. These issues are raised, with impartiality or otherwise, in the writings

of such authors as Bernard Lewis, Martin Kramer, and Judith Miller. See, for example, Bernard Lewis's article entitled: "Islam and Liberal Democracy," where democratic institutions are said to be absent in Islam:

> Nearly every aspect of Islamic government has an intense individualistic bent: There is no state, but rulers; no court, but judges. Even, there is no city as such, there is a conglomeration of neighborhoods with racial, religious, tribal, and kinship boundaries that is ruled by potentates and their appointed war lords.

Still, the Islamic civilization, Bernard argues, is better equipped for democracy than other non-Western cultures. See B. Lewis, "Islam and Liberal Democracy," *The Atlantic Monthly* (February 1993). Also see Martin Kramer's belligerent essay in *Commentary* (January 1993).

30. On this issue, the opinion of Frank Vogel (assistant professor of Islamic law at Harvard University) is particularly interesting. In response to the "misunderstandings" of Kramer and Miller, he states that the trouble with the Islamic law is that it has become, if anything, too "indeterminate." He also argues that the thesis of the religious mandate of the Islamic rulers is antithetical to religious decress and historical evidence. See Frank E. Vogel, "Is Islam Compatible with Democracy? A Comparative Perspective," in *Under Siege: Islam and Democracy* ed. Richard W. Bulliet (New York: Columbia University, 1994).

31. The contemporary Egyptian thinker Mohammad Ghazzali is not to be confused with the tenth-century philosopher and mystic Abu Hamid Mohammad al-Ghazzali.

32. The opinions of Mohammad Ghazzali are recorded in ʿ*Azmat al-Shoura* (Cairo, 1990.) It is noteworthy that Ghazzali, like Mohammad Iqbal Lahori, considers the gates of innovative jurisprudence (*ijtihad*) closed. The ideas of Mohammad Abdoh may be found in Hamid Enayat's *A Sojourn in the Arab Political Thought* (Tehran: Amir Kabir Publications, 1979):

> In adjusting the Islamic religion to the contemporary world, according to Abdoh, two principles should be taken into consideration: First, the principle of prudence (*maslahat* or *esteslah*) that is one of the precepts of the 'Maliki' Sunni school of thought. The principle warrants infringement of the strict religious deductions for the sake of preserving the common Good. The practical result of this provision is that if a regulation inferred from the Qurʾan and the Tradition proves deleterious to Moslems' well-being, it may be prudently suspended. . . . The second principle is fusion (*talfiq*). Through this principles Abdoh means to combine and reconcile the rulings of all four major Sunni schools of thought in order to better tackle social problems. (Ibid., p. 140)

Mohammad Khalil, dean of the faculty of *shariʿah* at the University of Khartoum, cites the opinion of the thirteenth-century jurist of the "Hanbali" school of thought, Najm al-Din al-Tufi: "The consideration of people's welfare is the most significant duty of the religious government." Hence, a stronger connection is forged between democracy and Islam. See Timothy D. Sisk, *Islam and Democracy* (Washington, D.C.: U.S. Institute of Peace, 1992), p. 19.

It is noteworthy that the people's best interests, according to some political theorists, has a mythical and nominal role in democracy and that it belongs to the antiquated definitions of democracy. For instance, Schumpeter in his book, *Capitalism, Socialism, and Democracy*, cites the old definition of democracy as follows: "The democratic method is that institutional arrangement for arriving at political decisions which realizes the common good by making the people itself decide issues through the election of individuals who are to assemble in order to carry out its will." However, according to the author, this definition amounts to no more than a myth. The new definition of democracy is as follows: "The democratic method is that institutional arrangement for arriving at political decisions in which individuals acquire the power to decide by means of a competitive struggle for the people's vote." In other words, democratic government is the government of the politicians not of the people. See Joseph A. Schumpeter, *Capitalism, Socialism, and Democracy* (New York: Harper, 1950), pp. 250, 269.

33. The resourceful jurisprudent, Hossein Ali Montazeri, in his detailed and scholarly book, *Fi Velayat al-Faqih va Fiq'h al-Dawlat al-Islamiyah* (On the Guardianship of the Moslem Jurisconsult and the Law of the Islamic State), deems the Islamic and the democratic states comparable on two major aspects. First, the ruler of the Moslems, whether elected or appointed, should be more virtuous and effective than the rest. Second, judicial, legislative, and executive functions of the Islamic government are discharged within the framework of Islamic laws and are, indeed, a form of theocracy. In this sense, the government belongs to the domain of the divine law, not to religious and clerical strata, as it was the case with the masters of the church in the middle ages, so that they may indulge in tyranny. (Ibid., vol. 1, p. 538, See Hossein Ali Montazeri, *Fi Velayat al-Faqih va Fiq'h al-Dawlat al-Islamiyah* (On the Guardianship of the Moslem Jurisconsult and the Law of the Islamic State) (World Headquarters for Islamic Teachings, 1408 HS).

34. The author is utilizing the double meaning of the term *fiq'h*, which denotes religious canon, or *shari'ah*, but etymologically means "comprehension." [Ed.]

35. A reference is to a verse from Rumi that encourages a more profound understanding of phenomena. [Ed.]

36. The statement is in Arabic in the original. [Ed.]

37. The reference is from a fable narrated by Rumi in which Moses rebukes a shepherd boy for his blasphemous but sincere prayer in which he invited God to enjoy the hospitality of his humble abode. God reproaches Moses for turning away a faithful, albeit naive, supplicant:

> We observe the interior and the inner states,
> Not the exterior and outward jests. [Ed.]

38. Iqbal Lahori, in his *The Reconstruction of Religious Thought in Islam* (p. 191), states:

> Islam has succeeded, through proper institutions, to create something like a social conscience and volition out of the heterogeneous mass of society. In the evolution of such a society, even the fixity of such commandments that deal with eating, drinking, and ritual purity and contamination have their own vital roles; for they endow the society with a particular flavor of spirituality. On the other hand, they promote the homogeneity of the inside and the outside of religion in the face of the hidden forces of discord.

39. The clerical rulers of the Islamic republic of Iran, in order to deal with legal, religious, and economic dilemmas that periodically plague the tenuous balance of the legislative decisions of the Iranian parliament (*majlis*) and the Council of Guardians or the high clerical body that oversees the legislature for possible infractions of religious law (Shoura-ye Negahban) have recently instituted a committee to discern the most prudent interests of the nation (Shoura-ye Tashkhis-e Maslahat) that may veto the rulings of the Council of Guardians. The author welcomes this necessary if reluctant clerical concession as a step in the right direction.

40. These constitute a major part of the Islamic jurisprudence. [Ed.]

41. See Max Weber's two seminal articles: "Science as a Vocation" and "Religious Rejections of the World and Their Directions," in Hans Gerth and C. Wright Mills (tr.), *From Max Weber* (New York: Oxford University Press, 1946). [Ed.]

42. This is what Durkheim called "pre-contractual solidarity," a moral sense of obligation upon which all the contractual economic, political, and legal arrangement are based. See Emile Durkheim, *Division of Labor in Society* (New York: Free Press, 1933). [Ed.]

43. Alexis de Tocqueville, *Democracy in America* (New York: Anchor Books, 1969).

44. Richard Niebuhr, "The Idea of Covenant and American Democracy," *Church History* 23 (1924): 154–55.

43. Thus Hafez reminds us:

Either do not befriend riders of elephants,
Or build a house worthy of elephants.
Either avoid the indigo dyers' mess,
Or drag an indigo finger over your own dress.

46. Let us not forget Hafez's warning:

Surely, the good news shall arrive, of a shelter from these sorrows,
If only a wayfarer keeps the pledge of returning what he borrows.
O wine-server, gauge the wine in the cup of justice, lest the poor
Are aroused to wreak havoc on the world. (Ghazal 186)

Chapter 10

1. The Persian calendar is unique, for although it takes as its point of departure the migration of the Prophet Mohammad from Mecca to Medina (like other Moslem countries), it remains a solar calendar. [Ed.]

2. The first day of the Persian new year and the first day of spring (March 21). There is no attempt even in the Islamic Republic to conceal the pagan (pre-Islamic) origins of this holiday. [Ed.]

3. Khadjeh Shams al-din Mohmmad Hafez Shirazi (1320–90), the most prominent master of the Persian Ghazal. It is said that there is no Iranian house in which a copy of Hafez's *Divan* can not be found. [Ed.]

4. Also known as Sheikh-e Ishraq, he was a neo-Platonist Persian/Islamic philosopher. [Ed.]

5. Mirza Fathali Akhound Zadeh (1812–77). An Azari dramatist who lived in the Russian Azarbayjan. [Ed.]

6. Reza Khan Mirpanj, later known as Sardar Sepah and Reza Shah (1867–1944) was the founder of the Pahlavi dynasty (1925–79). [Ed.]

7. Seyyed Ahmad Kasravi Tabrizi (1890–1945) was a jurist and historian who also wrote extensively on the necessity of religious reform. [Ed.]

8. Sadeq Hedayat (1903–51) was a renowned and highly original writer of modern Persian fiction. [Ed.]

9. Mohammad Reza Pahlavi (1919–80) was the last king of the Pahlavi dynasty. [Ed.]

10. The Persian pronunciation of "Plato" is *Aflatoun*. [Ed.]

11. A mythical character in Ferdowsi's *Shahnameh*. [Ed.]

12. "Aristotle" is pronounced in Persian as *Arastoo*. [Ed.]

13. The main hero of Ferdowsi's *Shahnameh*. [Ed.]

14. All of whom were the leaders of anti-Arab revolts in post-Islamic Iran. [Ed.]

15. The term was first used by the famous Heideggerian philosopher Dr. Ahmad Fardid in his lectures. Recognizing Fardid as the originator of the term, Al-e Ahmad proceeded to use it in a simpler context. But the original use was revived in postrevolutionary days by some of Fardid's disciples as an obscurantist attack on Western modernism and its political forms, including liberalism. The author will later in this essay distinguish the two usages while criticizing the philosophical usage as a deterministic as well as obscurantist attack on the Western component of the Iranian culture. [Ed.]

16. 1923–69. [Ed.]

17. The original words in *Gharb Zadegi* are: "zan sefat, hor hory mazhab, pa dar hava, bi takhasos, bi shakhsiyat, qerty, cheshm be dahan-e gharb." [Ed.]

18. Qurʾan 8:24.

19. Sheikh Muslih al-Din Saʿdi is the prominent and influential thirteenth-century Persian poet. His *Golestan*, a collection of highly polished prose and poetry, is said to compete with Hafez's *Divan* in popularity among Iranians. [Ed.]

20. The late martyr Motahhari in his instructive book, *Khadqmat-e Muteqabel-Me Iram wa Islam*, has enlarged and eminently elaborated the argument that an idea of foreign origin may still be considered as our own without causing a contradiction.

21. Milovan Djilas is the author of *The New Class* and *A Dialogue with Stalin*. An unrepentant communist and a serious critic of the communist regime, he suffered imprisonment and abuse at the hands of Yugoslav intellectuals. In his *A Dialogue with Stalin*, he states that Stalin was the greatest criminal in history; and let us hope he remains so, that is, that no one surpasses him.

22. Rites associated with the commemoration of the martyrdom of Imam Hossein, the grandson of Prophet Mohammad and the third Imam of the Shiʿa Moslems. Such popular exhibitions of piety as blade-beating, chain-beating, and breast-beating that are usually performed at this occasion have no justification in Islam but have been long tolerated by the religious authorities. [Ed.]

23. Imam Hossein was martyred along with seventy-two of his loyal supporters in an unequal battle with the forces of Yazid Ibn Moʿaviyeh, the second calif of the Umayyad dynasty, because he refused to recognize the legitimacy of his rule. This tragic event serves as the symbolic center of the Shiʿa Moslems celebrations of the months of Moharram and Safar in the Islamic calendar. [Ed.]

24. Rumi (*Mathnavi*, bk. 4) has the same view of water's cleansing abilities:

> When water battled [impurities] and became impure,
> To the point that the senses rejected its cure,
> God returned it to the immense sea,
> Washing it in his infinite mercy.
> The next year the water came back souring:
> Hey, wherefore are you? Of the sea the roaring!
> I was debased in this place but return sound,
> The highest took my garb; I returned to the ground.
> So come hither ye impure, come to me,
> For the Heavenly nature is held in me.

25. Esfandiyar is a hero of Ferdowsi's *Shahnameh*, but the author refers to the following poem by Sa'di:

> A thousand single twigs are each weak, slight
> Woven together, not even Esfandiyar can crush their might. [Ed.]

26. Let me briefly state what I have enlarged upon this somewhere else. The late Dr. Shari'ati who advanced his call for a return to the authentic self was well aware of the questions that would accompany such a call and went on to adjust and complement this idea with his call for the "excavation and refining of the cultural resources."

Chapter 11

This lecture was given November 1992 at the University of Isfahan. The occasion was the unification of the Hawzeh and the university. Hawzeh (literally, "circle") is short for Hawzeh ye Elmieh (the learning circle), which refers to the urban Shi'a religious seminaries in Iran and Iraq. The most important ones are in Najaf (Iraq), Qum, and Mash'had (Iran). In this article we will use the term "Hawzeh" as well as its translation, "religious seminary." "The university" refers to all secular institutions of higher learning that have been launched in Iran since the 1920s. [Ed.]

1. *The* cultural revolution was launched by the revolutionary council in order to revise the university's curriculum according to the revolutionary principles. The author was appointed as a member of the steering committee of cultural revolution. The results were mixed, and Dr. Soroush resigned his position after eighteen months. [Ed.]

2. 1800–1925.

3. This is an extraconstitutional and often powerful office in many of Iran's government institutions.

4. "Eating dubious food" refers to the Islamic maxim that ones earnings must be legitimate. One of the adverse side effects of shady economic practices is having to feed on dubious morsels, which is, in turn, hazardous for ones spiritual health. [Ed.]

5. The terms are *mufti* (the one who issues religious edicts, *modarres* (the professor in the religious seminaries), *mohtasib* (religious police), and *faghih* (jurisconsult).

6. At issue is the Fitr holiday, which marks the end of the month of fasting and heralds the new lunar year of the Arabic calendar. The holiday must be declared by Islamic jurists, who are inclined to quibble over whether the moon has been sighted and thus possibly delay eagerly awaited festivities. [Ed.]

7. *Menbar* is a high wooden podium on which the clergy sit while delivering their sermons. "To go on the *menbar*" is a trope that denotes giving a sermon in the mosque. [Ed.]

8. *The Eternal Martyr* (*Shahid-e Javid*) was written by a prominent clergyman (Mr. Salehi Najafabadi) in the early seventies. The book's historical account of the martyrdom of Imam Hossein and his apostles at the battle of Karbala challenges the popular Shi'a notion of the Imam's martyrdom as a predestined divine redemptive act. The author underlines the political motivations of all the parties involved and is at pains to show that the Imam's martyrdom was a consequence of earlier political decisions, not the enactment of a divinely planned self-sacrifice. The book scandalized the Hawzeh, but it must be noted that it was very much in synch with the revolutionary reinterpretations of Islam at the time. [Ed.]

9. Allameh Mohammad Baqer Majlesy was one of the most renowned clergymen of the Safavid period (1500–1722). He compiled the authoritative *Bihar al-Anwar*, which is an encyclopedia of holy traditions attributed to the prophet and the Imams. [Ed.]

10. The late Allameh Tabataba'i who died of natural causes at the outset of the revolution was the most renowned philosopher at the Hawzeh. His most famous work is an interpretation of the Holy Qur'an known as *Al-Mizan*.

11. Mohammad Iqbal Lahori is the Pakistani philosopher and poet and the author of *The Reconstruction of Religious Knowledge in Islam*. Although respected as a major revivalist and an early advocate of pan-Islamic views, he is not well received by the philosophically minded clergy of the Hozeh because of his irreverence toward "Islamic philosophy."

12. Although "Satanic question" or "forbidden question" have been suggested for *shobheh*, the closest English parallel for this concept is "scandal," especially in such biblical phrases as "to give scandal" or to "scandalize." The Greek "scandalous" originally meant to put an obstacle in the way of others, and in the Gospels, Jesus uses it in this sense. Although this usage is arcane, it seems prudent to revive and use it in the present context. [Ed.]

13. The former is a voluminous philosophical and theological treatise and with extensive commentary edited by Mr. Motahhari, while the latter is a short philosophical manifesto outlining Mr. Tabataba'i's philosophical approach. [Ed.]

14. The author is alluding to the popular verse by Hafez: "The monastics who so preen themselves in prayers and on Menbars / Do that other sort of thing when they retire to their chambers." [Ed.]

15. This is a book of prayers and hymns written toward the end of the Qajar dynasty in Iran. It owes part of its popularity to extensive commentaries by the compiler, who enumerates the benefits of reciting the prayers and recommends further invocations and mantras that are expected to pad one's ledger of good deeds and reduce, if not annihilate, ones sins. There are also invocations that promise to ensure good fortune, ward off evil, and cure ailments. [Ed.]

16. ". . . and it has similarly been conveyed that a piece of wood or iron must be placed on the aching tooth and the following spell must be cast seven times: [the spell is quoted]. It is very weird indeed that there is a worm in the mouth that

eats the bone and causes bleeding. I am the one who casts spell but only God heals."
The book of *Baqiat al-Salehat, Mafatih al-Jinan*, Sheikh Abbas-e Qumi, p. 287.

17. This is an honorary title meaning "the supreme one among all monotheists" for Mulla Sadra, the Islamic philosopher who synthesized various trends of the Islamic philosophy as well as a great deal of Shiʿa traditions. His magnum opus, *The Four Books (Asfar al-Arbaʿah)*, is taught at the highest level of philosophical training at the seminaries. [Ed.]

18. He was a renowned logician and the most famous commentator on Mulla Sadra.

19. The text of Mulla Sadra is as follows:

> . . . and (one of the providential creations of God on earth is the animal kingdom . . .) some of whom are for eating, some for riding and adornment. Some are beasts of burden and others are for elegance and comfort. Yet others are created for copulation. Others are used to furnish cloths and furniture.

Hajj Mulla Hadi Sabzevari adds in the following commentary on the margins of the above texts:

> There is a subtle point in the fact that Mulla Sadra has relegated women to the ranks of animals. This means that due to the general defectiveness of their reason, their weakness in perception of details and their inclination toward the trinkets of this world, the women are truly and justly ranked as dumb animals. They are often created with the character of domestic beasts but God has given them a human appearance so that men are not repelled by their appearance and will have intercourse with them. This is why men are empowered by the religious law in such matters as divorce and insubordination of spouses and the like. (*Asfar Arbaʿeh*, vol. 7, chap. 13, p. 136, published by Maktaba Mostafavi)

20. The Persian saying is a bit richer in connotation: "to leave the (broken) bone in the wound." This is the work of a wily but incompetent healer who closes the wound and saves the appearances without having properly addressed the causes of present and future pains. [Ed.]

21. A proto-Marxist Islamic organization that took arms against the Shah and was shortly in favor after the revolution. The Mojahedin were later outlawed because of a campaign of terror that they launched against the Islamic Republic of Iran. This group had been long associated with the popular and prominent clergyman, Mr. Taleqani, and attempted to remain close to him after the revolution. It is not clear that the latter supported the hard line of the organization, especially after the revolution. [Ed.]

Chapter 12

1. See Abdolhossein Zarrinkub, *"Tarikh dar Tarazou"* (Amir Kabir Publishers, 1976), p. 14

2. See Vico, *Opere Complete* (Milan, 1835–37), vol. 5, p. 147, as quoted in *Araʾ va Nazarriyehha dar ʿOlume Ensani*, translated by Muhammad Ali Kardan p. 16.

3. The author is referring to the famous verse of Hafez: "Repose by the brook and behold the water's voyage / Suffice us this metaphor of the world's passage." [Ed.]

4. This is quoted from the contemporary Italian philosopher Benedetto Croce. See E. H. Carr, *What Is History?* (New York: Knopf, 1962), p. 30.

5. The critique of the late Jalal Al-e Ahmad of Abbas Eqbal Ashtiyani. See *"Arzyabi Shetabzadeh."*

6. See Carr, *What is History?*

7. Arnold Toynbee's *A Study of History*, ed. D. C. Somerwell, vol. 1 (New York: Oxford University Press, 1947–57), p. 44.

8. R. H. G. Collingwood, *The Idea of History* (Oxford University Press, 1956), p. 20.

9. Qur'an 1:30. "'Behold,' thy Lord said to the angels, 'I will create a vice-regent on earth.' They said, 'wilt thou place therein one who will make mischief therein and shed blood? Whilst we do celebrate thy praises and glorify thy holy (name)?' He said 'I know what ye know not.'"

10. In Islamic apocryphal lore the Forbidden Fruit is identified as a grain of wheat. [Ed.]

11. Abu Lahab was one of the most notorious opponents of the Prophet Mohammad during his earlier years when he called people to Islam in Mecca. [Ed.]

12. Here the author is alluding the theological arguments of the late Ayatollah Motahhari in his *ʿAdl-e Elahi* (Divine Justice). This Leibnizian work aims to demonstrate the absolute goodness of the Almighty by explaining away the natural as well as social manifestations of evil. [Ed.]

13. Qur'an 70:19–22: "Truly Man was created very impatient. Fretful when evil touches him. And niggardly when Good reaches him. Not so those devoted to Prayer."

14. Qur'an 17:11: "The prayer that man should make for good, he maketh for evil; for man is given to Hasty (deeds)."

15. Qur'an 33:72: "We did indeed offer the Trust to the Heavens and the Earth and the Mountains. But they refused to undertake it, being afraid thereof: But Man undertook it—He was indeed unjust and foolish."

16. Qur'an 17:67: "When distress seizes you at sea, those that ye call upon—besides Himself—leave you in the lurch! But when He brings you back safe to land, ye turn away (from him), most ungrateful is man."

17. Qur'an 15:35–37: "(Iblis) said: 'O my Lord! give me then respite till the Day the (dead) are raised.' (Allah) said: 'Respite is granted thee—Till the Day of the Time Appointed.'"

18. Al-Ghazzali, *Ihya' al-ʿUlum al-Din*, vol. 3, "The Book of the Idiosyncrasies of the Heart," p. 29: "Verily Satan flows in mankind as does blood, but they may narrow his passageways by hunger."

19. Ibid., pp. 27–28: "There is not one of you but for whom there is an appointed Satan. They (the apostles) said: and for you too, O messenger of Allah? He said: and for I as well, but verily God helps me against him, so I surrender only to Him and do not command but to the good."

20. The article was published 1984. The prediction of the author was realized before the decade was out. [Ed.]

21. Qur'an 3:159: "It is part of the Mercy of Allah that thou dost deal gently with them. Wert thou severe or harsh-hearted, they would have broken away from about thee."

22. Qur'an 13:31: "Do not the Believers know that had Allah (so) willed, He could have guided all mankind (to the Right)?"

23. Qur'an 11:119–20: "If thy Lord had so willed, He could have made mankind One People: but they will not cease to dispute, except those on whom thy Lord hath bestowed His mercy: and for this did He create them: and the Word of thy Lord shall be fulfilled: 'I will fill Hell with jinns and men all together.'"

24. Qur'an 3:176: "Let not those grieve thee who rush headlong into Unbelief: not the least harm will they do to Allah."

25. Qur'an 6:108: "Revile not ye those whom they call upon besides Allah, lest they out of spite revile Allah in their ignorance. Thus have We made alluring to each people its own doings. In the end will they return to their Lord, and We shall then tell them the truth of all that they did."

26. Qur'an 27:80–81: "Truly thou canst not cause the Dead to listen, nor canst thou cause the Deaf to hear the call, [especially] when they turn back in retreat. Nor canst thou be a guide to the Blind, [to prevent them] from straying: only those wilt thou get to listen who believe in Our Signs, and they will bow in Islam."

Also Qur'an 30:53–54: "Nor canst thou lead back the blind from their straying: only those wilt thou make to hear, who believe in Our Signs and submit [their wills in Islam.]"

Also Qur'an 16:35–37: "But what is the mission of the messengers but to preach The Clear Message? For We assuredly sent amongst every People a messenger (with the Command), 'Serve Allah, and eschew Evil': Of the people were some whom Allah guided, and some on whom Error became inevitably (established). . . . If thou art anxious for their guidance, yet Allah guideth not such as He leaves to stray. And there is none to help them."

27. Qur'an 94:1–3: "Have We not expanded thee thy breast? And removed from thee thy burden? The which did gall thy back?"

28. Qur'an 10:62: "Behold! verily on the friends of Allah there is no fear, nor shall they grieve."

29. Qur'an 29:4: "Do those who practice evil think that they will get the better of Us? Evil is their judgment!"

30. Qur'an 25:20: "We have made some of you as a trial for others."

31. The author cites the following verse from Hafez to illustrate this argument: "Alas, the sweep of the oceans the fantasy envisions, / What swims in this impossibility-wishing droplet's visions?" [Ed.]

32. Rumi's *Mathnavi*, bk. 1, verses 273 and 1609. This poem is based on the alchemic lore where the qualitative differences of substances are attributed to various amounts of primary elements. The transubstantiation of matter is therefore a function of mixing the right amount of component elements such as earth, fire, air, etc. The author cites other poems as well to illustrate the argument, such as *Mathnavi*, bk. 3, verse 4418: "Day and night appear to oppose each other in hostility. / In truth they braid together, to create the same reality." And also *Divan-e Shams*, Foruzanfar, vol. 8, couplet 601 [Ed.]:

> Your soul shall be much taxed.
> You shall see your notoriety waxed.
> Get along with humans if you are human;
> If an angel, soar to the heavens, if you can.

Selected References

Ahmad Ashraf, entries in *Encyclopedia Iranica* (New York: Columbia University Press).

Mongol Bayat, *Iran's First Revolution: Shi'ism and the Constitutional Revolution of 1905–1909* (New York: Oxford University Press, 1991).

Daniel Bell, "The Return of the Sacred? The Argument on the Future of Religion," in *The Winding Passage: Essays and Sociological Journeys 1960–1980* (Cambridge, Mass.: ABT Books, 1980).

Robert Bellah, *Beyond Belief: Essays on Religion in a Post-Traditional World* (Los Angeles: University of California Press, 1970).

———, *Habits of the Heart: Individualism and Commitment in American Life* (New York: Free Press, 1985).

Peter Berger, *The Sacred Canopy: Elements of a Sociological Theory of Religion* (New York: Anchor Books, 1967).

———, *A Rumor of Angels: Modern Society and the Rediscovery of Religiosity* (New York: Anchor Books, 1969).

Mohammad Borghei, "Religious Knowledge and Rational Knowledge," in *Kankash: A Persian Journal of History and Politics* (Spring 1992).

Mehrzad Borujerdi, *Iranian Intellectuals and the West: The Tormented Triumph of Nativism* (New York: Syracuse University Press, 1996).

James Carrier, ed., *Occidentalism: Images of the West* (New York: Oxford University Press, 1995).

Mark Chaves, "Secularization as Declining Religious Authority," in *Social Forces* 27 (March 1994).

James Childress and David Harned, *Secularization and the Protestant Prospect* (Philadelphia: Westminster Press, 1969).

Roberto Cipriani, "Religiosity, Religious Secularism, and Secular Religion," in *International Social Science Journal* (June 1994).

Harvey Cox, *Religion in the Secular City: Toward a Postmodern Theology* (New York: Touchstone, 1984).

Grace Davie, "Completing Fundamentalisms," unpublished article, International Sociological Association, 1994.

N. J. Demerath III, "Rational Paradigms: A-Rational Religion and the Debate over Secularization," in *Journal for the Scientific Study of Religion* (March 1995).

Emile Durkheim, *Elementary Forms of Religious Life* (New York: Free Press, [1912] 1995).

————, *Sociology and Philosophy* (New York: Free Press, 1974).

Mohammad Faghfoori, "The Impact of Modernization on the Ulama in Iran: 1924–1941," in *Iranian Studies* (Summer 1993).

Michael Fischer, *Iran: From Religious Dispute to Revolution* (Cambridge, Mass.: Harvard University Press, 1980).

Charles Glock and Phillip Hammond, *Beyond the Classics? Essays in the Scientific Study of Religion* (New York: Harper and Row, 1973).

Andrew Greely, *Religious Change in America* (Cambridge, Mass.: Harvard University Press, 1996).

Jeffery Hadden, "Toward Desacralizing Secularization Theory," in *Social Forces* (March 1987).

Phillip Hammond, ed., *The Sacred in a Secular Age: Toward Revision in the Scientific Study of Religion* (Berkeley: University of California Press, 1985).

Michael Hughey, "The Idea of Secularization in the Work of Max Weber: A Theoretical Outline," in *Qualitative Sociology* (May 1979).

Mohammad Iqbal Lahori, *The Reconstruction of Religious Thought in Islam* (London: Oxford University Press, 1930).

Russell Jakoby, *The Last Intellectuals: American Culture in the Age of Academe* (New York: Doubleday Press, 1987).

Charles Kurzman, ed., *Liberal Islam* (New York: Oxford University Press, 1998).

Niklas Luhmann, *The Differentiation of Society* (New York: Columbia University Press, 1982).

David Lyon, "Rethinking Secularization: Retrospect and Prospect," in *Review of Religious Research* (March 1989).

David Martin, *A General Theory of Secularization* (New York: Harper and Row, 1978).

Martin Marty, *Modern Schism: Three Paths to the Secular* (New York: Harper and Row, 1969).

Roy Mottahedeh, *Mantle of the Prophet* (New York: Pantheon Books, 1985).

Tschannen Olivier, "The Secularization Paradigm: A Systematization," in *Journal for the Scientific Study of Religion* (December 1991).

Rudolf Otto, *The Idea of the Holy* (New York: Oxford University Press, 1950).

Talcott Parsons, *Sociological Theory and Modern Society* (New York: Free Press, 1967).

Ahmad Sadri, *Max Weber's Sociology of Intellectuals* (New York: Oxford University Press, 1994).

Mahmoud Sadri, "Reconstruction of Max Weber's Notion of Rationality: An Immanent Model," in *Social Research* 49, no. 3 (Autumn 1982).

Ahmad Sadri and Mahmoud Sadri, "Intercultural Understanding: Max Weber and Leo Strauss," in *The Living Legacy of Marx, Durkheim, and Weber: Applications and Analyses of Classical Sociological Theory by Modern Social Scientists* (New York: Gordian Knot Books, 1998).

Saint Augustine, *The City of God* (New York: Modern Library, 1994).

Wolfgang Schluchter, *Rationalism, Religion, and Domination: A Weberian Perspective* (Berkeley: University of California Press, 1989).

Steven Seidman, "Modernity and the Problem of Meaning: The Durkheimian Tradition," in *Sociological Analysis* (Summer 1985).

Georg Simmel, *Sociology of Religion* (New York: Philosophical Library, 1959).

————, *The Philosophy of Money* (London: Routledge and Kegan Paul, 1982).

Harry Smith, *Secularization and University* (Richmond, Va.: John Knox Press, 1968).

Bryan S. Turner, *Religion and Social Theory* (London: Sage, 1991).

Vala Vakili, *Debating Religion and Politics in Iran: The Political Thought of Abdolkarim Soroush*, Council on Foreign Relations, Occasional Papers, no. 2 (Fall 1996).

Max Weber, *The Sociology of Religion* (Boston: Beacon Press, 1956).

Max Weber, *Economy and Society* (Berkeley: University of California Press, 1978).

————, *From Max Weber: Essays in Sociology* (New York: Oxford University Press, 1946).

Deena Weinstien, "Rock Music," in *International Sociology* (June 1995).

David Yamane, "Secularization on Trial: In Defense of a Neosecularization Paradigm," in *Journal for the Scientific Study of Religion* (March 1997).

Index

modern theology, 12, 16, 20
modernity
  and secularism, 57–61
  and tradition, 54–56
  reaction against, xviii–xix
modernization, xvi, xviii–xix
Mohammad, 19
mohkam, 35
Mojahedin, x, 11, 14, 182, 202n.6,
  223n.21
monarchy, 55, 59, 63, 158
monavvarolfekr, x, xii
Montazeri, Hossein Ali, 218n.33
Moqaddam, Mohammad, 158
moral realism, 196
morality, 59, 105–121, 152–154, 211n.6
mores, 51, 109–110
morid bazi, 209n.5
Moses, 100, 208n.2, 218n.37
Moslems
  Qur'anic, 6
  Shi'ites, 5, 28, 82, 85, 172, 215n.18
  Sunnis, 82, 172
  See also Islam
Motahhari, Morteza, 4, 6, 11, 29, 168,
  177, 179, 180, 202nn.6–8, 205n.21,
  216n.19, 216n.27, 220n.20
moteshabeh, 35
Mulla Sadra. *See* Sadra, Mulla
mysticism, 17, 46

Nafisi, Said, 158
Nahj al-balaqeh (Soroush), 19
Najafabadi, Salehi, 176, 222n.8
names, 111–113, 212n.13
natural man. *See* human nature
natural order, 54–55
natural rights, 65
natural science, 57–58
nature, 65–66
Nazism, 93, 94
neo-Orientalists, xv
Niebuhr, Richard, 153
nominalism, 18, 208n.20
Nowrouz holiday, 167, 168

obligation, 68
opinion, 35
owl of Minerva allegory, 20

Pahlavi, Mohammad Reza Shah, 158
Paine, Thomas, 146
"Paradox of Islam and Democracy, The"
  (Paydar), 134, 135, 138
passion, 79–80
patience, 48, 205n.18, 205–206n.25
Paydar, Hamid, 134, 135, 137, 138, 140
perfection, 191
permanence, 28
Persian language, 157, 158, 159, 168, 179

philosophical anthropology, 189–197
philosophy
  ahistorical view of traditional,
    184–189
  Aristotelian, 10, 69
  of ethics, 18
  Greek, 65–66
  and human rights, 128
  Islamic, 4, 6, 69, 177–178
  and religion, 4, 14–15, 20, 69–73
  of science, 8–10, 15, 50
"Philosophy of Evil, The" (Soroush), 4
Philosophy of History (Soroush), 11
Plato, 158
pluralism, 145
politics, 64
  implications of secularism, 67–68
  in Iran, 5, 10–11
  and religion, 5, 60–61
  and society, 58–59
Popper, Karl, 9, 13, 15
populism, 180
positivism, 50
Post, Professor, 9
postmodernism, 45, 49–50
poverty, 46–49, 52–53
power, 101–102, 132–133, 146, 153, 174,
  179
pre-contractual solidarity, 219n.42
*Principles of Philosophy and the Method of
  Realism, The* (Tabataba'i), 6
prophets, 194–197
public speaking, 175
punishment, 67

qiblah, 213n.19
Qoshairi, Abol Qasim, 206n.25
questioning, 178–179
Quine, Willard, 15–16
Qum (Iran), xii, 20, 203n.13, 203n.21
Qur'an, xiii, 6, 7, 14, 100, 138, 176, 177,
  203n.14, 224nn.13–17, 224–
  225nn.21–30
Qur'anic Moslems, 6

radical laic modernism, xi, xviii–xix
rational metaphysics, 65
rationality
  and democracy, 149–152
  and faith, 71–72
  and freedom, 88–104
  and passion, 79
  and religion, 127–128, 154–155
Ravesh-e Realism (Tabataba'i), 179
Rayan, Alan, 18
Razi, Yahya bin Mo'az, 206n.25
Razziq, 'Abdol, 17
realism, 194, 196
reason. *See* rationality
"Reason and Freedom" (Soroush), 88–104

reasons, 214–215n.12
reform, xvi, xviii–xix, 26–38, 86–87
rejectionist revivalism. *See* anti-modern
    movements; revivalism
religion
    blessings of, 36–37
    change in, xvi, xvii–xviii, 15, 28
    and democratic government, 122–155
    and determinism, 56
    as distinct from religious knowledge,
        30–34
    and freedom, 97, 140–143
    and God, 64
    and humaneness, 124
    and human rights, 125–126, 128–129
    justifiability of doctrine, 74–87
    and knowledge, 16, 30–35, 71, 137,
        176
    language of, 62, 70–71
    modern theology, 12, 16, 20
    nature and social position of, 22
    and philosophy, 4, 14–15, 20, 69–73
    place in society, 21
    and politics, 5, 60–61
    and reason, 127–128, 154–155
    revivalists of past, 26–27
    revivalists of today, 27–30
    and salvation, 72
    and science, 4, 13, 14, 36, 60, 136–137
    and secularism, xvi, xvii–xviii, xix,
        56–57, 201n.20, 201n.22, 207n.14
    understanding of, 31, 33–34, 37, 142
    See also faith; Islam
revelation, 36–37, 127–128
revivalism, xvi, xviii–xix, 20, 26–38
Reza, Rashid, 29
right, 148
rights. *See* human rights
ritual, 147, 149, 202n.10
"Roof of Livelihood on the Pillar of
    Religion, The" (Soroush), 19
Rostam, 158
rouhaniyyat, 19
roushanfekr, x, xii
Rousseau, Jean-Jacques, xiv
Rouzbeh, Reza, 4
Rumi, 6–8, 10, 13–14, 17, 24, 41–44, 56,
    79, 85, 88, 93–95, 98, 102–104, 141,
    183, 202n.3, 203n.16, 204n.10,
    205n.15, 207n.4, 208n.2, 209n.9,
    210n.32, 212n.17, 215n.15, 218n.37,
    221n.24, 225n.32
Russell, Bertrand, 80, 95
Russia, x. *See also* Soviet Union

Sa'di, 4, 47, 48, 220n.19
Sabzevari, Mulla Hadi, 181, 223n.19
Sadra, Mulla, 8, 11, 82, 98, 99, 178,
    209n.19, 223nn.17–19
Sahabi, Yadollah, xii

Sahl Ibn 'Ata', Abol Abbas Ahmad Ibn,
    206n.25
Sajjad, Imam, 38, 62
salvation, 72
Satan, 192, 193
Saudi Arabia, 167
savior, 215n.18
scandal, 178, 180, 222n.12
Schumpeter, Joseph A., 218n.32
science
    Aristotelian, 8
    attacks on, 49–51
    and development, 49–53
    of history, 184–186, 188
    history of, 9
    impartiality of, 206n.30
    and liberalism, 214n.8
    modern knowledge, 57–58
    philosophy of, 8–10, 15, 50
    Quine on, 15–16
    and religion, 4, 13, 36, 60, 136–137
    science-centrism, 214n.8
    in university, 173
Science and Value (Soroush), 11
scientification, 207n.5
secularism, 40, 54–68, 201nn.20–22
    meaning of, 60
    and modern worldview, 57–61
    and relationship between rights and
        duties, 61–64
    and religion, xvi–xix, 56–57, 201n.20,
        201n.22, 207n.14
    roots in human mind, 65–66
    as scientification, 207n.5
    social and political implications of, 67–
        68
seminarians, 175
"Sense and Essence of Secularism, The"
    (Soroush), 18, 54–68
set theory, 9
Shabestari, Sheikh Mahmoud, 27, 55
Shahnameh (Ferdowsi), 159, 221n.25
shar', 127
shari', 15
shari'ah, 17, 18, 27, 31, 62, 134, 144,
    146, 218n.34
Shari'ati, 'Ali, x, xii, 7, 10–11, 14, 18,
    21, 29–30, 82, 162, 168, 202n.11,
    205n.21, 221n.26
Shenakht (pamphlet), 11
Shi'ites, xii, xv, 5, 28, 82, 85, 172,
    215n.18
Shirazi, Sadr al-Din. *See* Sadra, Mulla
Simmel, Georg, xvi
sin, 196, 197. *See also* evil
Sleepwalkers (Koestler), 13
Smith, Adam, 42, 59
social contract, 153
social justice, 30
social policy, 192–194

social sciences, 13, 16, 57–58
social transformations, 42
socialism, 214n.9
society, 57–61, 64
    morality in, 105–121, 211n.6
    and religion, 21
    See also democracy
socioeconomic development, 39–53
Sojourn in the Arab Political Thought, A
    (Enayat), 217n.32
Soroush, ʿAbdolkarim
    on Advisory Council on the Cultural
        Revolution, xi, 11–12
    childhood, 3
    combining of Islamic learning and
        science, 200n.7
    global context, xv–xix
    as icon, ix–xi
    as iconoclast, xi–xii
    interview with, 3–25
    opus of work, xii–xv
    poetry, 3–4
    public career, xi
    revisionist Islam of, xii–xv
    schooling, 4–5
    studies in philosophy of science, 8–10
    See also specific works
Souzani Samarqandi, 85, 86
Soviet Union, 5, 77–78, 116–117, 165–
    166
Stalin, Josef, 78, 116, 166, 220n.21
Story of Servitude and Love (Soroush), 19
Story of the Lords of Wisdom, The
    (Soroush), 17, 205n.21
Strauss, Leo, 65
Structure of Scientific Revolutions, The
    (Kuhn), 9
Sufism, 17, 174, 205n.21, 205–206n.25
Sunnis, 82, 172
superstition, 180
symbolic logic, 9

Tabatabaʾi, Allameh, 6, 8, 11, 176, 179,
    222n.10
tafsir, 203n.21
Talebof, xi
Taleqani, 182, 223n.21
Taqizadeh, xi
tariqah, 27
temporality, 33, 36
testability. *See* justifiability
textual interpretation. *See* interpretation
    of texts
theology. *See* kalam; religion
"Three Cultures, The" (Soroush), xiv,
    156–170

three-worlds theory, 13
Tocqueville, Alexis de, 153
Tolerance and Governance (Soroush), 19,
    131–155
tolerance, 138–140, 193
Toudeh Party, x, 5
Tradition, 34–35, 176, 177, 203n.14
tradition, 54–56, 180–181, 182
transparence of text, 35
"Treatise on Rights, The" (Sajjad), 62
Trotsky, Leon, 166
truth, 21, 59, 60, 211n.5
    and freedom, 91–92, 100
    and morality, 106, 112
    and reason, 89–90
Turner, Bryan S., 200n.17
tyranny, 101, 120, 138, 143

Umayyad dynasty, 84
universities, 12, 199–200n.6
    and the Hawzeh, 171–183
University of Tehran, 185
usul, 34, 203n.21

values, 39–45, 52
velayat, 210n.26
vice, 42–43, 52, 53, 67, 116, 212n.13
Vico, Giovanni, 185
violence, 112
virtue, 39–53, 67, 205n.21, 212n.13
Vogel, Frank, 217n.30

Warfare between Science and Theology
    (White), 81
wealth, 46–48, 52–53, 153, 205n.16
Weber, Max, ix, xvi, 149, 199n.1,
    200n.16, 201n.20
West toxication (*gharb zadegi*), 160–161
Western culture, xv, xvii, 159–162,
    168
What is Science, What is Philosophy?
    (Soroush), 11
"What the University Expects from the
    Hawzeh" (Soroush), xiv, 171–183
White, Andrew, 80–81
wisdom, 113–114
Wolff, R. P., 214n.8
women, 181, 182, 203n.12, 223n.19
World We Live, The (Soroush), 18
Wright, Robin, xv

Yazid Ibn Moʿaviyeh, 220n.23

Zadeh, Akhound, 158
Zobeidi, Morteza, 206n.25
Zoroastrianism, 157, 159